# HONG KONG in CHINA

## The Challenges of Transition

*Edited by*
**Wang Gungwu
& John Wong**

TIMES ACADEMIC PRESS

© 1999 Times Academic Press

First published 1999 by
**Times Academic Press**
An imprint of Federal Publications (S) Pte Ltd
*(A member of the Times Publishing Group)*
Times Centre
1 New Industrial Road
Singapore 536196
Fax: (65) 2889254
E-mail: fps@corp.tpl.com.sg
Online Book Store: http://www.timesone.com.sg/fpl

HC
470.3
, H668
1999

ISBN 981 210 148 9

Printed by
Percetakan Rina Sdn. Bhd. (31964–X)

# Contents

# CHAPTER 1

# INTRODUCTION

Wang Gungwu and John Wong

## An End to Post-handover Euphoria

On 1 July 1997, Hong Kong (HK) was returned to China to become its "Special Administrative Region" (SAR) based on the principle of "one country, two systems", which is backed by the Basic Law and the Sino-British Joint Declaration. Despite the continuing squabbles between Britain and China prior to this historic occasion, the event had proved to be a smooth handover after all. China did try everything possible to make the handover a success, and Hong Kong has been largely left to run its own affairs.

At the time of the handover, the Hang Seng stock index reached 15,000 (compared to the low of 10,000 in 1996).[1] Hong Kong quickly returned to "business as usual". Much of the pre-handover worries and polemics were soon brushed aside as post-handover euphoria rapidly gained ground amidst glowing reports of continuing economic prosperity. This culminated in Chief Executive Tung Chee-hwa's first policy address for the SAR in early October 1997, which was devoted to the "livelihood issue" of the HK people and promised to address Hong Kong's long-term problems, such as housing and education.[2] Tung's popularity index immediately soared to the record high of 89 percent while the Hang Seng index also climbed beyond the 16,000 level. In the immediate post-handover aftermath, Hong Kong was indeed in an exuberant "honeymoon" mood, apparently impervious to the financial turmoil that was then brewing in Southeast Asia.

However, barely two weeks after Tung's policy address, the Asian financial crisis spread to Hong Kong, with its "linked exchange rate", i.e. the US dollar "peg" coming under heavy speculative attack. In a matter of just a few days, the Hang Seng index plunged by 35 percent to about 10,000 level and its overheated property market plummeted by over 20 percent (currently, down by 40–50 percent) on account of the sharp rise of interest rates, which were introduced to defend the peg. Under such circumstances, the post-handover euphoric sentiments fizzled out almost immediately. In fact, the October 1997 attack on the HK dollar sparked off a serious economic recession for Hong Kong, with gloom and doom spreading rapidly from the financial and property markets to tourism and domestic retail sectors. As unemployment began to rise, the HK economy came increasingly under a cloud. As if economic and financial problems were not enough, Hong Kong had since been hit by a series of crises, including the much publicized "bird flu" and the disastrous opening of the new Chek Lap Kok (CLK) Airport.

In the event, the HK economy still ended 1997 with 5.3 percent and 6 percent inflation. In 1998, however, the HK economy plunged to a record 5.1 percent "negative growth" (contraction), with a creeping deflation.[3] Hong Kong had for years experienced full employment with acute labour shortages. By early 1999, unemployment had risen sharply to 6 percent, the worst in about three decades, and is still rising.[4]

# Things Fall Apart

Scarce in land and poor in natural resources except for its strategic location, Hong Kong has always depended on a booming economy as the *raison d'être* for its precarious existence. Now with such a spectacular collapse of its economic growth, Hong Kong is undermined by a serious crisis of confidence, and things seem to be falling apart on many fronts. Politically, the Tung Chee-hwa leadership is increasingly under fire from many quarters for its constant policy drifts and its lack of a clear direction. The civil service, previously noted for its operational efficiency and professionalism, is suffering from a serious decline in morale, especially after mounting public criticism for its ineptness in handling crises. Some observers would even add that Hong Kong's top economic bureaucrats (who are actually half an administrator and half a politician) lost their nerve when confronted with financial crises, citing as proof their hasty decision to intervene directly in the stock market in August 1998, when the HK dollar came under the second attack by international speculators.

Even Hong Kong's legal system, which Hong Kongers have so proudly treasured as a pillar of their justice and equality,[5] is not immune to crises. On 29 January 1999, the Court of Final Appeal delivered a controversial judgement to openly challenge China's National People's Congress (NPC) by restoring the right of abode of all mainland children, even if they have only one parent who is a Hong Kong resident, regardless of whether they were born in wedlock, or before their parents obtained residency rights. Furthermore, the judgement was "unequivocal" in asserting the right of HK courts to "examine whether any legislative acts of the National People's Congress or its Standing Committee ... are consistent with the Basic Law and to declare them to be invalid if found to be inconsistent."[6] This was initially hailed as a landmark ruling; but it almost touched off a constitutional confrontation with Beijing.

Shortly after the HK court's judgement, legal experts in China attacked the court for wrongly overruling the acts of the NPC, tantamount to placing the HK court above the national legislature, and is hence contrary to the Basic Law.[7] In the event, the SAR government, in a move to end this constitutional crisis, asked the Court of Final Appeal to clarify its right of abode decision, particularly concerning the legal supremacy of the NPC.[8] On 26 February 1999, the chief justice conceded that the original judgement "does not question the authority of the Standing Committee of the National People's Congress under article 158", and that "it cannot query the authority of the NPC and the Standing Committee".[9] With this clarification the matter was laid to rest.[10]

The upshot nonetheless serves to show that the HK court had obviously picked the wrong issue at the wrong time to assert Hong Kong's legal independence. The outcome of the court ruling could well be socially damaging to Hong Kong, as it would risk opening the floodgates to hundreds of thousands of mainlanders coming to settle in Hong Kong. At this time of deepening economic recession and rising unemployment, the issue was also naturally unpopular with many ordinary HK people.[11] Furthermore, any ruling on the "right of abode" involving such a large number of people is a matter of state policy or a political decision that should not be regarded as a purely legal matter to be decided by a handful of unelected high court judges. Hence the ramifications of the right of abode ruling, coupled with the earlier decision by the Secretary for Justice, Elsie Leung, not to persecute, on political grounds, the HK newspaper tycoon, Sally Aw, for a commercial offence, have much undermined public confidence in HK's judicial system.[12]

As the economic crisis deepens, social cohesion is weakened. Fault lines between Hong Kong's powerful and conservative business community and pro-democratic activists become more clearly drawn. In December 1998, Hong Kong's most prominent businessman, Li Ka-shing, threatened to abandon a HK$10-billion investment project because the HK business environment had deteriorated as a result of growing political tendency towards populism and welfarism. Several outspoken HK businessmen also joined in the chorus of attack and openly accused pro-democracy politicians of advocating populist or even socialist measures, like subsidies and minimum wages, in order to win votes.[13]

Meanwhile, Hong Kong's popular independent party, the Democratic Party led by Martin Lee, had also been polarized by the economic crisis. Lee had all along geared the party towards meeting the middle-class aspirations for greater democracy, and he wanted to achieve these goals through political debate and legislative changes in the LegCo. The more radical faction of the party, however, wanted to focus on the labour movement, and they wanted to take politics to the streets. In their view, with rising unemployment and worsening social conditions, the ordinary people in Hong Kong would naturally find the politics of "rice bowl" (livelihood issues) more appealing than the kind of democratic reforms advocated by westernized elite like Martin Lee.[14]

4

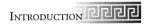

# A Robust Economy Tumbles

This is not to say that Hong Kong is in a state of disarray. However, the severe economic downturn has brought many of Hong Kong's latent political and social problems to the fore, which were further compounded by problems of post-handover transition. For an economy long used to high growth with full employment, a drastic change in economic fortunes would inevitably expose its political and social fault lines. The question can then be posed: Why should the HK economy have suddenly nose-dived so sharply in a matter of one year? Or, why has the HK economy so readily fallen victim to the Asian financial crisis?

On hindsight, it is quite simple to explain why the financial crisis should have struck Thailand, Malaysia, Indonesia and South Korea. But Hong Kong had much stronger economic fundamentals than these Asian economies, and by far, a stronger external balance: i.e. Hong Kong had a huge foreign exchange reserve and no foreign debt. Furthermore, Hong Kong is supposed to have a functioning legal system with effective and transparent regulations that are needed by international business. It had none of the Indonesian "*KKN*" (or corruption, cronyism and nepotism). As the region's foremost financial centre, Hong Kong's banks and financial institutions were well supervised and well regulated. In fact, as the reputable Political & Economic Risk Consultancy recently put it, "The banking system in Hong Kong is in better shape than any other economy in Asia and deserves its ranking as Number One".[15] Why then should the HK economy have such a low degree of immunity to the Asian financial crisis?

Hong Kong and Singapore are comparable in many ways: they are structurally quite similar, both are heavily dependent on external economic activities and hence are equally vulnerable to external fluctuation. Hong Kong is fortunate enough to have South China as its hinterland, which has not only remained relatively prosperous during the Asian financial crisis but also wants Hong Kong to prosper. With its hinterlands deep in an economic crisis, Singapore is comparatively less fortunate. The state of crisis in the neighbouring regions inevitably affected Singapore's trade adversely. Why then should the HK and not the Singapore economy (which experienced 1.5 percent growth in 1998), plunge so easily?

Economists have no trouble offering two standard explanations for Hong Kong's present economic predicament. The first is quite obvious. On account of its fixed peg to the US dollar, the exchange rate of the HK dollar had become too high *vis-à-vis* those of the regional economies; and it could not be flexibly adjusted downwards to keep the HK economy competitive. To offset its overvalued exchange rate, Hong Kong needs to undergo a large measure of asset deflation together with vigorous price- and cost-cutting measures. Second, Hong Kong's manufacturing sector had been extensively "hollowed out" to Guangdong. As a result, the HK economy had come to depend excessively on the export of services to China and the world. And service activities, from banking and finance to tourism, are most vulnerable to the regional financial crisis.

Clearly, the current economic woes in Hong Kong are not entirely due to the cyclical factors caused by the Asian financial crisis, but are also the results of far more serious and deep-rooted structural problems. Hong Kong has grown into a high-income and high-cost economy. In 1998, Hong Kong's per-capita gross national product at US$25,000 was the 13th highest in the world and higher than that of Britain (US$20,700). One year after the handover in mid-1998, Hong Kong was rated as the world's most expensive city in which to do business.[16] By the end of 1998, after a substantial asset deflation and domestic price adjustment, Hong Kong remained the third most expensive business centre, trailing only Tokyo and Osaka.

For a high-wage economy to keep growing, there must be a broad range of high value-added activities. Hong Kong's economic boom in the early 1990s was mainly driven by property and stock market speculation, which in any case cannot be sustained in the long run. In fact, on the eve of the handover, the HK economy had already developed many features of a "bubble economy". Now that the regional financial crisis has punctured the "bubble", this should present an opportunity to introduce the much-needed reforms and restructuring in the economy. To stay competitive, Hong Kong must find ways to contain or reduce business costs and take measures to maintain investor confidence. At the same time, it must chart a

new course and develop a new niche. In his second policy address on 7 October 1998, Chief Executive Tung Chee-hwa outlined a number of new initiatives for what may be called the third restructuring of the HK economy, aimed at developing several new niches such as information technology, the film industry and Chinese medicine.[17] The proposed development of a cyberport at HK\$13 billion, announced in March 1999 by Financial Secretary in the 1999–2000 budget, is another step in this direction.[18]

## The Peril of just another Chinese City

Meanwhile, Hong Kong faces a double challenge. For its continuing survival, Hong Kong would not only have to stay "competitive" as an international city, but would also have to meet its vital long-term strategic needs of staying "relevant" (i.e. complementary with) to China. Since the start of China's open-door policy 20 years ago, the HK economy has become closely integrated with China. After the handover, the future economic fortunes of Hong Kong will all the more be dictated by the *China factor*. Hong Kong's continued usefulness to China will depend on its ability to outcompete Shanghai or any other emerging Chinese cities on the China coast as a valuable service centre. This means that the HK economy should continue to cater to China's needs and exploit China's potential. At the same time, economically, Hong Kong must also retain its international orientation and, socially, its cosmopolitanism. By being a vibrant international city, Hong Kong will be a useful conduit for China's external operations. But it also needs to maintain its non-China source of economic growth. Should Hong Kong slowly deteriorate into just another Chinese city, its very survival would be at stake.

It is well known that Shanghai is aspiring to become the leading commercial and financial centre not just for China but also for the region in the long run. Recently, Shenzhen has also shown its ambition to develop into a science and technology hub for its Pearl River industrial hinterland.[19] As the current Asian financial crisis has left China relatively unaffected, the Chinese economy is likely to emerge from the crisis faster sooner. This means that Hong Kong might face serious challenges from its potential competitors in China earlier than expected.

On the whole, however, the threat of potential competition from China's own metropolitan centres, like Shanghai, is probably more apparent than real, at least in the short to medium term. Hong Kong's competitive edge over China in terms of institutional capability and experience on international capitalism should remain an asset for a fairly long time. China, on account of its sheer physical size, can quickly muster the required technological hardware; but it may not succeed as easily in developing the sophisticated "software" (e.g. management capability) required by international finance and high value-added tradable services. It is also *not* in the nature of dynamic economic competition to end up as a zero sum game whereby one party's gain is necessarily the loss for the other. In the course of time, Hong Kong can always adapt itself to work out a kind of economic symbiosis with its potential competitors in China which will benefit both parties.

## Economic Integration without Political Integration

In fact, since the late 1980s, Hong Kong has already built up a viable economic symbiotic relationship with South China which fuels each other's economic growth. What is lacking is an equally viable political and social symbiosis with China. The Basic Law and the Sino-British Joint Declaration have provided the political framework for Hong Kong to exist as the special administrative region for 50 years, under the broad principle of "one country, two systems". Eventually the "two systems" are supposed to become one, either with China and Hong Kong converging or with Hong Kong being absorbed into China's own institutional structure. The "convergence model" looks more realistic than the "absorption model". But there is neither a clear-cut institutional mechanism nor a firm timetable as to how this will come about.

It may be pointed out that there were also no formal institutional arrangements for Hong Kong's economic integration with China, and yet the HK economy has been moving closer to China by dint of the operation of market forces.

8

The same is true with Taiwan's economic relations with China, which have been fostered mainly by Taiwan's private sector initiative, sometimes aggravating the Taiwanese government. Taiwan's economic integration with China has also not been followed by any move towards closer political and social integration with the Mainland. The question remains: can HK sustain a growing economic symbiosis with China while keeping a big political and social distance from it, something as epitomized by the Chinese saying: *"Tongchuang yimeng"* — or "Same bed, different dreams"? It should be remembered that Hong Kong is not Taiwan; by international law, Hong Kong is already under China's sovereignty.

Most of Hong Kong's operating institutions — from the public administration, the legal system, financial and monetary regulatory authorities, the education system to the media and broadcasting — were long in existence before the handover. They were mainly the products of British colonialism, and as such they are worlds apart from their counterpart or equivalent operating systems in China. After the handover, one still finds no signs of Hong Kong's institutional structure being adapted in such a way as to facilitate closer political and social integration with China. Many events of the past two years, from the continuing use of Cantonese (rather than Mandarin) as the medium of instruction in schools to the recent Court of Final Appeal ruling on the right of abode issue, in open defiance of China's NPC, do not lend support to the convergence model.

The people in Hong Kong are apparently happy with their key institutions, even though these institutions are still heavily tainted with colonial characteristics. Hong Kong people specifically want to preserve such an institutional *status quo* to maintain their much treasured "Hong Kong way of life". Some institutions, like the legal system, are admittedly also critical to the maintenance of Hong Kong's competitive edge as a regional financial centre. But Hong Kong's preference to keep the *status quo* unchanged could also constrain it from developing a dynamic forward-looking outlook. It could undermine its ability as well to cope with new challenges. As one scholar points out, "The colonial legacy of Hong Kong and the peculiar circumstances of its post-colonial transition have placed

enormous emphasis on detailed continuity with the past —
something that would have been regarded as absurd under other
circumstances."[20] Hence a dilemma for Hong Kong.


## "One Country" vs "Two Systems"

Deng Xiaoping originally framed the "one country, two systems"
concept some 18 years ago in order to calm the HK Chinese of
their fears of communism — and also as an open gesture for
Taiwan. The British endorsed it for fear of outright Chinese
domination immediately after the handover of Hong Kong. Most
of the people in Hong Kong were keen on this proposal as it would
prevent the unwarranted intrusion of China's political and social
systems into their "Hong Kong way of life". Deng's highly
simplistic framework had no doubt served the immediate political
purpose of maintaining confidence in the run-up to the handover.
But such simplicity can be very "messy" in the long run because
it also imposes a high degree of institutional rigidity on Hong
Kong for its post-handover changes, something no other colonies
have ever experienced. To abide by the Sino-British Joint
Declaration, Hong Kong's institutions are not required to evolve
in such a way as to accommodate those from China while, at the
same time, Hong Kong itself is not supposed to develop a distinct
political identity of its own. Thus, Hong Kong finds itself
institutionally in limbo once the British left.

How would such a "static" institutional arrangement as the
"one country, two systems" effectively operate in the real world
of "dynamic" economic and social changes? Before the handover,
not many people in Hong Kong gave serious thought to this
matter. Optimists had originally pinned their hopes on the
continuing changes in both China and Hong Kong and on the
continuing pragmatism and flexibility on the part of both the
Beijing leadership and the people in Hong Kong. Since the early
1980s, China (particularly its economy and society) has, indeed,
changed beyond recognition. China is commonly slated to
become an economic superpower in the next 20 years with
further political and social openness. How and when will Hong
Kong's political and social systems be restructured in order to

accommodate China's, i.e. to move the "two systems" towards the "one country"? Admittedly, this is not a burning issue for Hong Kong now. Nor is it for China, at least not before the Taiwan question is settled. But clearly this matter cannot wait for 50 years. The next generation of leaders of both China and Hong Kong will have to start tackling this problem of the "same bed, different dreams".

Let us just take the first two years of the handover as an example. From the first day of the special administrative region, Beijing has behaved most correctly in its dealings with Hong Kong. The Chinese officials at the local levels have been strictly forbidden to interfere in the affairs of Hong Kong, and senior officials in Beijing have scrupulously avoided even making unnecessary public comments on HK affairs. Beijing has made an earnest attempt to show to the outside world that "HK people ruling Hong Kong" is for real, not a fiction. Yet Hong Kong has been beset with one crisis after another which did not emanate from China. And these crises have started to further divide HK society and polarize its elites. This suggests that Hong Kong's own system itself cannot remain "static" but it is also in need of "dynamic" adjustment and changes regardless of the Chinese side of the bargain.

In the immediate aftermath of the handover, "institutional continuity" was supposed to be the prevailing political orthodoxy in Hong Kong, with many international interest groups actually keeping a watchful eye on Hong Kong's major institutions to see if they are showing signs of giving way to pressures from China.[21] But the economic crisis has since called into question the actual viability of Hong Kong's pre-existing colonial institutional structure; and public pressures are already building up for institutional change and reforms, e.g. the call for the reform of the civil service.[22] The crisis has also intensified public debate in Hong Kong on many of its fundamental economic and social policies, e.g. government intervention in economic and monetary affairs, the public housing programme, the social welfare system, and the like.

So far the call for policy rethinking remains largely at the stage of public debate, which, except for the proposed civil service reform, has yet to translate into policy action for lack of consensus among the HK elites.[23] Suffice it to say that Hong Kong's major institutions are already under strong pressure to change and adapt to the new political environment. It would obviously be in the interest of Hong Kong to ensure that its institutional reforms and changes, while aimed at tackling Hong Kong's immediate problems, do not pose obstacles for future integration with China. In short, because of the economic crisis, Hong Kong may start moving the "two systems" towards "one country" sooner than it was originally envisaged.

## Learning How to Live with China

On Chinese New Year (16 February 1999), Tung Chee-hwa confidently predicted that the HK economy had stabilized and would soon recover from the financial turbulence of 1998.[24] Like the other East Asian economies, Hong Kong's economic recession may soon bottom out; but a sustained recovery cannot be assured especially since the Japanese economy is still in the doldrums and the Chinese economy is slowing down — Hong Kong's official forecast of economic growth for 1999 remains at the low 0.5 percent. More importantly, it would be difficult for the HK economy to return to its robust growth without addressing its structural malaise, like high costs and loss of competitiveness. Successful economic restructuring may well take many years.

In the process of recovery, Hong Kong's economic dependence on China will deepen and broaden. HK businessmen, still highly entrepreneurial, will be quick to capture new opportunities arising from expanding economic links with China, increasing economic interdependence further between Hong Kong and China after the recession. Economic symbiosis with China inevitably generates impetus for closer political and institutional integration with China, at least more pressures for a gradual or incremental political and institutional harmonization with China — e.g. measures to raise the consciousness of the Chinese identity of the HK people or more harmonization of education and professional standards between Hong Kong and China.

Harmonization smacks of convergence. Will this precipitate the untimely demise of the "one country, two systems" principle?

There is still one major obstacle. Most people in Hong Kong have little desire to see an earlier end to the "two systems" formula, perhaps because it is now only two years after the handover. Essentially, they are struggling with an identity crisis. Long-time HK residents who became Chinese nationals legally overnight, after 1 July 1997, are still asking themselves: Who am I?

In a meeting with the HK delegates at the recent session of the Ninth NPC in Beijing, President Jiang Zemin called on the HK people to "talk more about 'one country'" and the mainland people to "talk more about 'two systems'".[25] This will certainly facilitate working towards the convergence model. The mainland Chinese, generally having no direct interest in Hong Kong one way or other, have no difficulty in keeping the "two systems" going. But the problem lies mainly with the people in Hong Kong. They have to accept China before they will "talk more about the 'one country'". For most people in Hong Kong, they still have to learn how to live with China. This is no small challenge for them.

The question of Hong Kong's future political and social integration with China thus remains the most intractable part of the postcolonial transition for Hong Kong. There is still a great deal of uncertainty as to how this will come about exactly, inasmuch as China itself is also in a dynamic process of political and social change.

## Reflections on the Handover

In the run-up to the 1997 handover, a large volume of literature on Hong Kong had been produced, most trying to predict from specific angles what would happen to Hong Kong after it had reverted to China's sovereignty. Some were fairly optimistic while others were downright pessimistic (e.g. the *Fortune* magazine's June 1996 special HK edition, ominously entitled, "The Death of Hong Kong"). But most writings showed concerns over the political aspects of the HK transition, unduly worrying about Beijing's unwarranted intervention in Hong Kong's political and economic life, e.g. the possible suppression of pro-democracy politics, loss of political freedom, erosion of legal independence, and the like.

13

Few would have foreseen that one year after its return to China, Hong Kong actually found itself "all quiet on" the political front, and that the dominant concerns of the HK people were instead over economic affairs, such as the "rice bowl" issues of jobs and wage cuts. But then, few would have predicted the ferocity of the Asian financial crisis (which actually started in Thailand one day after the handover ceremony) and its relentless contagion effect. What has this upshot taught us? It is simply too hazardous to try to predict or define the future development of a place as dynamic as Hong Kong.

This volume could perhaps make a difference. First, it is based on a collection of essays written by established HK scholars in various fields of politics, economics, sociology and law. These scholars have been conducting research as recognized experts in their areas of specialization long before the handover. Second and more importantly, they wrote their papers *after* the handover when various problems in Hong Kong began to surface. As a result, we have been able to put together a fairly comprehensive picture of post-handover Hong Kong, covering the most recent political, legal, economic and social changes. This should provide a good starting point for an informed discussion of Hong Kong's problems and its challenges in the post-handover transition.

It should also be mentioned, if only for the record, that this volume is actually the product of an international conference on "Hong Kong in China: One Year After", organized by the East Asian Institute in Singapore from 29–31 October 1998. The conference was the first of its kind in Southeast Asia, with many eminent HK scholars brought to Singapore to interact with their counterparts not just from Singapore, but also from China, Taiwan, Japan, Indonesia, Malaysia and Thailand. After the conference, individual authors were asked to revise their papers in the light of the discussion, and to update their material when necessary.

# Post-handover Issues

The first two chapters by Kuan Hsin-chi and Lau Siu-kai are concerned with political changes. Kuan starts with the examination of the political backgrounds and various institutional implications of Deng's celebrated "one country, two systems" concept, which is to be the guiding principle for Hong Kong's postcolonial transition for the next 50 years. Kuan notes that more than one year after the handover, Deng's formula can be considered as having been successfully implemented because (a) Hong Kong has been able to preserve its previous institutional systems; and (b) Hong Kong has continued to manage its own affairs in a highly autonomous way, without unwarranted intervention from Beijing. While Kuan echoes how HK people are at present jealously guarding their autonomy under constant fears of "encroachment from the north", he emphasizes that the ultimate test of Deng's concept is how the HK system is to resonate harmoniously with that of the Mainland, i.e. the long-term problem of Hong Kong's political and economic integration with China, as pointed out earlier.

Lau, a political sociologist with special research interest on Hong Kong's political elites, focuses on the serious problem of "elite fragmentation", which came about in the run-up to the 1997 transition as both Britain and China were competing to occupy the political ground in its efforts to win over Hong Kong's elites. Hong Kong's last governor, Chris Patten, in his effort to woo pro-Britain elites, co-opted pro-democracy activists to support his democratic reforms and, at the same time, groomed selected senior civil servants as political successors. Beijing, in the meanwhile, used the cause of Chinese nationalism to court eminent business and community figures as well as grassroots leaders to support the smooth return of Hong Kong to China. Thus, on the eve of the handover in 1997, not only were Hong Kong's political elites fragmented, but no single group was able to prevail over the others. This is one of the most serious political legacies inherited by the SAR government. As Hong Kong's elites are deeply divided, it would be difficult for the Tung Administration to garner the needed political and social consensus to effectively come to grips with the economic crisis that is currently plaguing Hong Kong.

The next four chapters are concerned with economic transformation before and after the handover. At the time of the 1997 transition, most people in Hong Kong were worrying about political instability — years of prosperity had caused them to take

Hong Kong's continuing economic growth for granted. With the sudden collapse of economic growth one year after the handover, economic issues have risen to become the dominant concerns of the HK people. Liu Pak Wai explains what had gone wrong. The HK economy on the eve of the 1997 handover had actually developed into "one of the highest cost structures in the world" because of wage inflation and asset inflation. The former was caused by the tight labour market and the latter, by the overheated property market. The tight labour market itself was a result of Hong Kong's secular demographic trends towards lower fertility and rising emigration. Then the spillover of China's economic boom since the early 1990s added more fuel to Hong Kong's upward wage-cost spiral. Hence an unsustainable economic bubble for Hong Kong developed — it easily burst when Hong Kong was struck by the Asian financial crisis. Liu argues that the recession should provide the HK economy an impetus to carry out its third restructuring by developing new niches in higher value-added activities, such as the information industry and greater use of innovation and technology in manufacturing.

Tsang Shu-ki also brings out various structural imbalances in the HK economy, built up before the handover, and discusses how they were vulnerable to the Asian financial crisis. As a result of China's open-door policy, the HK economy has become increasingly integrated with China, leading to Hong Kong's rapid "de-industrialization": the manufacturing share of Hong Kong's gross domestic product declined from 23.7 percent in 1980 to a mere 7.2 percent in 1996. This, in turn, pushed Hong Kong down the path of what he calls "Manhattanization", rendering the HK economy excessively dependent on services, including property speculation and financial sector activities. While such a service economy is easily susceptible to external economic shocks, the Manhattanization process is basically inconsistent with the "one country, two systems" arrangement. According to Tsang, the HK economy needs to maintain some "coherence" in its own structure. He also pays additional attention to the problems caused by the linked exchange rate system (the US dollar "peg"), and critically examines the way the SAR government handled the currency crisis.

Y.C. Jao, a specialist on money and banking, discusses Hong Kong's financial centre in the wake of the Asian financial turmoil.

It is well known that the HK dollar "peg" with the US dollar had suffered two savage attacks by international speculators in October 1997 and in August 1998. The HK Monetary Authority had successfully fended off the attack in both cases, leaving its currency and banking system largely intact. However, Hong Kong's property and stock markets were badly bruised in the process. In fact, during the second attack, the HK government, in a radical departure from its past *laissez-faire* stance had stepped in to intervene directly in the stock market with the Exchange Fund. This move has since become very controversial in Hong Kong; but Jao finds the government intervention technically necessary and morally acceptable. "Criticizing Hong Kong's 'interventions' is like criticizing a victim of an act of robbery ... for trying to defend himself". Jao has also discussed the future prospects of Hong Kong as an international financial centre in the Asia–Pacific region, including potential challenges from Singapore.

Hong Kong owes much of its economic growth and prosperity to the *China factor*. Sung Yun-wing's chapter on Hong Kong's growing economic integration with China is devoted to this important aspect of its economic life. He discusses the origins and development of the growing Hong Kong–Guangdong economic nexus and how it has thrived on the back of powerful economic, geographic and cultural factors. Traditionally as Hong Kong's immediate hinterland, Guangdong benefited much from the relocation of Hong Kong's manufacturing bases across the borders. But shifting comparative advantage has taken place in China's coastal regions over the years. Since the early 1990s, Hong Kong's "economic wing" in China has expanded northward. In response to new opportunities, Hong Kong's trade and investment links have now spread beyond Guangdong to Shanghai, Fujian, Zhejiang, Jiangsu and Shandong. But for the foreseeable future, the HK–Guangdong economic nexus will continue to dominate Hong Kong's economic activities in China. The "HK connection" has enabled Guangdong to develop its export-oriented industrialization successfully, so much so that the Guangdong economy is now also vulnerable to the Asian contagion effect.

There are three chapters on the social changes in Hong Kong. The first, by Wong Siu-lun, begins with the discussion of identity crisis in Hong Kong created by the handover. Needless to say, such a drastic political change as the reversion of Hong Kong's sovereignty to China after 150 years of colonial rule has driven many long-time HK residents into a dilemma leading them to ask questions such as: Who am I? The problem was further complicated by the artificially constructed "one country, two systems" formula, which allows a HK Chinese to become Chinese national overnight, legally, right after the change of flag and, at the same time, retain the practical day-to-day life of a HK resident as in the past. Based on his interviews with 30 HK families, Wong constructs four prototypes of HK identities (which he labels as the loyalist, the local, the waverer and the cosmopolitan) and analyses their complex responses to the reality of transition. Most of those interviewed wanted to emigrate, if possible; and the desire to emigrate is linked with their individual sense of identity. Wong particularly highlights an emerging breed of increasingly cosmopolitan HK Chinese, who, combining "cultural affinity with economic rationality", no longer consider China their home.

While many permanent HK residents have emigrated abroad in anticipation of the 1997 transition, many mainland Chinese have been migrating to Hong Kong over the years, both legally and illegally. However, most mainland immigrants, including those who came in legally, were unable to bring their whole family to settle down in Hong Kong because of the SAR's stringent immigration control. Along with the new phenomenon of HK men marrying mainland wives or keeping mainland mistresses in China, this has resulted in a sharp rise of involuntary separation of families creating a whole host of social problems, such as the dysfunctional family. Kuah Khun Eng analyses these split families, their changing lifestyle and family patterns, and the overall social implications for Hong Kong. She also sheds light on the mainland mistresses, and brings to attention the tribulation and hardship of the children separated from either one or both their parents. The recent Court of Final Appeal ruling, in extending the right of abode to these remaining family members, could put an end to the hardship of these split families, but at a higher social cost to Hong Kong.

Lee Ming-kwan addresses the important issue of what had happened to Hong Kong's rising middle class before and after the handover. In the run-up to the handover, the politics of identity dominated political debate in Hong Kong, with battle-lines clearly drawn between the "pro-China" and the "pro-democracy" (or "pro-Patten") camps. It was the political community, rather than the social classes, that was in conflict. After the handover, while many old social tensions remained, new sites of social conflict emerged. As the political anxiety over the handover subsided with China honouring its word to leave Hong Kong alone, the politics of identity had given way to potential class conflict, which has increasingly become the new battleground for organized labour, business interests and the middle class. As economic recession set in, interclass conflict began to sharpen over the shrinking economic pie. This new development has, in fact, caught the middle class unprepared. Little organized and badly divided, as Lee argues, Hong Kong's middle class seems set to lose out to organized business and organized labour.

The last two chapters are concerned with legal development after the handover. The creation of the SAR as a legal entity was unprecedented in any colonial transition and legal safeguards were thus necessary to ensure its integrity and autonomy. This is also the issue that is vital to Hong Kong's economic survival as a prosperous international financial hub — the situation is closely watched by the international business community as well. In discussing the legal aspects of the SAR's new identity in its first year, Johannes Chan starts with the controversy surrounding the creation of the Provisional Legislative Council and its legality. He emphasizes that while the Basic Law may be the most important legal document for the SAR, it is legally not sufficient to protect its autonomy and integrity as a separate system. From the viewpoint of international law, China as a sovereign power is competent to create whatever authority to govern Hong Kong, pre-handover promises notwithstanding. Fortunately for Hong Kong, Beijing has thus far left it alone. As for the judiciary (which is crucial for the executive-led SAR government), Chan tells us that the courts have acquitted themselves reasonably well, despite a few bad judgements.

The reversion of Hong Kong's sovereignty to China marks the shift of *Grundnorm* (basic norm) of Hong Kong's legal system, which was previously identical to that of Britain and is now to be derived from the Chinese Constitution. In simple terms, the Basic

Law has replaced the English Common Law as the new *Grundnorm* of Hong Kong's legal framework. Albert Chen, in discussing the birth of the SAR's legal system, has gone into the various legal implications of this transition, including the differences in their respective legal traditions. He notes that since the Basic Law also provides for "a high degree of *continuity* for Hong Kong's pre-existing laws and judicial institutions", HK has been able to fulfil the basic conditions for the rule of law after the handover.

Another important issue brought up by Chen refers to the application of the mainland laws to the SAR, which is mainly confined to national defence and foreign affairs, as stated in Annex III of the Basic Law. Accordingly, the "smaller the scope of application of these Annex III laws, the higher is the degree of autonomy of the SAR's legislative system". However, the Standing Committee of the NPC may still add or delete items in the Annex III after consultation with the SAR government. This explains why the recent attempt of the HK Court of Final Appeal to challenge the legislative powers of the NPC in interpreting the Basic Law had created a great hue and cry from Beijing's legal experts.

## NOTES

1. Hong Kong's well-known China commentator, Willy Wo-Lap Lam, declared in Tokyo in November 1996, "If the Hang Seng stock index doesn't rise beyond 15,000 by July 1997, Jiang Zemin will be in trouble". "The prospects for post-1997 HK: The Chinese perspective", *The Nikkei Weekly*, Tokyo, 18 November 1996.

2. Tung's policy address consisted of 156 paragraphs, out of which 37 percent concentrated on housing and education, 21 percent on business policies and IT development, 13 percent on social issues, and 14 percent on the judiciary and public administration. "Building Hong Kong for a New Era", address by the chief executive, Tung Chee-hwa, at the Provisional Legislative Council Meeting on 8 October 1997 Hong Kong SAR government.

3. "The 1999–2000 Budget: Onward with New Strengths", speech by the Financial Secretary, 3 March 1999.

4. "Jobless rate may top 8pc", *Hong Kong Standard,* 16 March 1999.

5. As Chief Secretary Anson Chan recently declared in Legco, "The rule of law to Hong Kong is not a cliché or a slogan. It is the very foundation on which the community has been built." *South China Morning Post,* 12 March 1999.

6. In the Court of Final Appeal of the Hong Kong Special Administrative Region FACV No. 14, 15, 16 of 1998. (Date of judgement: 29 January 1999, Hong Kong).

7. "China says change Hong Kong ruling", *Washington Post*, 13 February 1999.

8. "Judges asked to clarify right abode decision", *South China Morning Post*, 25 February 1999. This at once touched off new controversies as the Court is supposed to have legally performed its function and hence no longer has jurisdiction to re-open or examine its judgement already delivered.

9. "Judges say they never intended to question NPC, *South China Morning Post*, 26 February 1999.

10. "Experts welcome CFA's clarification": NPC describes HK court's statement as "a necessary step", *China Daily*, 1 March 1999.

11. The eligible number of mainlanders could well rise to 3 million within 10 years. *Ming Pao*, Hong Kong, 24 February 1999.

12. Sally Aw Sian, a publishing tycoon of the Sing Tao group, was investigated, along with three of her senior colleagues, for conspiracy to default. But the Secretary for Justice, Elsie Leung, decided not persecute Aw and she explained her decision to the LegCo on 4 February 1999 as follows: "If the group should collapse, its newspapers would be compelled to cease operation. Apart from losing employment, the failure of a well-established important media at that time could send a very bad message to the international community". "Advice was spurned", *South China Morning Post*, 11 March 1999). The case led to the tabling of a no-confidence motion at the LegCo on 11 March 1999. Finally, Tung had to lobby very hard for the motion to be defeated. "Justice Secretary survives vote despite attacks on competence" and "The price of victory", *South China Morning Post*, 12 March 1999.

13. "SAR 'moving from capitalism to socialism'", *South China Morning Post*, 24 December 1998; "Business chiefs join attack", ibid., 24 December 1998; "Tien warns against populism", *Hong Kong Standard*, 9 January 1999; and "Hong Kong's politics worry tycoons", *Washington Post* , 7 February 1999.

14. "Democrats at the crossroads", *South China Morning Post*, 30 December 1998. Also, "Parties weakened by waning public trust", *South China Morning Post*, 5 January 1999.

15. *Asian Intelligence*, Hong Kong, no. 530, 10 March 1999, p. 3.

16. "The cost of living, worldwide", *Asiaweek*, 10 July 1998.

17. "From Adversity to Opportunity", address by the chief executive, Tung Chee-hwa, at the Legislative Council Meeting, October 1998.

18. "The 1999–2000 Budget: Onward with New Strengths", speech by the financial secretary, Donald Tsang, 3 March 1999, Hong Kong. The cyberport received a strong boost from Bill Gates of Microsoft, who signed a joint deal with HongKong Telecom to allow HK computer users access

to the new technology of downloading news, films, music, games and texts at a fast speed. "Tech stocks jump as Gates backs cyberport", *South China Morning Post*, 10 March 1999.

19. See "Premier calls for Shenzhen take-off", *South China Morning Post*, 22 February 1999.

20. Christopher Howe, "The Political Economy of Hong Kong since Reversion to China", JPRI Working Paper No. 52, Japan Policy Research Institute, Tokyo, December 1998, p. 8.

21. E.g. The American National Democratic Institute is watching closely to see if Hong Kong's democracy is retreating; the American Heritage Foundation is watching if Hong Kong's *laissez-faire* economy is slipping; and the International Commission of Jurists is watching if Hong Kong's legal integrity has suffered. And there are also various human rights groups looking for signs of abuses. Suffice it to say that all these international interest groups have their own agendas, which may not correspond with the majority interest of the Hong Kong people. The case in point is the recent Court of Final Appeals ruling on the right of abode. See Paul Ye Guohua, "Breaking out from the old fences for a new era", *Lianhe Zaobao*, Singapore, 28 February 1999.

22. See, e.g. Bretigne Shaffer, "Hong Kong's Quest for Accountability", *Asian Wall Street Journal*, 22 September 1998.

23. Shortly after the 1999 Budget, the SAR government released a consultancy document entitled "Civil Service into the 21st Century", to prepare public opinion for revamping the civil service of 180,000. But the task will not be easy as the fundamental question concerning the political role of top civil servants has not been resolved. See, e.g. "Civil service reform lauded", *Hong Kong Standard*, 13 March 1999.

24. "Tung's New Year vote of confidence", *Hong Kong Standard*, 18 February 1999.

25. "Tung well-placed to garner trust for civil-service reform", *Hong Kong Standard*, 10 March 1999. This is certainly an effective way to bring about "social integration".

CHAPTER 2

## IS THE "ONE COUNTRY, TWO SYSTEMS" FORMULA WORKING?

Kuan Hsin-chi

## Introduction

How do we assess if the formula "one country, two systems" is working? A convenient way is to start with the benchmark set by the former governor, Chris Patten, who proposed, in his last policy address in October 1996, 16 criteria for judging the implementation of "one country, two systems." One year after the handover, Jonathan Braude, a journalist for *South China Morning Post* evaluated the formula on the basis of Patten's benchmark.[1] The results (for details, see Appendix) are quite positive, except for the performance of the Provisional Legislative Council and the exclusion and marginalization of democratic politicians. There are also other kinds of assessment, including a few critical ones.[2]

This chapter aims to offer a more comprehensive and longer-term view of the issues involved. Unlike many other contributions of the kind, this one does not dwell so much on the analysis of events. Instead, this chapter takes an institutional view in order to demonstrate how the formula of "one country, two systems" is being institutionalized as norms for conduct of behaviour. No attempt is made here to analyse why "one country, two systems" has succeeded so far. The chapter will also discuss the issue of "preservation" and "autonomy" *vis-à-vis* integration, moving from the "two systems" to the "one country". The discussion here is necessarily limited, with an emphasis on the cultural sense of the matter.

## The Conceptual Essence of "One Country, Two Systems"

The idea of "one country, two systems" was first developed as a proposal to solve the problem of national unification with Taiwan. It turned out that Hong Kong instead became the first test case for its workability. The test can begin with the concept itself. As enunciated in speeches of top leaders in China, the concept of "one country, two systems" is both straightforward and ambiguous. It is straightforward in that it allows the co-existence within a unitary state of two different systems, one socialist and the other capitalist. Such an allowance is supposed to alleviate the fears of many people that the Hong Kong ways of life would be destroyed once China resumes her sovereignty over the territory. The ambiguities, however, work in the other direction. First, the co-existence of the two systems is wrapped in the asymmetry of political power. The weaker power has to live under the constant fear of intervention by the stronger one. In terms of institutional norms, the powers enjoyed by Hong Kong Special Administrative Region (HKSAR) are derived by delegation of the central government. The region has no residual power. In addition, there is no institutional arrangement for the resolution of conflicts between the two systems, such as a constitutional court, in which the region is represented on an equal footing as the other system. Justice has to depend on the self-restraint or pleasure of the bigger power. Second, there is a tension between diversity as represented by the two different systems and unity as required by the "one country". Would there be a day when "one country"

24

requires some kind of standardization at the expense of diversity between the "two systems"? Thirdly, there is a time factor in the applicability of "one country, two systems", i.e. the guarantee of "no change" is confined to 50 years only. This time frame has been written in the Basic Law for the HKSAR (Art. 5). On the one hand, it conveys a seemingly certain commitment of the Chinese central government not to impose the socialist system on Hong Kong. On the other hand, the specification of a time frame necessarily invokes a sense of uncertainty for the future. To our relief, 50 years may be a period long enough to eschew any kind of forecasts. One implication of these conceptual ambiguities may be that "one country, two systems" defies any easy institutionalization.

There is another way of understanding the concept of "one country, two systems". This is to read it in the light of the history of the Hong Kong policy of the Beijing government. This policy can be summed up by the dictum of "consider the long term, while fully [utilizing Hong Kong]". This policy consistently withstood the urge to settle accounts with the colonial power, the mocking by the Soviet Union, and the nationalist excesses of the Great Cultural Revolution. It could be expected to last longer were there no expiry date to the lease of the New Territories in 1997. Seen in this light, the formula of "one country, two systems" is an ingenious tool to meet the historic necessity of taking over Hong Kong in 1997 while retaining the utility of Hong Kong to keep pace with the modernization efforts of China. In one word, the essence of "one country, two systems" is pragmatism.

There are two risks inherent in this pragmatism. For one thing, pragmatism smacks of political convenience. It is the motivation and will of the top leaders that matter, not institutional norms or other principles. For another, the pragmatism of "one country, two systems" may be faulted for its ideological deviation from socialism, thus subjecting it to the exigencies of politics on the Chinese Mainland. Hence, its strength can only be vindicated in its practice. This is tantamount to saying that "one country, two systems" works so long as the government in Beijing remains pragmatic in the context of the decline of socialism. The record is, as everybody can see, so far so good.

# The Legal Parameters of "One Country, Two Systems"

If the conceptual analysis of the idea of "one country, two systems" suggests the risk of political convenience, a legal analysis should provide some assurance that there is something more reliable in this proposed system. What is the Basic Law for the HKSAR proposing to achieve when it translates "one country, two systems" into constitutional arrangements?

There are two major objectives pursued by the Basic Law: to preserve the existing systems in Hong Kong and to guarantee a high degree of autonomy for the HKSAR. Should the two objectives come into conflict under certain circumstances, the Basic Law grants the preservation of the existing systems the higher priority over the guarantee of autonomy. Indeed, in the process of drafting the Basic Law, the large area of autonomy demanded was often justified by the need for Hong Kong to preserve its complex capitalist system.

In order to assure the people of Hong Kong that their way of life would not be affected by the handover, the Basic Law set out to preserve the existing socio-economic systems. The assurance is two-fold. While the Basic Law prescribes that the socialist system will not be practised in Hong Kong, a number of provisions specify that "previous systems" of economy, law, civil service and principles of public policies should be retained. These existing systems and established policy principles are seen in the Basic Law largely in economic terms, with all serving to preserve the capitalist system.

However, there are certain provisions within the Basic Law which give cause for concern. The prescription of "previous systems" and related provisions is a legal injunction, which will curtail the autonomy of the HKSAR when dealing with the necessary changes. There is also another important implication: the central government of China has the legitimate right to intervene should the HKSAR violate the Basic Law requirement of preserving the previous systems. The Beijing government did exercise such a right in connection with the establishment of the Provisional Legislative Council.

The autonomy enjoyed by the HKSAR under the Basic Law is both substantial and restricted. While the HKSAR has more powers than many autonomous regions or federal units, the exercise of these powers is subject to closer scrutiny and supervision than powers elsewhere.[3] All autonomous powers of the HKSAR are allocated by means of delegation. And, there are specific provisions governing the ways these powers are exercised. The central government has, therefore, the right to supervise and enforce the Basic Law-imposed restrictions on regional autonomy.

In the light of the above, the Basic Law offers two yardsticks for judging the success of the "one country, two systems": whether Hong Kong has been able to maintain its old systems and whether it has been able to retain its autonomy in the management of its affairs, without unlawful intervention from the central authorities. The analysis of the Basic Law has highlighted the fact that in the minds of the drafters of the Basic Law and probably also the government in Beijing, the preservation of the capitalist system is more important than the granting of a high degree of autonomy to the HKSAR. If given the choice, the people of Hong Kong would have probably wished that autonomy is given higher priority, so that the freedom to maintain or to change whatever systems that serve Hong Kong best is retained by the HKSAR.

## The Preservation of Systems

The exact meaning of "previous" or "existing" systems in the Basic Law or in the common understanding of the formula of "one country, two systems" is never clarified. Do they refer to the systems in 1984 when the Chinese and the British government signed the Joint Declaration, to the systems on the eve of the handover in 1997, or to something else? Uncertainty in the answer allows different interpretations of the extent to which the formula of "one country, two systems" has worked. All systems in Hong Kong have been changing, especially since the early 1980s. Yet, there is in the Basic Law a hierarchy of systems to be preserved where the economic system of capitalism is paramount. If we then submit that capitalism is deemed to have been preserved, so long

27

as its core values such as property rights and the principle of free market have not been abandoned even if other peripheral aspects have changed, "one country, two systems" has indeed survived without flying colours.

There is some concern that the style of governance has changed. Compared with the previous colonial administration, the government under Tung Chee-hwa has become more interventionist and planning-prone. Critics may say that socialism has crept in through the backdoor and even the language used sounds similar to that used in Beijing. The most pertinent indicators are the enforcement of the target of 85,000 housing units per year and the government's intervention in the stock market. These policies are admittedly controversial, however, the system implications of these policies are far from obvious.

In the short span of one year after the handover, there has been no occasion where the value of preservation clashes with that of autonomy, thereby subjecting the relationship between Beijing and Hong Kong to an acid test. The case of the government's intervention in the stock market does reveal a potential conflict between preserving the existing currency board system and having the power to change it. The intervention has been justified by the need to defend the currency board system whereby the Hong Kong dollar is pegged to the US dollar. In the discussion on alternative solutions, it was noted that the option of using the US dollar as the local currency in place of the Hong Kong dollar may be in violation of the Basic Law. Here, we seem to have a case in which the freedom of the HKSAR government may be restricted by a provision in the Basic Law. However, the case should not be exaggerated since, apart from the possibility of interpreting the relevant provision in the Basic Law differently, the core values of the capitalist system are not affected.

## Autonomy and Institutional Boundaries

Efforts have been made to maintain the boundaries between the two systems when new organizations were established or old ones restructured. To design boundary rules is an integral part of the process of institutionalizing "one country, two systems." At least three offices are involved: the Hong Kong Branch of the New China News Agency (HKNCNA), the Commission of the Foreign Affairs Ministry in Hong Kong (CFAMHK) and the Hong Kong and Macao Office (HKMAO). How they define and perform their role *vis-à-vis* the HKSAR certainly has important bearings on the region's autonomy. It is apparent that the authorities concerned have been very judicious in their words and actions so as not to create any suspicion of an interventionist attempt.

The objectives of the CFAMHK are well defined: to manage those foreign affairs related to the HKSAR; to assist the region in its autonomous external relations and to carry out any other instructions by the central government and the Ministry of Foreign Affairs. In his work, the Commissioner of the Ministry of Foreign Affairs in HK seems the most liberal, open-minded and pragmatic among mainland Chinese officials in Hong Kong. When he assumed duty, he promptly announced four working principles, which were well received.[4] Pragmatism is further reflected in a few decisions. For instance, expatriate officials from the HKSAR government were allowed to participate in international organizations as members of the Chinese delegation. Another example is the willingness to present the report on the human rights situation in Hong Kong on behalf of the HKSAR government, although China is not a signatory to the international covenants concerned. The commissioner commented publicly that he would not intervene in the issue of the "national" flag of Taiwan, or in the May elections to the Legislative Council. There is a press report that the commissioner refrained from making decisions whether dignitaries from foreign countries might visit the region and in what manner, referring to this as matters within the jurisdiction of the region. All in all, the CFAMHK was able to quickly establish a credible image in the region against the original fear of a second centre of power.

The record for the HKMAO is not bad either. The office had redefined its post-handover roles much earlier as one of a gatekeeper, a coordinator and a service provider. Later on, after Liao Hui took over the directorship, a policy of "three No's" were announced.[5] The HKMAO has, indeed, done a lot to propagate the Basic Law in the Mainland, such as assuaging critiques against special treatments meted out to the HKSAR, and restraining ministries, bureaus or local governments from arbitrarily setting up offices in Hong Kong. Yet, the gatekeeper role is double-edged. On the positive side, it serves to insulate the region against potential interference from mainland Chinese organs. On the negative side, the freedom of the HKSAR government to deal directly with those organs is restricted. It is because of the bridging role of the HKMAO that the establishment of the Liaison Office of the HKSAR in Beijing had to be delayed.

The HKNCNA did not start with a clean record. It had to shed the legacy of being the second centre of power in Hong Kong before the handover. Its downsizing and restructuring gave some comfort to the people of Hong Kong. The change of the director from Zhou Nan to Jiang Enchu also helped. The HKNCNA's roles were redefined as follows. First, to promote mutual trust and understanding between the people of Hong Kong and those on the Mainland. Second, to strengthen communication and exchange between Hong Kong and the Mainland. Third, to support the work of the HKSAR government while refraining from interfering with its autonomous affairs. With these objectives in mind, the HKNCNA has now a very low profile compared with the period before 1997. Unlike in the elections of 1991 and 1994, there was no attempt to coordinate cooperation among the leftist political forces in the elections of May 1998. United front work, however, continues unabated. The HKNCNA seems quite active in promoting pro-China associational life. It is also noticeable that all pro-China press has supported the policies of the HKSAR government unconditionally, probably under the instructions of the HKNCNA. All these activities can hardly be labelled as intervention in the region's affairs.

To complete our discussion of delineating institutional boundaries, we need to mention three very important institutions: the National People's Congress of China (NPC) and the Chinese Communist Party (CCP or the Party) and the People's Liberation Army (PLA).

Hong Kong delegates attend the NPC. Their role after 1997, however, has been a subject of concern. In representing the interests of the people of Hong Kong, they have yet to resolve the extent to which they can get involved in any matters that may involve the autonomy of the HKSAR. A process of soul-searching and learning already began before the handover. The first issue was whether the Hong Kong delegates should establish an office in Hong Kong to provide logistic support and to receive enquiries and complaints from the local residents. After a long struggle, it was decided not to establish any office. The next major issue centred on Xu Simin's attack against the Radio Television Hong Kong in early March 1998. The event which will be analysed in the next section contributes to an immediate clarification by top Chinese leaders of the role of the Hong Kong delegates in both the NPC and the Chinese People's Political Consultative Congress. (See the section on "The Exercise of Autonomy: Other Sectors".) The role of the delegates is confined to participation in national affairs; they have no powers whatsoever with respect to any Hong Kong affairs. In addition, more concrete rules to back up the principle of non-intervention in the autonomous affairs of the HKSAR were developed in subsequent months. These rules include, for instance, the exclusion of the HKSAR government from the inspection of the NPC delegates and the non-transferability of citizens' complaints against the HKSAR government.

The last difficult subject refers to the role of the underground CCP in Hong Kong. Little is known about its activities, although it is safe to speculate that it has grown in membership and remained active in organizing and developing pro-China forces in the region. It would not have crossed people's minds had it not been the elections of the Hong Kong delegates to the National People's Congress. In defiance of the public opinion in Hong Kong, Jiang Enzhu contested and won a seat in the organ of the highest power in the People's Republic of China (PRC). He even became the chairman of the Hong Kong delegation. The event vividly reminded the people of Hong Kong that under the principle of the leadership of the Party, it is as natural in the region as in the Mainland that Hong Kong should be represented in the NPC by the secretary of the local branch of the Party. The suspicion is thus sustained that there is an invisible hand directing the HKSAR government in the management of the affairs of the region.

The stationing of the PLA in Hong Kong was controversial. For the central government, it is an expression of Chinese sovereignty. For the people of Hong Kong, it reminds them of the Tiananmen incident in 1989. From the very beginning, therefore, the PLA adopted a very low profile. There was no occasion when its services were called for. As time went on, it began to participate in social life and even staged an open day to improve its image.

## The Exercise of Autonomy by the HKSAR Government

The ideal test for a region exercising autonomy can be seen in the following scenario: in a situation where there is an apparent conflict of interest or preference between the regional government and the central authority, the will of the region ultimately prevails. This author is unaware of any such case to date.

Looking at it objectively, the HKSAR can still be regarded as having a fair amount of autonomy when it gets what it wants most of the time even though there is no serious conflict of interest involved between the centre and the periphery. A case in point is when the chief executive of the HKSAR, Tung Chee-hwa, was granted the flexibility he wanted in designing the electoral system for the Legislative Council against the dominant preference of the members of the Preparatory Committee for the Establishment of the HKSAR.[6] The case reveals that the central government has an interest in boosting the authority of the new SAR government. This necessarily contributes positively to the maintenance of the region's autonomy.

A third scenario about the extent of autonomy refers to cases where the central government attempted to exert influence indirectly on the HKSAR. Again, no concrete case, if any existed, has come to light. Nevertheless, an interesting event did hint at the existence of indirect influence. When Anson Chan, the chief secretary, returned to Hong Kong from her overseas trip on 17 June 1998, she was asked the following question at the airport:

> Mrs Chan, how do you actually feel about "one country, two systems" in the past year or so? Can you tell us whether in the past year when you made policies related to Hong Kong there are officials from the central authorities or the Mainland

explicitly or implicitly who told you what to do? Or have you sought their views?

She answered as follows:

> There may be hints. But everyone who understands me knows I know my role very well and how I carry out my responsibilities.[7]

The information official, Choi Kit-yu, immediately clarified with Chan and told the reporters that Chan had meant "some Hong Kong people" may have hinted at what she should do, but this did not refer to either the central government or officials from the Mainland. The clarification is significant in its own right. It can, however, also be interpreted as confirming that the central authorities are sensitive enough so as not to directly tell the HKSAR government what to do, but there are local people who can do the job for Beijing, whether on instruction from or by ways of second-guessing Beijing. In the strict sense of the word, the autonomy of HKSAR government is not infringed upon.

As mentioned earlier, the spirit of pragmatism in the "one country, two systems" principle can only be vindicated in its practice. It is, therefore, important that, apart from the legal parameters of the Basic Law and the institutional boundaries analysed in the preceding section, government officials on both sides constantly watch their actions. Seen in this light, "one country, two systems" as a reality is less a legal straitjacket, but rather an equilibrium of interactions between the HKSAR government and the government on the Mainland, in which both sides respect each other's own turf.

## *The Exercise of Autonomy: Other Sectors*

The issue of autonomy goes beyond the freedom of the HKSAR government in managing its own affairs. Other sectors may be affected by the development of "one country, two systems" as well. The first sector of great significance is the press. Is the press in Hong Kong still free? Is there any institutional development in this area? The answers are probably already well known. There is no evidence of direct intervention from Beijing. There were some changes in press ownership which is now in pro-China hands. A few "unfriendly" journalists from Hong Kong were barred from entering China for reporting. All these are minor. The greatest worry is the extent of self-censorship. Articulate critics, such as Emily Lau, has consistently sounded the alarm bell. Yet, according to the annual report of the Hong Kong Journalists' Association, *Questionable Beginnings*, self-censorship was no worse a year after the handover. In fact, the threat of self-censorship or accusation of such seemed to have the opposite effect of making Hong Kong journalists more assertive in their reporting. This is at least true in the eyes of the officials of the HKSAR government.[8] The crux of the issue is that self-censorship applies to news reporting on China, but not on Hong Kong. The HKSAR government has never interfered with the freedom of the press, although it has retrogressed on its path to open government.[9] In terms of institutional development, it has been precisely the sensitivity of the issue of press freedom that has hindered the development of a press council that might entail the enforcement of professional ethics on the press.

An important event may have incidentally contributed to the temporary strengthening of press freedom in Hong Kong. In early March 1998, Xu Simin, a Hong Kong delegate to the Chinese People's Political Consultative Congress (CPPCC), bombarded the Radio Television Hong Kong (RTHK), at a meeting of the CPPCC, for having failed to fulfil its obligation as a government station to support government policies in its programmes. Li Wai-ting, an NPC delegate from Hong Kong, echoed similar sentiments at a meeting of the NPC. He charged that some people in Hong Kong had violated the principle of "one country" by propagating that the anti-China activities tolerated and encouraged under the colonial era could continue after the handover.

Xu's remarks drew an immediate rebuttal from Anson Chan, who pointed out that freedom of the press is respected in Hong Kong and any criticism against the government or government departments should be conducted in Hong Kong, but not on the Mainland. Otherwise, such criticism could be construed as an attempt to invite the Beijing government to intervene in the affairs of the HKSAR. Chan's views were widely shared by the general public and the opinion leaders. Polls conducted in those days revealed that the majority of the respondents supported the editorial independence of the RTHK and regarded Xu's remarks in Beijing as having adversely affected the confidence in press freedom in Hong Kong as well as in the "one country, two systems".

The handling of the event by the central government is laudable. On three consecutive days, top leaders came out in public to reiterate the Beijing government's determination to maintain the "one country, two systems", to warn Hong Kong delegates to the NPC and CPPCC not to meddle in the affairs of the HKSAR. Li Ruihuan, Chairman of the CPPCC, clarified that under the principle of "one country, two systems", the Hong Kong delegates have no right to exercise power of the CPPCC in Hong Kong. According to him, CPPCC is a structure that belongs to the Mainland's socialist system. Hong Kong is under another system where the CPPCC does not have a role. It is, therefore, inappropriate for Hong Kong delegates to talk much about Hong Kong at the CPPCC. Jiang Zemin also commented that Hong Kong delegates to the NPC only represent the compatriots of Hong Kong as participants in the management of national affairs, they should not interfere with any matter pertaining to the HKSAR government.

The effect of the event on press freedom is positive, at least for the time being. The swift reaction of the public against the danger to press freedom and the resolute defence of the RTHK by Anson Chan have restrained those forces in the government who do share Xu's views that the RTHK, as a publicly funded organization, should submit to the government. From now on, those critics of the RTHK have to think of other means to bring the station into line. The tenure of the director of the RTHK seems less threatened precisely because of the event. It is expected that a review of the station may be called for in the near future. The RTHK itself developed a set of more elaborate guidelines, along those lines used by the BBC, for its programming as a self-imposed means to ensure political neutrality. Those guidelines have been adopted by other media organizations. All in all, the event has indirectly contributed to the institutional development of the mass media in Hong Kong towards more professionalism.

The role of the judiciary in Hong Kong in upholding the autonomy of the region is another important issue in the framework of "one country, two systems". Two court cases and a piece of legislation in the year reveal the difficulty in maintaining the autonomy of Hong Kong in cases where the Mainland and the region interact with each other.[10]

The first court case, HKSAR v. David Ma Wai Kwan & Others, arose from a common law offence of conspiracy to pervert the course of public justice. The charge was made in 1995 but carried into the post-handover year. The respondents argued among others that the Provisional Legislative Council had no legal basis, and that the offence was no longer part of the law of the HKSAR since there had been no formal act of adoption by the NPC or its Standing Committee. In its judgement, the court of appeal concluded that the HKSAR courts had no power to question the validity of decisions made by the NPC. The reason given is that the NPC is sovereign and it is not permissible for a regional court to challenge the acts of the sovereign. An analogy was drawn between the NPC and the British parliament, whose decisions could not be challenged by the colonial courts in Hong Kong before 1997. The Hong Kong courts is said to have inherited the same restriction on their jurisdiction by virtue of Article 19 of the Basic Law.[11] The implication of this ruling amounts to the establishment of a new and potentially indeterminate source of law, beyond the prescription of the Basic Law. The judgement has aroused grave concerns among legal scholars in the region.[12] Legal scholars, however, regard the analogy made by the judge as wrong for several reasons.[13] For the purpose of this chapter, the implication of the case lies in the timidity of the courts in Hong Kong in exercising their judicial powers, thereby undermining the high degree of autonomy promised to the region.

Another court case, Cheung Lai Wah (an infant) & ORS v. Director of Immigration, has cast doubt on the exercise of rights as enshrined in the Basic Law but the restriction of the autonomy of the region is not unconstitutional. The case concerns the right of abode of children of Hong Kong residents who were born in mainland China and had been arrested for entering or staying in Hong Kong illegally. The crux of the problem involves the interpretation of both Article 24(3) of the Basic Law that confers on those illegal immigrant children the right of abode in Hong Kong, Article 22(4) that requires people from other parts of China to apply for entry into the HKSAR, and the Immigration Amendment (3) Ordinance passed by the Provisional Legislative Council that requires proof of the status of permanent residence and the certificate of entitlement. The legal issues involve among others the legality of the Provisional Legislative Council, and the constitutionality of the No. 3 Ordinance. The political issue pertains to leaving the exercise of a basic right in the hands of the mainland authorities that control the quota system governing the exit of Chinese nationals into the HKSAR. The illegal immigrant children lost their case both in the first instance and in the appeal. The respective judges concluded on both occasions that Article 24(3) must be construed in the light of Article 22(4) and that the latter qualifies the former, and therefore the No. 3 Ordinance is not incompatible with the Basic Law. It is a limitation on the autonomy of the HKSAR, nonetheless, but it is lawful.[14]

The legislation that touches the boundary between the two systems under the scheme of "one country, two systems" is the Adaptation of Laws (Interpretative Provisions) Ordinance. It seeks to change colonial definitions in all the laws of Hong Kong, substituting terms such as the "the Crown" with "the State". The Ordinance prescribes that no law in Hong Kong shall in any manner whatsoever affect the right of or be binding on the State unless it is therein expressly provided or unless it appears by necessary implication that the State is bound thereby. The Ordinance defines "State" as the HKSAR government and the central authorities of China or their subordinate organs. It attracted attention only after the public learned that HKNCNA is one of those subordinate organs exempted from the laws of Hong Kong. It so happened that HKNCNA had broken the Personal Data (Privacy) Ordinance before the promulgation of the Adaptation of Law (Interpretative Provisions) Ordinance by not responding within 40 days to the request of a member of the Legislative Council, Emily Lau, made in December 1996 to reveal the files HKNCNA held on her. HKNCNA replied to Lau a year later that it held no files on her. The Privacy Commissioner conducted an investigation confirming the breach of the law and passed the case to the Department of Justice for possible prosecution. HKNCNA was not prosecuted because the offence was, according to Tung Chee-hwa, "a technical breach, not a substantive breach". The legislation reveals that what began as straightforward and technical amendments turned out to be issues of fundamental consequences for the relations between the central government and the region. The government argued that the new law merely puts it beyond doubt that Hong Kong laws do not apply to state organs in the way it would not have applied to British government bodies before 1997. Legal scholars, however, regarded the government's position as operating on "the mistaken assumption that Hong Kong is a colony of China".[15]

# The Issue of Integration

The concept of "one country, two systems" goes beyond the preservation of the two different systems and the exercise of autonomy. The idea is to accommodate "diversity" in "unity". Therefore, while our attention is necessarily focused on the most urgent issue of maintaining the boundary between the two systems, the final test lies in how successful the problem of "suspended" unity is to be solved. It is a long-term issue of full integration[16] preceded by increasing interactions between the two systems on all fronts. The issue is not just the coexistence of the two systems, but how much each is valued and respected by the other and how both "partial" systems contribute to the emergence of the new "whole" in future, to which people in both systems feel a sense of belonging. In other words, it is about the evolution of common institutions and identity.[17] This is no easy task and any judgement today is surely premature. The experience of German reunification may offer some hints for the development of "one country, two systems" in China. It has been 10 years since the Wall of Berlin was taken down, but West and East Germany still exist in the socio-economic, and especially cultural sense. The imposition of a single political framework cannot ensure a full integration of the Germans in the two parts of the country which had been politically divided and had experienced divergent socio-economic development for four decades (1949–89). (See Wong Siu-lun, Chapter 8, on the subjective identities of the people of Hong Kong which remain as complex and diverse as ever, with the handover in 1997, and show no signs of rupture or conversion.)

The building of common institutions to promote integration has barely started. To the extent that they existed at all, such as the Hong Kong Mainland Major Infrastructure Co-ordinating Project Committee, all mechanisms are geographically confined to the promotion of cooperation between Hong Kong and Guangdong. Even in this limited area, entrenched interests and mutual mistrust has held up progress. It seems that in the case of Hong Kong—Mainland integration, institutional development requires prior changes in attitudes.

Attitudes do not change simply because of increasing interactions. They have actually given rise to ideologies unfavourable to the cause of integration. Among the people of Hong Kong, there exist two major, competing ideologies: "northbound colonialism" and "encroachment from the north". "Northbound colonialism" denotes the chauvinist ideology of the people of Hong Kong in terms of a sense of superiority grounded in economic success and a sense of mission to lead their fellow countrymen in the Mainland to modernization. The ideology has been promoted primarily through songs, movies and novels.[18] In comparison, the fear of encroachment by the north is a more recent phenomenon. It refers to a concern that after the reunification of Hong Kong with China in 1997, the demand for nationalist education and other pressures will promote "the culture of the central plateau" at the expense of the local, vernacular culture. The distribution of these attitudes among the Hong Kong population has not been subject to any systematic research. As far as impression goes, industrial and commercial entrepreneurs are interested in colonizing the Mainland, while intellectuals are concerned about the imperial intentions of the mainlanders.[19] As the above discussion is confined to Hong Kong's own image of "integration", it would be interesting to ascertain the corresponding image of the mainland Chinese.

# Conclusion

To recapitulate, the concept of "one country, two systems" is ambiguous, but what counts is its spirit of pragmatism. In terms of the law, the principle of "one country, two systems" becomes more concrete but is still not free of contradictions. From the perspective of this chapter, the principal contradiction pertains to the relationship between the preservation of the "previous systems" in Hong Kong and the granting of a high degree of autonomy to the HKSAR. When in conflict, the law makes sure that the first objective prevails. In terms of political practice, the Chinese government should be commended for its efforts to refrain from interfering with the work of the HKSAR government or from any actions that may create any misunderstanding of intervention. Minor defects abound, such as the rubber-stamp image and the conservative legislation of the Provisional Legislative Council, the timid attitude of the Hong Kong courts in using their power of judicial review, and the lingering self-censuring of the press against the principle of "one country, two systems". Yet, the overall picture must be judged to be satisfactory.[20] Short-term satisfaction has not buried long-term worries. It is a matter of whether the good start will stay and whether a full integration of the two diverse systems as a new entity under one country can ever succeed.

A critic may argue that the satisfactory landscape may prove illusory and the crackdown may come one or two more years later as it happened in Shanghai after 1949. The implication is that we must wait longer before we are certain that Hong Kong has successfully retained its autonomy. However, what is clear is that Hong Kong today is not Shanghai yesterday. For one thing, in the early 1950s, China was experiencing a revolution. Right now, she is undergoing reforms and seeking entry into the world capitalist system. For another, China's stake in Hong Kong responding successfully to its modernization efforts seems larger than that of Shanghai in 1949. Does Hong Kong not deserve a better fate?

A more subtle argument may pitch informal influence against formal intervention. The Beijing government has not intervened in the internal affairs on Hong Kong primarily because it has put firmly into place people it can trust.[21] It can also expect its informal influence to increase in time when mainland-based firms control the local economy, when pro-China tycoons own most of the mass media, and the increasing number of new immigrants from China changes the demographic structure of the Hong Kong population. Therefore, the Beijing government can afford to be patient.

However, it is difficult to take on this kind of argument. There is evidence that the Beijing government does take a patient, long-term view of its Hong Kong policy,[22] working through local "patriotic" forces it has tried to groom for local leadership in preference to blatant intervention. But so what? We are talking about an open-ended context of intensifying interaction between Hong Kong and the Mainland in many fields. There are many ways in which political influence can be exercised given the possibilities of mutual influence, i.e. Carl Friedrich's rule of anticipated reaction. It is often difficult to say who really influences whom and how in complex situations. Therefore, in the final analysis, it boils down to what one stands for in a subtle power struggle and whose influence stays. There should be no regret, if, in a peaceful evolution, the values of one system prevail over those of the other system.

This should not be regarded as an invitation to complacency. In the context of no blatant, obvious intervention, the risks come from within. The questions are then whether those risks are exposed and values that are treasured have been reaffirmed. In fact, they are, as alluded to earlier. When Xu Simin attacked the RTHK, public opinion in Hong Kong reacted strongly. When Tung Chee-hwa over-committed himself to the cause of "one country", there were warnings to remind him of the requirements of the "two systems".[23] On the whole, it seems that the society still has the critical ability to stand for the values that Hong Kong represents.[24] Therefore, there is still hope.

## Notes

1.  Jonathan Braude, "Pass for Pattens' Benchmark Test," *South China Morning Post*, 30 June 1998.

2.  See, for instance, Jean Philippe Beja, "Hong Kong Politics One Year On: Worst Case Scenario Fails to Materialise," *China Perspective*, no. 18 (July/ August, 1998), pp. 6–11.

3. The above analysis is based on Yash Ghai, *Hong Kong's New Constitutional Order, The Resumption of Chinese Sovereignty and the Basic Law,* Hong Kong: Hong Kong University Press, 1997.

4. The four principles are mutual support, mutual respect, mutual trust and close cooperation.

5. They are "don't criticize the HKSAR officials", "don't criticize any HKSAR policies", and "don't harp on the bureaucratic links between HKMAO and the HKSAR".

6. Lau Siu-kai, "The Making of the Electoral System for the 1998 Legislative Council Elections," a paper presented to the conference on "The 1998 Legislative Council Elections" on 24 September 1998, organized by Hong Kong Institute of Asia-Pacific Studies, The Chinese University of Hong Kong.

7. *Ming Pao,* 18 June 1998, p. A8; also in *Hong Kong Economic Journal,* 18 June 1998, p. 7.

8. Chris Yeung, "Tung's Attitude Problem", *South China Morning Post,* 25 January 1998.

9. See the reported findings of the survey of journalists on the issue in the *Ming Pao* or *Hong Kong Economic Journal,* on 9 February 1998. See also the joint annual report by the Hong Kong Journalist Association and the 19th Article, as reported in *Economic Daily,* 29 June 1998.

10. This chapter is concerned with the behavioural practice of the courts only. For a general analysis of the judiciary, see the chapter by Johannes Chan in this volume.

11. Article 19 states that "the restrictions on their jurisdiction imposed by the legal system and principles previously in force in Hong Kong shall be maintained."

12. See for example, Yash Ghai, "Dark Day for our Right", *South China Morning Post,* 30 July 1997.

13. First, the Basic Law is a written constitution that has listed all sources of law for Hong Kong and decisions of the NPC do not constitute one of them. Second, the doctrine of parliamentary supremacy is a specific doctrine of the United Kingdom and is not applicable to the HKSAR. Third, the doctrine of judiciability of parliamentary acts does allow the regional or local courts to review the constitutionality of acts of the national legislature. The *Hong Kong Law Journal* devotes a special issue on the case, i.e. vol. 27, part 3, 1997, pp. 374–404. The above and other arguments can be found there.

14. Gerard McCoy QC, *Hong Kong Cases,* 1998 Part 6 (30 March 1998), Hong Kong: Butterworths Asia, 1998, p. 638.

15. Yash Ghai, "False Analogies," *South China Morning Post,* 5 April 1998. Professir Ghai further submitted that the origins of the rule that the government is not bound by the law lie in feudalism. It has no place in a

modern state, which is committed to the rule of law. Instead, the rule should be all laws bind the government unless it is expressly and necessarily exempted from it. In contrast to Yash Ghai, Albert H.Y. Chen, in his chapter in this volume, is more lenient when he argues that since it is a common law tradition for legislation not to bind the Crown, "it would be extremely difficult to justify to the Central Government in Beijing any abolition or curtailment of the presumption as part of an exercise in adaptation of laws or even in law reform."

16. The discussion on integration in this section is limited to the political and cultural aspects. The author is not competent to talk about economic integration. There is a rich literature on increasing interaction and interdependency in economic terms between Hong Kong and the Mainland. Some of the issues involved are addressed in the chapter by Sung Yun Wing in this volume. The author is sceptical of the common claim concerning the high degree of economic integration between Hong Kong and the Mainland, in view of the fact that there has been no common economic institutions, factor mobility across the border, and common policies. In this regard, the new trend of policy coordination mentioned by Sung is a welcome development.

17. Anson Chan is right in saying that the ultimate question for the people of Hong Kong is one of identity.

18. For a perceptive discussion on the basis of the novels by Leung Fung-yee, see Kung Ho-fung, "Preliminary Investigation of Northbound Colonialism," in Chan Ching-kiu (ed.), *Cultural Imagination and Ideology*, Hong Kong: Oxford University Press 1997, pp. 53–88. (In Chinese.)

19. As an example, music commentators were critical of the "Symphony 1997: Heaven, Earth and Man" played as the central piece of the handover concerts on 1 July 1997. The symphony is full of imperial symbols and can be interpreted as sounding a death bell to the Cantonese culture. See Yu Shiu-wah, "The Revitalization of Imperial Symbols in the 1997 Reunion of Hong Kong with China," in *Hong Kong Cultural Studies Bulletin*, no. 8–9 (Spring/Summer 1998), pp. 84–91. It may be added that the decision of not using Cantonese at all at the handover ceremony also evoked some ill feelings among the general public in Hong Kong.

20. The general public in Hong Kong finds the working of "one country, two systems" satisfactory too. According to a survey conducted in July 1998, 74 percent of the respondents reported "satisfied" to the question "Are you currently satisfied or dissatisfied with the performance of the PRC government in dealing with Hong Kong affairs?", whereas 11 percent said "dissatisfied" and 15 percent "don't know". This indeed compares very favourably with 45 percent, 41 percent and 15 percent respectively, recorded in June 1997. Statistics provided by the "Hong Kong Transition Project", as reported in Michael E. DeGolyer, "Public Opinion and Participation in the 1998 Legco Elections: Pre/Post Colonial Comparisons," paper presented to the Conference on the 1998 Legislative Council

Elections, organized by Hong Kong Institute of Asia–Pacific Studies, The Chinese University of Hong Kong, on 24 September 1998, Table 1, p. 7. In another survey conducted in January 1998, it was found that 51.8 percent of the interviewees were "optimistic" or "very optimistic" with the prospect for "one country, two systems", against 25.8 percent who were "pessimistic" or "very pessimistic". See Wong Ka-ying (Timothy), *Exchanges and Interactions among the Three Areas across the Taiwan Straits: Tendencies of Popular Attitudes in Hong Kong*, Hong Kong: Research Centre on Relations among the Three Areas across the Taiwan Straits, Research Monograph no. 1, 1998, p. 9. (In Chinese.)

21. See the chapter by Lau Siu-kai in this volume on how Beijing took pains to set up new institutions with the explicit purpose of fostering the rise of pro-China leaders before 1997. In Lau's judgement, the central government has not succeeded in the grooming of political collaborators in the transitional period.

22. See for example Lu Ping, "On the Problem of Reunion of Hong Kong with China," in Selected Reports of The Central Party School, no. 122, issue 6 of 1998 (6 October 1997), pp. 2–17. (In Chinese.) On the Hong Kong policy of the Chinese government, consult Kevin P. Lane, *Sovereignty and The Status Quo: The Historical Roots of China's Hong Kong Policy*, Boulder: Westview Press, 1990, and Lau Siu-kai, "The Hong Kong Policy of the People's Republic of China, 1949–1997," *Journal of Contemporary China*, vol. 9, no. 23 (March 2000) forthcoming.

23. See for instance, Danny Gittings, "The Danger in Tung's Hard Line," *South China Morning Post*, 30 November 1997.

24. This is despite the many allegations of press censorship, officials second-guessing Beijing, businessmen courting the favour of Mainland cadres, and so forth.

# Appendix

# How do the Patten benchmarks rate?

The questions                                (Marks out of 100)

---

1.  Is the civil service still professional and meritocratic? Are its key positions filled by individuals who command the confidence of their colleagues and owe their appointments only to their abilities?

    ( 80%)

2.  Is the SAR Government writing its own budget, or is it under pressure to respond to Beijing's objectives?          (100%)

3.  Is the Monetary Authority managing the Exchange Fund without outside interference?          (100%)

4.  Is Hong Kong behaving in a truly autonomous way in international economic organisations?          (80%)

5.  Is the legislature passing laws in response to the aspirations of the community and the policies of the Government, or is it under pressure from Beijing?          (50%)

6.  Are the courts continuing to operate without interference?

    ( 90%)

7.  Is the Independent Commission Against Corruption continuing to act vigorously against all forms of corruption, including cases in which China's interests may be involved?          (80%)

8.  Is Hong Kong continuing to maintain its own network of international law enforcement liaison relationships?          (100%)

9. Is the integrity of the Hong Kong/Guangdong border being maintained? (80%)

10. Is the Hong Kong press still free, with uninhibited coverage of China and of issues on which China has strong views?

(70%)

11. Are new constraints being imposed on freedom of assembly? Are the annual commemorations and vigils of recent years still allowed?

(80%)

12. Are foreign journalists and media organisations in Hong Kong still free to operate without controls? (100%)

13. Is anybody being prosecuted or harassed for the peaceful expression of political, social or religious views? (90%)

14. Are Hong Kong's legislators, at successive stages of the transition, fairly and openly elected, and truly representative of the community? (20%)

15. Are democratic politicians continuing to play an active role in politics, or are they being excluded or marginalised by external pressure? (50%)

16. Is the Chief Executive of the Special Administrative Region exercising genuine autonomy in the areas provided for in the Joint Declaration and Basic Law? (80%)

CHAPTER 3

# FROM ELITE UNITY TO DISUNITY: POLITICAL ELITE IN POST-1997 HONG KONG

*Lau Siu-kai*

As far as the character of Hong Kong's post-1997 political elite is concerned, the unique manner the former British colony becomes decolonized has played a predominant role in its formation. The rare process of "decolonization without independence" that took place in Hong Kong had produced a fragmented layer of political elite with limited mass support. The first year of the Hong Kong Special Administrative Region (HKSAR) — which came into existence on 1 July 1997 — had seen even further elite fragmentation and discord. Growing elite fragmentation was the breeding ground of intense conflicts within the elite. In turn, it spawned increasing political cynicism, political disillusionment and public mistrust of political authorities in society. By the time the first anniversary of the HKSAR was celebrated, it was fairly evident that Hong Kong was saddled with a problem of ungovernability. Admittedly, this problem has much to do with the heavy blow suffered by Hong Kong brought about by financial instability and economic recession of late 1997 as well as a slew of natural and man-made disasters (the avian flu and the new airport being the most glaring examples). The HKSAR government — under the leadership of Chief Executive Tung Chee-hwa — was, however, widely blamed for making Hong Kong's difficulties more complicated by its incompetence, lack of resolution and arrogance. The ineffectiveness of the HKSAR government was the result of elite fragmentation and the elite-mass gap that appeared in the last years of colonial rule. At the same time, it can be argued that the political incompetence of the HKSAR government was also a major cause of further elite fragmentation and the political alienation of the people.

Thus, unlike many former colonies — which saw a unified political elite taking over the reins of government from the departing colonizers at the time of independence, the unique path of decolonization of Hong Kong had seen the obverse. To understand the political predicament now facing Hong Kong, it is necessary to describe the effects of Hong Kong's "decolonization without independence" on the formation of the political elite in pre-1997 Hong Kong. The way the Tung administration had exacerbated the predicament also needs to be analysed in order to understand better the current political difficulties of the HKSAR government.

# The Unified Political Elite under Colonial Rule

As late as the early 1980s, a ruling class dominated Hong Kong under British rule, which was unified and self-perpetuating. The political arena basically resembled a colonial bureaucracy, headed by a governor appointed by the British Crown. Unlike many British colonies where indirect rule through political intermediaries (often landlords and tribal chiefs) was practised, colonial rule in Hong Kong was direct rule imposed upon a population of immigrants who fled from China to seek political safety and economic improvement. Politics in Hong Kong was essentially elite politics since there were extremely limited opportunities for popular political participation. As public acceptance of colonial domination was in large measure the result of Hong Kong people's rejection of Chinese rule — communist rule in particular, colonial rule was generally taken for granted and even cherished. There had been no significant anti-colonial or independence movement throughout Hong Kong's history. In contrast with other colonies where the struggle for independence provided the crucible for the rise of popular and charismatic leaders, anti-colonial political leaders with strong mass support had failed to appear in Hong Kong. Moreover, both the nationalist and communist governments in China were adamantly against the political separation of Hong Kong from the motherland. For the sake of avoiding trouble with China, Britain had all along used all means to forestall the rise of autonomous or antagonistic political leaders in Hong Kong. Since the idea of independence for Hong Kong had never been seriously contemplated by Britain, it therefore did not see the need to cultivate indigenous leaders in the territory for that purpose. The "theory of preparation" — a much exaggerated view of Britain's sincere intention to prepare its colonies for eventual independence even before the colonial subjects asked for it — was therefore not applied to Hong Kong.[1] Colonial rule, nonetheless, became more benign after the Second World War in response to anti-colonialism abroad and the rise of nationalistic fervour in China. In the wake of the social disturbances of the mid-1960s — which revealed deep-seated political alienation in society, the colonial government began to take a more lenient position on political dissent. Consequently, the people of Hong Kong were granted more freedom to articulate grievances and launch protest actions — which were often directed towards the government. Pressure groups and single-issue groups mushroomed to overload the government with specific demands pertaining to social and livelihood issues, rendering the process of governance more complicated. Yet, no credible opposition politicians emerged as potential challengers to the colonial regime.[2]

Until the early 1980s, the indigenous political leaders that appeared in colonial Hong Kong were the products of colonial political largesse. Their political influence was derived from their colonial masters. Their relationship with their political overlords was one of dependence, deference and supplication. In the eyes of the colonial regime, these indigenous leaders were employed primarily to legitimize colonial rule, to enhance its understanding of the colonial subjects and to serve as the transmission belt between the government and the governed. Most relevant to the development of indigenous political leadership was the government's elaborate strategy, involving the co-option of established and emergent Chinese elite (mostly businessmen and conservative community leaders) into the colonial regime as its complementary but subsidiary components. Through appointing them to the Executive Council, the Legislative Council, numerous advisory bodies and para-administrative organizations, and rewarding them with various titles dispensed by Britain, the colonial regime obtained for itself a team of collaborators. The job of co-option by the colonial government was facilitated by the process of westernization which assimilated the Chinese elite into English culture, the convergence of interests between the colonial regime and the Chinese elite, the cravings of the mercantile Chinese elite for political protection and recognition by the colonial authorities, and the lack of a traditional literati-scholar class who would be more resistant to the co-optive tactics of an alien government.

Over time, the system of elite co-option perfected by the colonizers became more or less institutionalized, and the colonial government was also flexible enough to adapt the system to changes in the social and political environment. By the early 1980s, the co-optive system had developed to such a stage that a system of political mobility was available to the political aspirants among the Chinese elite. Under the system controlled by the colonial government, there was a hierarchy of political appointments with the corollary gradations of status and influence. To the Chinese elite, it was possible to pursue a quasi-political career on the condition that they identified with the colonial system. Though the colonial government had not been successful in stamping out all forms of dissent through co-option, the co-optive system had been highly successful in bolstering colonial rule.

A most significant feature of the co-optive system lies in the fact that it was basically the individual rather than the group who was co-opted into the political system. It was as individuals that the elite was recognized by the colonial government, and they were basically accountable to the government who awarded them the appointments. The co-optive system hence activated intense individual competition among the Chinese elite for colonial favours. A major outcome was the fragmentation of the Chinese elite and their detachment from the masses. Nevertheless, notwithstanding elite fragmentation, the fact that the Chinese elite derived their political status and influence from the colonial government and that there was a well-defined pecking order among them ensured that a unified political elite dominating Hong Kong was the name of the game. Moreover, this elite was by and large detached from and unchallenged by the masses.[3]

# The Breakdown of the Unified Elite in the Transitional Period 1984–97

The co-optive system of elite recruitment started to break down in the early 1980s when the political future of Hong Kong was settled by the Sino-British Joint Declaration signed at the end of 1984. The integrity of the co-optive system hinged upon a monopoly of political power by the colonial government. Under these circumstances, the colonial government could ensure that only a single channel of access to power was made available to the politically ambitious Chinese elite.

The onset of the transitional period in 1984 was marked by the gradual disintegration of the unified structure of the political elite in Hong Kong. The increasing fragmentation and disunity which set in were a result of several crucial factors: the erosion of the authority of the departing colonial regime, the depreciation in value of its political awards, the intrusion of China as a powerful political actor, the incessant tug-of-war between China and Britain over transitional matters, the enlargement of the political arena following democratic reform, and the entry into politics by the masses through various channels. These momentous political changes in the transitional period demolished the colonial regime's monopoly of power and replaced the hitherto single channel of political recruitment with multiple channels of political recruitment. The new channels of political recruitment, however, were ill defined and far from institutionalized. Furthermore, they overlapped with one another in complex ways.

51

What is most noteworthy is that while the significance of the old channel of political recruitment had vastly depreciated, it is difficult to ascertain the real value of the new channels of political advancement, for each of them carried its own benefits and risks. In any case, in the transitional period, instead of a unified elite under the control of the colonial regime, different elite competed with one another for political spoils and status. The breakdown of the elite hierarchy crafted by the colonial regime had resulted in warring elites, none of whom would recognize any status hierarchy among them. A semblance of order within the Chinese elite was only maintained with much difficulty by China and Britain — as the respective new and old dispensers of political favours — particularly the latter.

The decline in the political prestige and power of the colonial regime triggered off a stampede among long-time political collaborators who pulled away from their former political patron. Most of them moved towards China — the future sovereign of Hong Kong — in order to court political favour, while others became the colonial regime's opponents or simply called it quits politically. With the rapid contraction of the elite support base, the colonial regime was spurred to take steps to bolster its political legitimacy and authority in order to avert the crisis of ungovernability. In addition, both Britain and the colonial regime deemed it essential that public opinion in Hong Kong be on their side if Chinese interference in Hong Kong's affairs was to be thwarted. The colonial government took the most significant step to achieve its political purposes: it announced political reforms in Hong Kong even before the Sino-British Declaration was formally signed. Though China's opposition had forced a substantial scale-down of the reforms eventually undertaken, the attempt by the colonial government to establish a "representative government rooted in Hong Kong" — centring upon a phased transformation of the legislature into a fully elected body — nonetheless drastically changed Hong Kong's political landscape.[4] The direct (read *popular*) election of a portion of the legislators, in effect, provided a great impetus to mass political participation. The sudden expansion of the mass political arena in Hong Kong greatly facilitated the rise of politicians who appealed vigorously to the public as anti-communists, democratic activists, social welfarists, labour rights advocates or plain populists. The enlargement of the mass political arena also enabled non-politicians, such as journalists, scholars and professionals — who were able to articulate their views on public issues in the mass media — to obtain increased political influence as opinion leaders in a rapidly politicizing society.

In the early years of the transitional period, the colonial government targeted its long-time political collaborators as its successors who will govern Hong Kong after British withdrawal. It believed that, after the handover in 1997, for the sake of their self-interests, they would stand firm against Beijing and determinedly safeguard Hong Kong's autonomy as solemnly promised by China. In this respect — in the colonial government's attempt to groom its collaborators into its successors — Hong Kong's experience can be likened to that of other former British colonies in the early phases of decolonization.[5] However, it did not take long for the colonial government to have second thoughts on the matter with the flagrant and swift transfer of allegiance from Britain to China on the part of its political collaborators, their obsequious behaviour towards Beijing, the antagonistic stance adopted by some of them towards Britain, and their stiff resistance to the democratic reforms introduced by the departing colonial regime. In the last years of colonial rule, particularly after the Tiananmen incident (the military crackdown of the student movement on 4 June 1989) in Beijing, the colonial government decided to rely more on public support to counter the ever-growing influence of Beijing and its political collaborators in Hong Kong — to bolster colonial authority. The last colonial governor, Chris Patten, accelerated democratic reform and sought political alliance with the democratic activists. As the democratic activists were both anti-communist and anti-colonialist, the colonial government found it impossible to accede fully to their demands. Consequently, this political alliance was uneasy and fraught with conflicts. In any case, since the colonial government reckoned that the democratic activists — who were popular with the Hong Kong people — should be more capable than the pro-China politicians to look after Hong Kong's interests after 1997, it was prepared in the eleventh hour of colonial rule to groom them as a counterforce to China. Accordingly, the democratic activists, who used to be sidelined by the colonial government, were granted more opportunities to participate in the making of public policies, though the colonial government stopped short of granting them the status of a junior partner in colonial governance. In fact, apart from issues related to human rights and democratic reform, the colonial government and the democratic activists were constantly at loggerheads with each other. At any rate, on the eve of the handover, the political clout of the democratic activists was tremendously boosted. The unprecedented reliance on popular support as a pillar of effective governance in the last years of colonial rule contributed further to the political significance of the expanding ranks of opinion leaders in Hong Kong, who in turn worked actively and successfully to build up public opinion as a major political force in the rapidly changing political scene.

Throughout the transitional period, the colonial government played a largely defensive game to slow down the irreversible decline of its authority. Arguably, Britain's influence in grooming its successors in most of its former colonies was quite limited. Since colonial rule in Hong Kong had not been conducive to the formation of popular leaders, and as the intrusion of China as a powerful political actor in Hong Kong severely undermined any possible efforts on the part of the colonial government to hand-pick its successors, the only alternative available was to promote the civil service as the mainstay of the post-1997 polity. In any case, in view of the facts that its long-time political collaborators became increasingly unreliable and that its last-minute alliance with the democratic activists was only an exercise in expedience, the colonial government had perforce to make the senior civil servants, who were still under its control and a product of British cultural influence *par excellence*, its political successors.

Britain was astutely aware of the significance of the civil service in the "executive-led" government which China envisaged for post-1997 Hong Kong. It also understood very well that China — which had no capable and popular administrators at its disposal to take over and operate the bulky bureaucracy left behind — had no alternative but to depend on the service of the colonial civil servants in spite of their untested and uncertain political loyalty to Beijing. The last years of colonial rule saw strident efforts by the colonial government to turn senior officials

54

into politicians. In pursuit of this end, the process of localization of the upper echelon of the civil service — which was much neglected before the early 1980s and very slow even after — was accelerated. With the exception of the governor and the attorney-general, by the time of British departure, all the top posts in the colonial government were occupied by local Chinese.[6] Senior officials took on the high-profile duties of explaining and defending government policies, mobilizing and organizing political support for the government, countering the critics of the government aggressively and even combating Beijing's initiatives. Though not all senior officials were comfortable with their new political roles, some of them were able to develop into prominent politicians with distinctive political personalities. Admittedly, the most senior civil servants could become only partial politicians, for they were prohibited from joining political parties or civic groups. They were also not allowed to have their own political agenda. Nevertheless, the selection of senior civil servants as its political successors by the departing colonial regime is an unprecedented *démarche* in colonial history. The end result was that the senior civil servants acquired an enormous sense of political self-importance and had considerably honed their political skills. During colonial rule, when career bureaucrats basically governed Hong Kong, senior civil servants saw themselves as the natural rulers of Hong Kong as well as the rightful custodian of public interests.[7] They tended to see the newly formed politicians — particularly the mass-oriented politicians — as contemptible political upstarts seeking to advance partisan interests. The introduction of the "representative" government by the colonial regime in its last years had transformed the political mentality of the civil servants to some extent, but still the sense of superiority of the civil servants was only thinly disguised.[8] On the eve of the handover, instead of a civil service which was politically prepared to serve the new sovereign dutifully, the senior civil servants of Hong Kong became highly politicized and were poised to fight hard for their individual and collective ascendancy.

As a powerful political actor in the transitional period, Beijing should presumably be in an unrivaled position to groom political leaders to its liking for post-1997 Hong Kong. Nevertheless, theoretically it should have no reason to do so, as the promise of "Hong Kong people governing Hong Kong" means that China should automatically give its blessing to the leaders preferred by the Hong Kong people. In fact, given Hong Kong people's anti-communist propensity and their tendency to side with Britain and the democratic activists in their conflict with China, Beijing naturally wanted to have its hand-picked leaders taking up the reins of the HKSAR government in order to safeguard its interests. To that end, China originally sought the assistance of Britain. Britain was asked to incorporate pro-China figures into the colonial administration so that they could obtain the much-needed training in administration as well as exposure in politics. Not surprisingly, Britain refused the request. Apart from the fact that granting Beijing's request would undermine Britain's own efforts at leadership grooming, Britain was also very much concerned about the further erosion of colonial authority and, what was worse, the presence of Trojan horses inside the colonial government. Consequently, China had to take on the task of leadership cultivation single-handedly. Intensified Sino-British confrontation after the 4 June event accelerated China's efforts in that direction. The half-decade before the handover saw China taking great pains to set up new institutions with the explicit purpose of fostering the rise of pro-China leaders. Previously, Beijing used to appoint local people, who were loyal to the communist regime, to central political bodies in China, among which the most prominent were the National People's Congress and the Chinese People's Political Consultative Conference. The work of these bodies was, however, confined to Mainland affairs. Since the signing of the Sino-British Joint Declaration, a number of political bodies concerned with Hong Kong affairs were set up to prepare the territory's for transition to Chinese sovereignty. Among the most notable were the two bodies related to the drafting of the post-1997 mini-constitution of Hong Kong: the Basic Law Drafting Committee under the National People's Congress and the Basic Law Consultative Committee — supposedly a local body. Nevertheless, these organizations had a clearly defined agenda and only a small number of people could sit on them. Since 1992, however, the pace of leadership formation picked up. Initially, China introduced the scheme of Hong Kong Affairs Advisers to co-opt eminent community figures into the pro-China camp. These advisers were supposed to render advice to Beijing on matters with respect to Hong Kong, though in essence the appointments were largely honorary. In total, four batches of Hong Kong Affairs Advisers had been appointed: 44 on 11 March 1992, 49 on 1 April 1993, 49 on 26 May 1994 and 45 on 28 April 1995. When Governor Chris Patten expressed his intention to strengthen democratic reform in Hong Kong, disregarding China's vociferous protest, China vowed to dismantle his reforms after the British were gone and "set up a new stove" to replace it. To demonstrate China's determination to go it alone, the Preliminary Working Committee (PWC) was set up on 2 July 1993 by the National People's Congress to advise China on the preparation for the establishment of the HKSAR. The PWC had a membership of 57, among whom 30 were Hong Kong members and 27 mainland members. The PWC was subsequently slightly enlarged to 70 by the addition of 8 Hong Kong and 5 mainland members on 2 July 1993. When the PWC gave way to the Preparatory Committee — a powerful body set up by the National People's Congress — on 28 December 1995, the number of eminent community figures co-opted by Beijing further expanded. As a body with real decision-making power and responsible for preparing the establishment of the Hong Kong Special Administrative Region and prescribing specific methods for forming the first government and the first Legislative Council of the HKSAR, the Preparatory Committee was extraordinarily large, with 150 members (94 from Hong Kong and 56 from the Mainland). On 2 November 1996, the Preparatory Committee functioned as an electoral college to elect the 400 members of the Selection Committee which, in turn, elected the first chief executive of the HKSAR on 11 December 1996. It goes without saying that the total number of major community figures co-opted by China through various channels was large, even after taking into account overlapping membership in those political bodies.

China's effort at leadership formation was not confined only to the territory-wide elite, for grassroots leaders were also the targets of China's co-optive strategy. Throughout the transitional period, China had achieved more success in wooing grassroots leaders — who were less educated, more susceptible to nationalistic appeals and more deferential to authority — than in courting the upper elite. While major community figures were appointed to important political bodies, the lesser figures were never neglected. The Hong Kong Branch of the New China News Agency — the *de facto* Chinese embassy in Hong Kong — started appointing the first batch of 274 District Affairs Advisers on 4 March 1994. Thereafter two more batches of District Affairs Advisers were named: 263 of them on 9 January 1995, and 133 on 13 July 1995. Like the Hong Kong Affairs Advisers, the District Affairs Advisers were honorary positions indicating a form of political recognition by Beijing.

The major goal of the co-optive strategy of China was to construct a united political front in support of China in the pursuit of its Hong Kong policy and in its tussle with the British during the transitional period. Moreover, the united front was to be the breeding ground for Hong Kong's post-1997 political leaders as well as the firm support base of the future HKSAR government. In retrospect, however, the leadership strategy of China was by and large a failure. The major achievement of the strategy, if any, was the slight reduction in the threat of political opposition to Beijing in Hong Kong before the handover. China, however, was unable to build a broad united front of political leaders in its support and to do its bidding. By the time of the handover, the "pro-China" label was considered an albatross around the neck of any political leader who wanted to be popular with the people.[9] As a result, a post-1997 government led largely, if not exclusively, by pro-China political figures would not be able to gain the trust of the Hong Kong people and guarantee Hong Kong's stability and prosperity.

Frankly, China's failure to groom political collaborators in the transitional period is no surprise at all. Inasmuch as the Hong Kong people had strong mistrust of China and were only minimally susceptible to nationalistic and patriotic appeals, China suffered from a congenital disadvantage in its efforts at grooming leaders. As China was preoccupied with countering British "conspiracies" and offensives during the transitional period, the policy of grooming leaders was unfortunately subordinated to short-term considerations and tactical calculations. Depending on the situation, different types of leaders were approached and their support sought. During the

Sino-British negotiations over Hong Kong's future in the early 1980s, China made intense nationalistic and anti-colonial appeals to the Hong Kong people in order to deprive Britain of public support. At that time, China even wooed democratic activists with nationalistic proclivities in its battle with Britain and the pro-British elite. After the future of Hong Kong was settled and the issue of the future political system came to the fore, China then undertook to rally support from the conservatives (including the pro-British elements whose interests would be adversely affected by democratic reform) and the pro-China forces to thwart the intentions of Britain and the democratic activists. When Sino-British conflict and anti-communist sentiments among the Hong Kong people reached a new level of intensity in the wake of the Tiananmen incident, China had no alternative but to rely exclusively on itself and the small number of ardently pro-China leaders to limit its losses in a largely defensive battle against Britain. The strategic retreat of Britain in the last one-and-a-half years of the transitional period and the ensuing warming up of the Sino-British relationship induced China to dump the extreme pro-China figures, to embrace the moderates in the pro-China camp and to adopt a more receptive stance towards the pro-British leaders (many of them had by then resigned themselves to the reality of Chinese sovereignty).

In all, China and Britain's obsession with the threat from the other side had undoubtedly driven both of them to adopt a short-term, exploitative and divisive approach to leadership formation. Both were heavily involved in Hong Kong's transitional affairs making their declared intention to groom indigenous leaders for post-1997 self-governance a mockery. The perennial confrontation between Beijing and London in the transitional period inevitably led to the vicious competitive mobilization of local elites on their part, resulting in the pervasive discrediting of Hong Kong's fledgling leaders. The shortage of indigenous political leaders before the early 1980s was, therefore, not resolved in the long transitional period.

On the eve of the handover in 1997, Hong Kong faced a glaring political irony. While China's promise of "a high degree of autonomy" and "Hong Kong people governing Hong Kong" was apparently sincere, the territory had to draw upon the service of only a thin layer of fragmented political elite. Generally speaking, the political elite suffered from poor prestige and had only weak support from the people.[10] This was particularly true with respect to the pro-China elite. The democratic activists, because of their anti-communist and populist orientations, enjoyed better popular recognition. Nevertheless, Hong Kong people were sceptical about their political effectiveness because they were not accepted by the new sovereign. In this leadership vacuum, the highly politicized senior civil servants became the most visible and eligible political leaders in post-1997 Hong Kong. It can thus be said that compared to China, Britain had achieved a greater measure of success in determining who were going to run Hong Kong after the end of colonial rule.

# Elite Fragmentation and Discord in Post-1997 Hong Kong

Pervasive elite fragmentation on the eve of the handover was a major reason — though not the sufficient reason — for the selection of Tung Chee-hwa (a shipping tycoon with limited political experience and a disdain for politics) as the first chief executive of the HKSAR. In the context of pervasive intra-elite mistrust and jealousies and popular aversion to elite rivalries, Tung's political inexperience, non-involvement in political networking and fatherly image were a breath of fresh air in local politics. The warring elites were willing to accept him as a compromise candidate, for none of them was able to put their candidate in the top post. Even though Tung was basically a political unknown to the elite and people of Hong Kong, they were nevertheless led by his modesty, sincerity and good manners into believing that he had the personality, open mind and social skills to mediate among the disparate elite to build a cohesive governing coalition and to bridge the gap between the political elite and the people. At the time of Tung's accession to the position of chief executive at the end of 1996, Tung had accumulated a fairly large number of well wishers.[11] In any case, in a context of soaring economic optimism and diminishing political anxieties which characterized mid-1997, nobody foresaw crises of any kind that would severely tax the political ability of this "good guy" to bring people together to deal with common difficulties.

By the time the HKSAR celebrated its first anniversary in 1998, Hong Kong found itself not only in dire economic straits, but also saddled with more debilitating elite fragmentation and discord. Very much contrary to general expectations, Tung had failed to promote elite unity in the first year of office, and elite disunity had reached an alarming stage which not only greatly narrowed his support base within the elite, but also threatened his ability to govern a society which had been severely tormented and destabilized by financial turmoil, economic recession, escalating unemployment and a series of mishaps (notably the avian flu and the new airport fiasco).

Right from the very beginning, Tung proceeded to build only a narrow and exclusionary governing coalition. As a conservative, paternalistic and authoritarian politician, and with a view to politically appease Beijing, Tung obviously did not induct the democratic activists, anti-communists and people who fell out of favour with Beijing into his government. Likewise, Tung was suspicious of those elite figures who were reasonably popular with the people and who acted as public opinion leaders. Tung's elitist propensity is evident in the composition of his 15-strong Executive Council — the highest consultative-cum-policymaking body of the HKSAR — which was appointed on 24 January 1997. Except for the three principal officials, the rest of the members of the council were overwhelmingly businessmen and professionals from the business sector who had limited political skills and minimal public appeal. In Tung's perception, the Executive Council was primarily his closet advisers and was not supposed or expected to play a high-profile political role in society. Consequently, the Executive Council could not serve as the nucleus for a broad-based governing coalition and the chief mechanism for Tung to mobilize public and media support for the new regime whose authority and credibility had yet to be secured.

Tung's exclusionary approach can be seen in another instance. As the victims of the Sino-British row over democratic reform in Hong Kong, the 18 District Boards and the 2 municipal councils (the Urban Council and the Regional Council) — which were popularly elected in 1994 and 1995 respectively — were dismantled at the time of the handover. For the sake of stability, the Preparatory Committee decided that all the original members of these bodies could be re-appointed to their temporary replacements — the Provisional Urban Council, the Provisional Regional Council and the Provisional District Boards — in the HKSAR. In addition, the chief executive was empowered to appoint new members to these district organizations with the provision that they could not exceed 20 percent of their membership. The intention of the Preparatory Committee was to use the newly appointed members to dilute the political clout of the democratic activists and populists in these bodies.

On 11 June 1997, Tung dutifully announced that 469 persons were appointed as members of the 18 Provisional District Boards (373 were originally directly elected members of the existing District Boards and 96 were new members). At the same time, 100 members were appointed to the two provisional municipal councils (80 were members of the existing municipal councils and 20 were newly appointed).

The exclusionary character of Tung's coalition-building programme is baldly evident upon a close scrutiny of the new appointees. Among the 96 newly appointed members of the Provisional District Boards, none of them were members of the Democratic Party — the flagship organization of the democratic activists. About 20 percent (18) of the new appointees were defeated candidates in the 1994 District Board elections. Ten were members of the Democratic Alliance for the Betterment of Hong Kong — a pro-China political party with a grassroots bent. One was a member of the Liberal Party — a pro-business political party who also had an eye on contesting direct elections, and 5 were members of the Hong Kong Progressive Alliance — a pro-China political party catering to the needs of small- and medium-sized business firms. Fifty were District Affairs Advisers to the Chinese government and 41 were appointed members of District Boards before the 1994 District Board elections. Similarly, among the 20 new members of the two provisional municipal councils, 10 were Selection Committee members, 5 were Hong Kong Affairs

Advisers, 4 were members of the Preparatory Committee, 2 were deputies of the National People's Congress, 2 were members of the Chinese People's Political Consultative Conference, and 2 were members of the Heung Yee Kuk — a rural consultative body dominated by conservative rural leaders. Four were members of the Hong Kong Progressive Alliance, and one each from the Liberal Party and the New Hong Kong Alliance (a small political group made up of pro-China figures).[12]

As Beijing decided to retain the structure and personnel of the hundreds of advisory committees in Hong Kong after the handover, Tung's ability to tamper with the composition of these committees was limited in his first year of office. Nevertheless, it can easily be seen in the small number of key appointments and re-appointments, which Tung had made so far, that the policy of exclusion was practised consistently and doggedly. This was particularly true with respect to the two advisory committees which were supposed to give substance to Tung's long-term vision and to allow him to get new policy ideas outside of the civil service — the Commission on Strategic Development and the Innovation and Technology Commission. The kind of political allies whom Tung preferred is also clear from the list of people who were honoured by the HKSAR government under a new system of honorary titles which it created. On 2 July 1997, 12 recipients were awarded the Grand Bauhinia Medals — the highest honour conferred by the HKSAR government — by Tung. On the first anniversary of the HKSAR, 4 more people were given the Grand Bauhinia Medals together with 226 others who were awarded lesser honorary titles or recognition. Yet another example is the government's decision in May 1998 not to renew Frederick Fung Kin-kee's — an outspoken democratic activist with long-time experience in public housing — appointment to the Housing Authority upon when it expired.

A caveat is in order though. While the Basic Law reserves enormous powers in the hands of the chief executive, Tung was, however, very much constrained in his ability to shape his governing coalition. As mentioned earlier, as a result of Hong Kong's unique colonial history and decolonization experience, Tung simply did not have a large pool of political talent to draw upon to build his leadership team. Secondly, the absence of active political and community involvement on Tung's part in the past means that Tung had no reliable and competent political allies to speak of. He therefore had to turn largely to his business associates and close friends for help. Unfortunately, many of these people also did not command political experience and public trust. Thirdly, even though the governing coalition envisaged by Tung was narrow and exclusive, the state of elite fragmentation in Hong Kong still means that Tung had to bring into his government a diverse selection of elite in order to reflect a decent spectrum of elite interests. This balancing act on Tung's part can be clearly seen in the make-up of his Executive Council. The council, as the chief executive's top advisory body, should display great coherence, camaraderie and unity. Unfortunately, it faithfully mirrored the state of fragmentation of Hong Kong's elite which comprised previously pro-British loyalists, staunch pro-China figures, apolitical professionals, "representatives" of big business, pro-business professionals and a lonely trade unionist. As a result, the Executive Council was a recipe for political disarray at the centre of the government from the outset. Fourthly, Tung had to pay heed to Beijing's views and to incorporate people it trusted into his government even though they might not owe him any allegiance and even have their own political agenda. A few such people were widely believed — or suspected to say the least — to serve as Beijing's eyes and ears in Tung's government, though no hard evidence had ever been produced. Last and most significantly, the lack of trustworthy pro-China leaders in Hong Kong on the eve of the handover and the strengthened political leadership role of senior civil servants in the last few years of colonial rule left Tung — and Beijing in that regard — with no alternative but to leave the civil service intact and allow it to continue as the mainstay of the new regime. Thus, when Tung nominated 23 principal officials to the central government for appointment on 20 February 1997, except for Elsie Leung — the Secretary of Justice,[13] all were incumbent civil servants of the colonial government.[14] The wholesale induction of senior civil servants into the new government was done notwithstanding Tung's and — more crucially — Beijing's knowledge that quite a number of the senior officials had been deliberately groomed by Chris Patten for top positions in post-colonial Hong Kong.

Despite Tung's apparent efforts to appease all the elite whom he deemed as the indispensable foundation of his government, it turned out that his governing coalition was too narrow even to placate the elite. As Hong Kong's elite was not organized and there was no legitimate hierarchy among them, it was not possible for Tung to mete out political appointments and rewards to representative leaders of the elite. Instead, the political spoils dispensed by Tung went primarily to individuals. The limited number of political appointments and rewards unavoidably left many people frustrated and discontented. Particularly significant among the aggrieved were a number of influential pro-China figures who felt betrayed after so many years of loyal service to Beijing which had, in turn, earned them opprobrium among the Hong Kong people. In general, large proportions of the pro-China elite were offended by their exclusion from the political rewards to which they thought they were entitled. This state of affairs was at odds with Beijing's original plan of having the pro-China camp as the political bedrock of the new regime. The Tung administration had also alienated the intellectuals, who had begun to play an increasingly conspicuous political role in the last years of colonial rule and who used to be major players in traditional and modern Chinese politics. None of the important political appointments made by Tung had gone to the intellectuals, resulting not surprisingly in widespread resentment in intellectual circles. Moreover, conservative grassroots leaders felt slighted by the new government, which appeared to them to be paying too much attention to the interests of the upper elite. Quite obviously, the narrow governing coalition built by Tung in his first year of office had considerably alienated the elite whose support he desired to obtain and sown the seeds of further elite disunity.

Insofar as elite fragmentation and discord in the HKSAR is concerned, the disgruntlement of the pro-China elements was only a minor problem in comparison with the uneasy coexistence between the senior civil servants on the one hand, and Tung and his political associates on the other. The latter was the *casus belli* of not only a factious governing coalition from the very beginning but also a major factor in exacerbating the fragmentation of the elite.

Beijing's incessant and sincere efforts to court the civil servants, the fact that senior civil servants commanded more public trust and respect than any other categories of political leaders, and the fact that senior civil servants had more opportunities than others to develop political skills before the handover had momentous consequences for the elite infighting and the lack of cohesiveness within Tung's governing coalition. In the first place, the sense of self-importance of the senior officials had vastly expanded to the point that they — who owed their positions to their superiors more so than through election by the people — saw themselves as the rightful and most qualified successor to the colonial rulers. They held little regard for Tung as a political leader and public administrator and were intent to "control" him as the way to perpetuate their supreme role in governance. They saw Tung's pro-China advisers as not only incompetent in policymaking but also morally corrupt. From the very beginning of the HKSAR, there were perennial conflicts between Tung and some of his senior officials on the one hand, and between some of Tung's advisers and the senior officials on the other. Though none of them would admit that there were any serious problems in their relationship, the large number of gossips reported in the press were however rarely denied by the individuals concerned. To complicate matters, both Tung's advisers and some of his senior officials stab each other in the back by giving off-the-record briefings to the press, and, in doing so, give the journalists many a field day.

An incomplete list of the conflicts among Tung, his advisers and his senior officials would give a rough idea of the internal dissension at the centre of the new government. Even before the handover, disagreements between Tung and his newly appointed principal officials had erupted on a number of matters: whether to set up a Hong Kong office in Beijing, whom to appoint as the head of the Central Policy Unit (the in-house think-tank of the government),[15] the future of the Land Fund after it was turned over to the HKSAR government by Beijing, the amendment of the Public Order and Societies Ordinances,[16] and the problem of the permanent residence legislation.[17]

After the handover, the more visible conflicts between Tung, his advisers and his senior officials were:

(1) In October 1997, individual members of the Executive Council were rumoured to have tried to interfere with the electoral boundaries drawn by the Electoral Affairs Commission. The public saw this as a blatant and improper interference of the government in the work of an independent statutory body charged with the responsibility of conducting a fair Legislative Council election on 24 May 1998. It was widely believed that the principal officials in the Executive Council leaked this piece of information to the press to tarnish the public image of the members concerned.

(2) In October 1997, Tung decided to hold a small party at Government House (the former official residence of the colonial governors) to celebrate the eightieth birthday of Chung Sze-yuen (an elderly politician and the most trusted of Tung's advisers) with public money. An uproar against the decision set in when the people learned about it. As Chung was a prominent collaborator of the colonial regime before he went over to the pro-China camp, he was a highly controversial figure in Hong Kong. In all likelihood the news of Tung's decision was leaked out by the principal officials in the Executive Council in order to embarrass not only Chung, but also Tung himself. Though Tung eventually reversed his decision with much reluctance, his political image, together with that of some of his close advisers, was damaged.

(3) In March 1998, Xu Ximin, an outspoken member of the Chinese People's Political Consultative Conference, lambasted Radio and Television Hong Kong (RTHK), a government body in Beijing, for its anti-communist and anti-government radio and TV programmes, and urged Tung to take appropriate action. Xu's comments greatly aroused public fears that press freedom in Hong Kong would be curtailed. In order to placate the pro-China figures, Tung — coincidentally also in Beijing at the time — said blandly that "while freedom of speech is important, it is also important for government policies to be positively presented."[18] However, Tung failed to forcefully defend freedom of expression in Hong Kong, further fuelling fears for the independence of the RTHK. To make matters worse, his chief secretary of

administration, Anson Chan, issued a ringing rebuttal against Xu in Hong Kong and won loud applause from the public. On his return to Hong Kong, Tung was thus forced to declare that the editorial independence of RTHK was not under threat, and that its future was a matter for the Hong Kong people to decide. He further said the government welcomed criticism from RTHK and the media, and hoped the media would continue to play the role of watchdog over government policies.[19] The different positions expressed by Tung and his top principal official hurt Tung's prestige but left Anson Chan's popularity soaring.[20]

(4)  Since the onslaught of the financial turmoil in Hong Kong, the government had been bombarded by strong demands coming from various affected interests to intervene in the economy to relieve economic pains and to stimulate economic growth. The principal officials were steadfast against modifying the time-honoured practice of economic non-interventionism which they believed constituted the foundation of Hong Kong's past economic success. Tung, however, had a more activist conception of the government's role in Hong Kong's economic future. Persistent resistance by the senior civil servants, however, did not prevent Tung from gradually moving Hong Kong towards an economy increasingly managed by the government. On several significant occasions, public declarations of the government's economic policy by individual officials were swiftly and bluntly refuted by Tung, who would then promulgate a contrary policy position. Such *coups* on Tung's part further strained his relationship with the principal officials and further damaged the credibility of the government.

The never-ending strife within the leadership core of the HKSAR government reflected not only insufficient mutual trust within it, but also the wide divergence in the political orientation, policy position, decision-making style and practical interests of its members. Apparently there exists a debilitating deadlock between Tung and his advisers on the one hand, and the senior officials on the other. Tung and his advisers complained that the senior civil servants had no long-term vision and were paralyzed by a hidebound bureaucratic mentality. On the other hand, senior civil servants resented Tung's disrespect for long-established bureaucratic procedures, ignorance of administrative rationality, personal arbitrariness and vulnerability to persuasion by sectional interests. Neither party, however, was able to prevail over the other. Hong Kong's experience is thus quite unlike that of many other former British colonies. In other places, the civil servants were more willing to subordinate themselves to their new political masters whatever their opinion. More frequently, it was the new political masters — being popular leaders with solid bases of mass support gained through anti-colonial struggles — who insisted that the civil servants be indoctrinated with new ideologies in keeping with the new political situation.[21] In the HKSAR, the senior civil servants, despite their tremendous bargaining power, actually lacked a sense of political security. As former colonial officials, they were not sure about Beijing's trust in them. Many of them considered their jobs as only temporary in nature, believing that sooner or later pro-China politicians would replace them. Thus, when Tung announced on 21 March 1997 that he had appointed three members of the Executive Council — Antony Leung, Leung Chun-ying, and Tam Yiu-chung — to study policy issues related to education, housing and the problem of the elderly respectively, this was interpreted by the senior officials as the prelude to a "ministerial system" which would relegate the civil servants to only a subsidiary position in the new administration. Needless to say, the three appointees subsequently encountered insuperable difficulties in getting their job done.

Politically speaking, when a governing coalition lacks an organized and broad mass support base, its internal unity becomes even more critical in maintaining effective governance. The incoherent leadership of the Tung administration was further plagued by the narrowness of the governing coalition and the fragmentation of the elite. Under these circumstances, policymaking and policy implementation were destined to be difficult, if not impossible. Since late October 1997, the financial turmoil, economic recession, rising unemployment, sagging economic confidence, together with the natural and man-made disasters, had made the situation even worse. The Tung administration was not only unable to rise to the challenge, its ability to handle the economic downturn in Hong Kong was much weakened by its internal friction. The "crisis" of ungovernability was increasingly a problem of public concern.

The ineffectiveness of the Tung administration, which was amply exposed in the first year of the HKSAR, in turn exacerbated the fragmentation and discord of the political elite. The contraction of the economic pie engendered by economic recession inevitably resulted in intensified conflict of interests among the elite. The ineptitude of the government in handling Hong Kong's economic woes had hurt the interests of the elite, particularly the business elite, very hard. Almost all social sectors suffered from the economic downturn and the natural and man-made disasters, which crowded the first year of the HKSAR, and they had not failed to blame Tung and his government for their distress. Occasionally, Tung was even criticized for favouring particular interests at the expense of others. Consequently, Tung and his government's popularity plummeted, further depleting his elite and mass support base and exacerbating the "crisis" of ungovernability in Hong Kong.

## Concluding Remarks

Elite unity in Hong Kong before 1997 was achieved primarily because of the authoritarian nature of colonial rule. A certain degree of elite disunity is bound to appear when Hong Kong is no longer a British colony and instead becomes a partial democracy in China. Nevertheless, while acknowledging that elite contestation is a "healthy" political phenomenon, "too much" elite disunity threatens social and political stability. Arguably, elite disunity in Hong Kong after 1997 has reached such an extent that the ability of the HKSAR government to govern is seriously undermined and the Tung administration suffers from low popularity. Elite disunity has become a major political problem, which in turn exacerbates the many problems which have been created by the economic downturn in Hong Kong since October 1997.

In all likelihood, Hong Kong's economy will remain in the doldrums for a while, and there is no light yet at the end of the tunnel. At a time of widespread depression and anxieties, it is imperative that the government is able to inspire hope and confidence in society if effective governance and constructive problem-solving can be attained. In view of the constraints of the Basic Law and the opposition of the business community, speeding up the process of democratization as a means of reducing elite disunity is non-existent. Hence, it is imperative that Tung takes steps to rectify the situation. Apparently, the first priority of the Tung administration is to rebuild a governing coalition, which is broad-based and cohesive. This is needed not only to reverse the trend of continuing elite fragmentation, but also to bridge the enlarging elite-mass credibility gap. Nevertheless, before any of these things can be done, it is most important that Tung re-orients himself politically and gives politics its proper emphasis. While acknowledging that it is inordinately difficult for Tung himself to change his political personality, however, it is arguably the only way that Hong Kong can pull itself together and cope with its unprecedented economic as well as political crises.

## NOTES

1. B.B. Schaffer, "The Concept of Preparation: Some Questions about the Transfer of Systems of Government," *World Politics*, vol. 18, no. 1 (October 1965), pp. 42–67.

2. Lau Siu-kai, "Social Change, Bureaucratic Rule, and Emergent Political Issues in Hong Kong," *World Politics*, vol. 35, no. 4 (July 1983), pp. 544–562.

3. See Lau Siu-kai, "Colonial Rule, Transfer of Sovereignty and the Problem of Political Leaders in Hong Kong," in *The Journal of Commonwealth & Comparative Politics*, vol. 30, no. 2 (July 1992), pp. 223–42; and Lee Ming-kwan, "Politicians", in Y.C. Wong and Joseph Y.S. Cheng (eds.), *The Other Hong Kong Report 1990* (Hong Kong: Chinese University Press, 1990), pp. 113–30.

4. See Lau Siu-kai, "The Unfinished Political Reforms of the Hong Kong Government," in John Langford and K. Lorne Brownsey (eds.), *The Changing Shape of Government in the Asia–Pacific Region* (Victoria: The Institute for Research on Public Policy, 1988), pp. 43–82; idem., "Hong Kong's Path of Democratization," *Swiss Asian Studies*, XLIX, 1 (1995), pp. 71–90; idem., "Decolonization à la Hong Kong: Britain's

Search for Governability and Exit with Glory in Hong Kong," *The Journal of Commonwealth & Comparative Politics*, vol. 35, no. 2 (July 1997), pp. 28–54; and Kathleen Cheek-Milby, *A Legislature Comes of Age: Hong Kong's Search for Influence and Identity* (Hong Kong: Oxford University Press, 1995).

5. See, for example, Brian Lapping, *End of Empire* (London: Paladin Grafton Books, 1985); Trevor Royle, *Winds of Change: The End of Empire in Africa* (London: John Murray, 1996); and John Keay, *Last Post: The End of Empire in the Far East* (London: John Murray, 1997).

6. The most significant civil service appointments made by the colonial government in this respect were the appointment of Anson Chan — Secretary for the Civil Service — as Chief Secretary to succeed David Ford on 29 November 1993, and the appointment of Donald Tsang Yam-kuen to succeed Hamish McCleod as Financial Secretary on 1 September 1995.

7. The "gentlemanly mode" cherished by the Indian civil service before India's independence can be easily applied to Hong Kong's Chinese civil servants. Its major features include: (1) the identification of *public service* as *morally virtuous*; (2) the high value placed on *confidence* in one's own judgement and, allied to that, the low value placed on servility to one's superior and hence the powerful gentlemanly norm of *courageous self-discipline*; (3) the celebration of the *amateur* and the conception that gentleman amateurs were *generalists*. See David C. Potter, *India's Political Administrators 1919–1983* (Oxford: Clarendon Press, 1986), pp. 66–75.

8. A study of the senior civil servants by Cheng and Lee has this to say: "The senior civil servants are changing from classical bureaucrats to political bureaucrats who are willing to accept the increasing interference of politics in bureaucratic performance ... The bureaucrats obviously agree with the legislative politicians in their value and perception towards economic prosperity, political stability and a more open and accountable government process ... The senior civil servants accept that there is increasing criticism and interference from the legislative members." However, senior civil servants still thought that it was they who were in charge of governance. And legislators were only assigned the role of the subsidiary watchdog. See Joseph Y.S. Cheng and Jane C.Y. Lee, "The Changing Political Attitudes of the Senior Bureaucrats in Hong Kong's Transition," *The China Quarterly*, no. 147 (September 1996), p. 932. See also Lau Siu-kai and Kuan Hsin-chi, *Chinese Bureaucrats in a Modern Colony: The Case of Hong Kong* (Hong Kong: Centre for Hong Kong Studies, The Chinese University of Hong Kong, 1986).

9. See for example Lau Siu-kai, *Democratization, Poverty of Political Leaders, and Political Inefficacy in Hong Kong* (Hong Kong: Hong Kong Institute of Asia–Pacific Studies, The Chinese University of Hong Kong, 1998); and Jamie Allen, *Seeing Red: China's Uncompromising Takeover of Hong Kong* (Singapore: Butterworth–Heinemann Asia, 1997).

10. See Lau Siu-kai, "Institutions Without Leaders: Hong Kong Chinese View of Political Leadership," *Pacific Affairs*, vol. 63, no. 2 (Summer 1990), pp. 191–209; idem., "Social Irrelevance of Politics: Hong Kong Chinese Attitudes toward Political Leadership," *Pacific Affairs*, vol. 65, no. 2 (Summer 1992), pp. 225–46; idem., *Public Attitude toward Political Parties in Hong Kong* (Hong Kong: Hong Kong Institute of Asia–Pacific Studies, 1992); idem., "Public Attitudes toward Political Leadership in Hong Kong: The Formation of Political Leaders," *Asian Survey*, vol. 34, no. 3 (March 1994), pp. 243–57; idem., "Democratization and Decline of Trust in Public Institutions in Hong Kong," *Democratization*, vol. 3, no. 2 (Summer 1996), pp. 158–80; and idem., "Political Order and Democratization in Hong Kong: The Separation of Elite and Mass Politics," unpublished paper, 1996.

11. Lau Siu-kai, "The Search for Political Legitimacy by the Hong Kong Special Administrative Region Government," unpublished paper, 1998.

12. A person could belong to two or more of the categories mentioned. Even so, the fact that the new appointees were dominated by pro-China and conservative figures was clearly evident.

13. The post of Secretary of Justice in the HKSAR government is equivalent to the post of attorney-general in the colonial government. The attorney-general was an expatriate up to the last minute of colonial rule.

14. All of the principal officials, except for Elsie Leung, were to assume office only on 1 July 1997.

15. It was rumoured that the civil servants wanted one of them to be appointed the head of the Central Policy Unit, while Tung's advisers preferred an outsider. Eventually, the civil servants won the battle when on 28 July 1997, Tung named Gordon Siu Kwing-chue — a senior civil servant — as the head of the Central Policy Unit.

16. In April 1997, the HKSAR government proposed to amend the Societies Ordinance and the Public Order Ordinance, adding "national security" as a ground for the government to prohibit the formation of societies and the holding of parades. This amendment was made to set the heart of Beijing — who was apprehensive about the occurrence of anti-communist actions after the handover — at ease. A number of principal officials, however, had deep reservations about this attempt to curb the freedom of expression in postcolonial Hong Kong.

17. On 9 July 1997, the Provisional Legislative Council passed the Immigration (Amendment) (No. 5) Bill 1997, which provided that children who claimed the right of abode in the HKSAR under Article 24(2) (3) of the Basic Law must produce proof of their rights by way of a certificate of entitlement or other acceptable proof of identity. The bill had retrospective effect dating from 1 July 1997. The purpose of the bill was to prevent a deluge of these children into Hong Kong. Certain principal officials, on the other hand, were of the opinion that the bill was in contravention of the Basic Law.

18. *South China Morning Post*, 5 March 1998, p. 1.

19. *South China Morning Post*, 7 March 1998, p. 1.

20. In fact, Tung's popularity rating always trailed behind that of Anson Chan's before and after the establishment of the HKSAR. This was deeply embarrassing to the chief executive.

21. Singapore offers a case of the new rulers taking the initiative to remould the mentality of the civil servants. The Singapore civil service at the time of independence was largely uninfluenced by nationalistic sentiments and Singapore's aspirations to achieve independence. In the opinion of the leaders of the People's Action Party (PAP), the civil service had to be tutored to develop a thorough commitment to a multiracial Singapore. "For this purpose, soon after they first assumed power in 1959, the PAP leaders set up a Political Study Centre with the chief purpose to impart political education to civil servants and raise their consciousness and understanding of the problems facing Singapore. The PAP rulers had little interest in the theoretical notion of a politically neutral civil service that served different political masters as and when they assumed power and owed a basic loyalty only to the state." Raj Vasil, *Governing Singapore* (Singapore: Mandarin, 1992), p. 137.

India, on the other hand, represents a case that saw the civil servants willingly taking a cooperative stance towards the new masters. According to Potter, the Indian Civil Service (ICS) realized at independence that political administrators do not last long if they become isolated from the political leadership of the state and dominant social classes in society. "The ICS tradition of administration survived the 1940s because there was continuing political support for it from first the British Government and then the Congress Government. Also, its continuation did not pose any threat to the dominant classes at the time. Although this broad *structure* of support is important in explaining why the ICS tradition survived, so also is the *agency* of Indian ICS initiatives in actively cultivating the support of leading politicians during the 1940s." David C. Potter, *India's Political Administrators 1919–1983*, p. 126.

CHAPTER 4

# THE ASIAN FINANCIAL CRISIS AND THE HONG KONG ECONOMY

Liu Pak Wai

## Introduction

In the 1990s as Hong Kong prepared for the changeover of sovereignty in 1997, the society was embroiled in the endless conflict between the Chinese government and the Hong Kong government (under British rule) over issues such as the financing of the new airport, container terminal no. 9, the political system, direct election and interpretation of the Basic Law. According to the scheme of the Chinese government, Hong Kong is to maintain stability and prosperity under the "one country, two systems" arrangement after 1997. During the transitional period, the political conflict, at times rather ferocious, raised doubts as to whether there would be stability in Hong Kong and whether the mainland government would honour its pledge of giving Hong Kong a high degree of autonomy after 1997. Economic prosperity was taken for granted whereas political stability was the main cause of concern. Indeed, it was the major push factor behind the emigration of Hong Kong residents.

It is ironic that after the changeover of sovereignty in July 1997, political stability faded away as an issue of main concern but the economy became the major focus. What many Hong Kong people and international observers feared about intervention by the Chinese authorities did not happen. The Chinese government has gone out of the way to rein in central and provincial government officials from intervening in Hong Kong affairs, so much so that they have refrained from making comments on Hong Kong in public, in sharp contrast to the days of political struggle against the British colonial government before 1997. The "one country, two systems" arrangement took off with an auspicious start. Quite unexpectedly, economic prosperity which most people took for grant after long years of high and steady growth, abruptly gave way to a sharp recession following the outbreak of the Asian financial crisis. One year into the Asian financial crisis, the picture of what went wrong in the Hong Kong economy becomes clear.

## Structural Problems Causing Inflation

Before the outbreak of the Asian financial crisis, Hong Kong has one of the highest cost structures in the world reflected in its property prices, office rentals and wages. Table 1 shows the average office rental cost of several cities in Asia and Australia.

The high cost structure was built up after a decade of high inflation in Hong Kong. Inflation accelerated since the mid-1980s as a result of rapid economic restructuring. Following the opening up of China in 1979, Hong Kong manufacturers took advantage of the low labour and land costs in South China, which were only a fraction of those in Hong Kong, and moved their labour-intensive low value-added production operations across the border into South China, leaving the front-end and back-end manufacturing processes, such as sourcing, merchandizing, marketing and design, in Hong Kong. These are the higher value-added processes which require different skills from those of assembling. Products of these outward-processing activities of Hong Kong manufacturers in South China are mostly re-exported through Hong Kong. This stimulates a fast growth in the re-export trade in Hong Kong,

*Table 4.1*

**Average Office Rental Costs in June 1997, Selected Cities**

| Location | Average cost per sq. m. (US dollar) | Location | Average cost per sq. m. (US dollar) |
|---|---|---|---|
| Hong Kong | | Sydney | |
| Central | 1,153 | Central | 477 |
| Wanchai | 825 | | |
| Causeway Bay | 789 | Taipei | |
| | | Min-Sheng | 478 |
| Shanghai | | Tun Hwa South | 456 |
| Huangpu | 1,063 | Nanking-SC | 401 |
| Singapore | | Tokyo | |
| Raffles Place | 938 | Maronouchi | 1,123 |
| Shenton Way | 801 | Toranomon | 1,036 |
| Orchard Road | 760 | Shinjuku | 926 |

*Note:* Average of highest and lowest rental cost

*Source: Hong Kong 21*

and demand for services to support these activities, including transportation, storage, business services, insurance and trade financing, expands rapidly. The economy of Hong Kong rapidly restructures itself to become service-oriented. What is unusual about the economic restructuring of Hong Kong in the 1980s is its speed. From 1981 to 1991 the share of manufacturing in employment fell from 41.3 percent to 28.2 percent. An index of sectoral shift in employment measuring the minimum proportion of workers who have to change sectors as a result of sectoral shift in 1987–92 for Hong Kong is 8.90 as compared with 3.27 for Singapore, 6.50 for Korea, 2.22 for Japan and 2.16 for the United States (Suen, 1995).

To understand how the structural adjustment process worked to generate inflation, it is useful to think of the economy as producing two types of products: traded and non-traded. Manufactured products in Hong Kong are usually traded. Services include both traded and non-traded products but as a whole they are less tradeable when compared to manufactured products. The outward expansion of manufacturing activities into South China led to a growth in income from foreign sources for Hong Kong that is not recorded in gross domestic product figures. This increase in wealth boosted consumption. While tradeables can be imported, consumption of non-tradeables have to be met by increased production at home. Given Hong Kong's linked exchange rate system, the prices of traded products are determined in world markets; their rates of inflation have to follow international levels. The prices of non-traded products are determined domestically; their rates of inflation depend on the excess of demand over supply.

## Wage Inflation

On the supply side the cost of producing non-tradeables, or specifically services, has increased due to the slow down in the growth of the labour force which ultimately led to a labour shortage in 1987–94. The slowdown in the growth of the labour force was caused by a number of factors. Following the abolition of the so-called "reached-base" policy in immigration in October 1980, illegal immigration ceased to be a major source of supply of cheap labour, as it had been in the last three decades. Since the policy change, illegal immigrants were no longer able to obtain residence status by illegal entry into Hong Kong. Employing illegal immigrants who had no identification documents also became a criminal offence. This effectively cut off the supply of unskilled labour.

Reduction in the inflow of immigrants alone has a major effect on slowing down the growth of the labour force. This effect is exacerbated by a number of other factors. These are the declining rate of natural population increase, the changing age structure of the population, the declining labour force participation rate, and the rising outflow of emigrants.

## Declining Rate of Natural Population Increase

The rate of natural population increase in Hong Kong has declined substantially over the last decades as a result of the rather rapid decline in fertility in Hong Kong. In 1965, Hong Kong's total fertility rate was 4.93. By 1990 it had fallen to 1.21 which was lower than that of virtually all North American, European and Asian countries. For instance, in 1990 the total fertility rates of the US was 1.88 (1989 figures), Sweden 2.14, the United Kingdom 1.84, Switzerland 1.59, Australia 1.90 (1989 figures), Japan 1.54 and Singapore 1.83 (Kono, 1996).

## Changing Age Structure of the Population

Since the labour force is drawn mainly from the population within the working age of 15 to 65, a shift in the age composition, in particular, from the younger age bracket to the older age bracket, will have a significant impact on the size of the labour force. The age group 15–24, being the youngest group in the labour force which will provide manpower for the economy for many years to come, shrank from 1.2 million in 1981 to about 886,000 in 1996. In contrast, the age group 55–64, which is due to retire from the labour force, grew in size from about 410,000 to 513,000 over the same period. The ageing of the population reduces the supply of labour over time.

## Declining Labour Force Participation Rate

Both the male, female and overall labour force participation rates reached a peak level in 1981 because the wave of illegal immigration in 1978–80 brought a massive influx of young illegal immigrants from the Mainland who by self-selection were mostly potential participants in the labour force. Since 1981 labour participation rates has declined (see Table 2), thus reducing labour supply over time.

The decline in overall labour participation rate is mainly due to the fall in the participation rate of the youngest and the oldest age groups in the labour force. The drop in the participation rates among youngsters of age 15–19 and 20–24 is the result of the rapid expansion of secondary and tertiary education in Hong Kong in the 1980s which provided more educational opportunities,

*Table 4.2*

## Labour Force Participation Rates in Hong Kong

| | Labour force participation rates (%) | | |
|---|---|---|---|
| Year | Male (%) | Female (%) | All (%) |
| 1976 | 80.7 | 45.0 | 63.3 |
| 1981 | 82.5 | 49.0 | 66.3 |
| 1986 | 80.5 | 48.9 | 65.1 |
| 1991 | 78.8 | 47.8 | 63.4 |
| 1996 | 76.0 | 47.8 | 61.8 |

*Source:* Economics Database, Department of Economics;
  *Hong Kong Monthly Digest of Statistics.*

causing many youngsters to defer entry into the labour force. As for workers in the age group 55–64 the decline in their participation rate can be attributed to their retiring earlier than before. The rise in the real wage of workers increases their income, which induces them to allocate more time to leisure and retire earlier.

## *Rising Outflow of Emigrants*

Much of the 1980s and the early 1990s were underpinned by the rising tide of emigration. The number of emigrants was between 18,000 and 22,000 throughout the first half of the 1980s. It picked up in 1987, and rose sharply in 1990 following the Tiananmen incident of 4 June 1989 in Beijing. The number of emigrants peaked at 66,000 in 1992 before moderating to a lower level following the tightening of quotas in major recipient countries like Canada and Australia (See Figure 4.1).

Emigration hit the service sectors hardest. Table 4.3 shows that a disproportionately large number of the employees who have emigrated were from the service sectors. This contrasts sharply with the experience in the manufacturing sector. Experienced and skilled personnel who emigrated had to be replaced by junior

*Figure 4.1*

## Total Estimated Emigrants, 1989–97

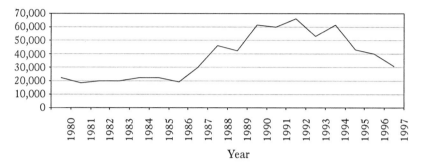

Year

*Source*: *Hong Kong Monthly Digest of Statistics* 1980 (January)–1998 (April)

*Table 4.3*

## Occupation of Emigrant Employees, 1988

| | |
|---|---|
| Professional | 33.6% |
| Administrator/Manager | 16.2% |
| Clerical | 13.4% |
| Sales | 13.1% |
| Services | 10.6% |
| Production | 9.0% |
| Others | 4.0% |

*Source:* Census & Statistics Department, and Consulates/High Commissions.

staff with less experience. As a result, labour productivity growth in the service sectors was slowed down more than in the manufacturing sector.

The combined effect of the above factors slows down the growth of the labour force. Since the abolition of the "reached-base" policy, the growth rate of the labour force has fallen to 1–3 percent p.a. (See Figure 4.2). The tightness of the labour market in the late 1980s to early 1990s had the effect of smoothening the structural unemployment problem which could have emerged from economic restructuring.

Manufacturing workers released by industries moving north were readily absorbed into the service sector. In fact during the period of most rapid economic restructuring in the late 1980s when sectoral shift in employment from manufacturing to service was the largest, the labour market was so tight that there was a period of labour shortage in 1989–94. Unemployment rate fell to a historical low of 1.1 percent in 1989 (see Figure 4.3).

*Figure 4.2*

**Labour Force Growth 1976–97**

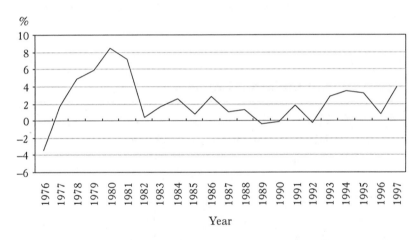

*Source*: *Hong Kong Monthly Digest of Statistics* 1980 (January)–1998 (April)

In response to labour shortage the Hong Kong government introduced a modest programme of importation of semi-skilled and unskilled labour in 1990. At the peak of the programme only about 27,000 workers were imported including those working on the construction of the new airport (but excluding domestic helpers). However, political opposition made it difficult for the government to expand the programme. By 1995, the labour market had eased and the unemployment rate rose. The

*Figure 4.3*

## Quarterly Unemployment Rate, 1987–98

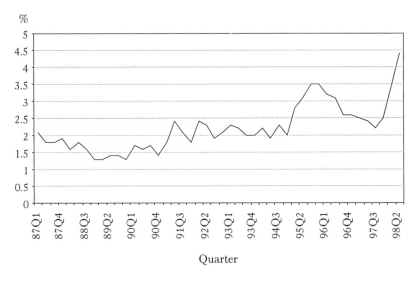

Quarter

**Source**: *Hong Kong Monthly Digest of Statistics*
1988 (January)–1998 (September)

government was obliged to replace the General Scheme of Labour Importation with a Supplementary Scheme 1996 which imported only 2,000 workers. The opportunity to ease the tight labour market and to moderate wage rise, from mid-1980s to mid-1990s, with labour importation was not fully exploited.

The consequence of an increased demand for labour, in particular in the service sector running against a slow growing labour force was dramatic. Wages rose rapidly (see Figure 4.4). The net effect of slower productivity increase but faster nominal wage growth in the service sector than the manufacturing sector is that production costs were pushed up faster in the former than in the latter. The rapid transformation of the economy that took place within the context of a slow growing labour force and the linked exchange rate combined to accelerate inflation. This explains why the domestic rate of inflation has been higher than international levels since 1986.

**Figure 4.4**

**Wage Growth vs Inflation 1967–97**

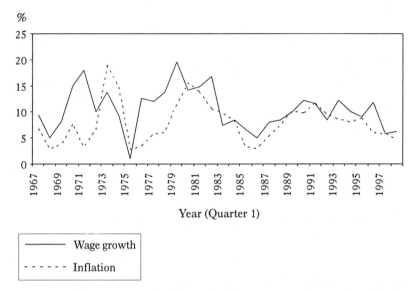

*Source*: *Hong Kong Monthly Digest of Statistics* 1967 (January)–1998 (April)

# Asset Price Inflation

The inflationary pressure in the product market is also reflected in input markets other than the labour market. Capital which is internationally mobile is less subjected to inflationary pressure from economic restructuring. Residential land is a relatively non-traded resource. Hence its value rises significantly.

The period of strong demand for land inauspiciously coincided with a period of restriction on the supply of new land. According to the Sino-British agreement on the future of Hong Kong signed in 1984, a Land Commission with representatives from the two governments was set up to approve the sale of new land up to 1997 subject to a limit of 50 hectares per annum. The Chinese government was very suspicious that the British Hong Kong government would sell as much land as possible before 1997 and repatriate the reserve, thus depriving the future Hong Kong

SAR government of a very valuable resource after 1997. This conspiracy theory led the Chinese government to insist on writing into the Sino-British agreements a restriction on the sale of land. Unfortunately the limit of 50 hectares was set in 1984, a year when the property market was at the lowest point after the crash in 1981. The limit was set too low as the projection of future demand for land was undoubtedly influenced by the actual demand at that time as well as the suspicion of British conspiracy.

The 50 hectares per annum encompass land for all use including residential, commercial, community and infrastructure, except public housing. In practice if the Hong Kong government was able to put up a case for more land, the Land Commission could approve more than 50 hectares. Given the atmosphere of mistrust and conspiracy which prevailed throughout the period of transition towards 1997, the Land Commission was not likely to be willing to approve much more than the 50-hectare limit. A request much beyond the 50 hectares put up by Hong Kong government representatives would cause suspicion and antagonism of the Chinese government representatives. Consequently, with the exception of special requests for the construction of major public facilities like the new airport, the new land supply approved by the Land Commission was about 50–100 hectares a year. The actual disposal of government land for residential property construction from 1985 to 1994 was about 20–30 hectares per annum. Only in 1995–97, when property prices already reached a very level, did the Land Commission approve about 60 hectares per annum (see Figure 4.5). It is interesting to contrast the annual supply of residential land over the last ten years with the planned supply of the Hong Kong SAR government in the first five years after the changeover as an indication of the possible large shortfall in the supply of land before 1997. In his first policy address in October 1997, the chief executive, Tung Chee-hwa, announced a policy to cool down the overheated property prices with increased supply of new residential land. The planned average annual supply of new residential land is 76 hectares which is about two to three times the actual supply in 1985–94.

The strong demand and the restricted supply of land pushed up property prices to an unrealistic level. Figure 4.6 shows that residential property price index increased sharply by sevenfold

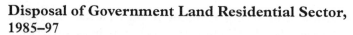

*Figure 4.5*

## Disposal of Government Land Residential Sector, 1985–97

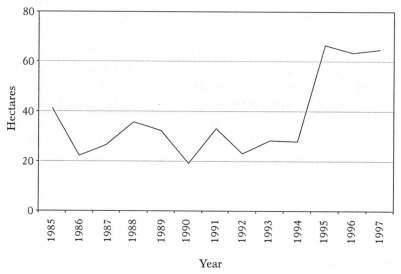

*Source*: *Hong Kong Monthly Digest of Statistics* 1985 (January)–1998 (April)

*Figure 4.6*

## Property Price Index 1987–98

(Base Year 1989=100)

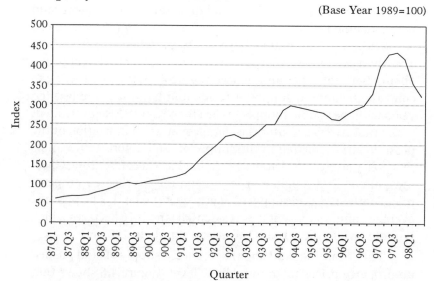

*Source*: *Hong Kong Monthly Digest of Statistics*
1989 (January)–1998 (September)

in the last 10 years before the market crashed in late 1997. Residential property prices in Hong Kong overtook Tokyo and all major cities to become the highest in the world by a wide margin. Commercial property prices and office rental followed more or less the same pattern.

To summarize, the analysis presented here offers an explanation for a wide array of phenomena in Hong Kong. First, we have an explanation for high inflation caused by rapid structural transformation of the Hong Kong economy that created a continuous excess demand for non-tradeables. Second, the opening of China generated an enormous boom in economic activity in Hong Kong, especially in the service sectors. The rapid growth in demand for labour ran against a slow growing labour force, leading to a situation of over full employment. Third, the slow growing labour force and full employment imposed capacity constraints on the economy. This is consistent with the observation of slow GDP growth. Fourth, the increase in wealth that accrued to Hong Kong from investments in China explains why despite slow GDP growth, asset prices in Hong Kong have risen faster than inflation. In the decade before the Asian financial crisis, the Hong Kong government failed to address the structural problems of the economy to remove labour and land supply bottlenecks. Wages and property prices rose to unrealistic levels. A bubble economy was taking shape.

# The Bubble Economy

The high cost structure of Hong Kong had been sustained for a decade before the onslaught of the Asian financial crisis. The opening up of China and its rapid economic growth generated plenty of high value-added economic activities in Hong Kong which are very profitable. It is estimated that the re-export margin which Hong Kong earns from the re-export of products from the Mainland is as high as 21.1 percent to 35.3 percent in 1990–94.[1]

For reasons explained earlier, property prices soared, bringing huge windfall profits to property developers. Related industries, such as construction, surveying and engineering, also reaped huge benefits from the property boom. The wealth of property investors, speculators and homeowners alike expanded rapidly as their assets appreciated through capital gain. The property market boom attracted an inflow of speculative capital from Southeast Asia and the Mainland. Credit lending of Hong Kong banks also contributed to the boom. Mortgage loan and property-related lending became the major and probably the most profitable business of banks. As property prices rose for over a decade, bad mortgage loans were almost non-existent. Even though the Hong Kong Monetary Authority (HKMA) has a guideline for banks that no more than 40 percent of their loan portfolios should be property-related, in practice, many banks exceeded the guideline. Mortgage loans were the most lucrative business, and in the last couple of years before the Asian financial crisis, banks competed fiercely for mortgage borrowers by lowering their mortgage interest rate to as low as prime rate plus 0.25 percent, even though historically the benchmark rate is around prime rate plus 1.5 percent.

The interest rate of Hong Kong followed the US interest rate because the Hong Kong dollar is linked to the US dollar at 7.8. As a result, throughout most of the ten-year period of high inflation in Hong Kong, the real interest rate (prime rate) was negative (See Figure 4.7). Negative interest rate, easy credit for mortgage loan, inflow of speculative capital, rising demand for land and property, and the shortage in the supply of new land were elements that contributed to the bubble in the property market. Residential property prices rose sharply. By mid-1997, the price of a first-rate luxurious condominium has risen to HK$20,000 per square foot (about US$2,600 per square foot). Medium-sized flats for the middle class in urban locations were selling at HK$8,000 per square foot (about US$1,000 per square foot). The wealth effect of asset price inflation fed into the retail, restaurant and other consumption-related sectors. The boom enabled these sectors to sustain their high cost of operation. Property prices inflation also helped to push the Hang Seng Index of the stock market to a historical high in August 1997. The bubble economy was ready to burst.

*Figure 4.7*

## Nominal Interest Rate vs Real Interest Rate, 1981–98

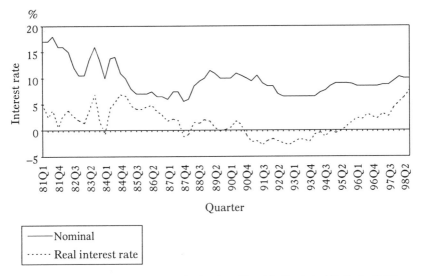

*Source*: Hong Kong Monetary Authority: *Monthly Statistical Bulletin* 1993 (January)–1993 (September); *Hong Kong Monthly Digest of Statistics* 1981 (January)–1998 (September)

# The Asian Financial Crisis and Cost Deflation

In the last few years concerns had been raised by many foreign investors and local businesses on the high cost of business operations in Hong Kong. There were warnings that Hong Kong would lose its competitiveness as its costs continued to inflate. However, because Hong Kong is located in the centre of the high growth region of East Asia, and is the gateway to rapid growing China, the profit and potential profit of investing in the region have attracted local and overseas businesses to continue to invest, despite the high cost.

The Asian financial crisis began with the depreciation of the Thai baht in July 1997, at the time of the changeover of sovereignty of Hong Kong. Hong Kong was caught by the contagion effect on 23 October 1997 when currency speculators attacked the Hong Kong dollar linked with the US dollar after Taiwan depreciated its currency. In defending the currency link, HKMA bought Hong Kong dollars unloaded by the speculators and the clearing balance accounts of the banks at HKMA were depleted. The overnight interbank rate shot up to 280 percent. The Asian financial crisis had swept into Hong Kong.

From 1 July 1997 to the end of January 1998, a number of Asian currencies had depreciated substantially with respect to the US dollar, the Indonesian rupiah by 79 percent, the Thai baht by 51 percent, the Korean won by 42 percent, the Malaysian ringgit by 41 percent, the Philippines peso by 28 percent, and the Taiwan dollar by 16 percent, and the Singapore dollar by 14 percent. The Hong Kong dollar link with the US dollar remained steady at 7.75. As a result all these Asian currencies depreciated with respect to the Hong Kong dollar.

The relative high cost structure of Hong Kong business operations gauged in US dollar was accentuated by currency depreciation of other Asian countries. Hong Kong abruptly lost competitiveness *vis-à-vis* its neighbouring countries in competing goods and services. The sector that was hit quickest and hardest is tourism. The decline in tourism began two months before the changeover. Travelling to other Asian countries became much cheaper than to Hong Kong after their currency depreciation. The fall in tourism demand due to the relative price effect was aggravated by the income effect as a number of source countries including Japan slipped into recession. In the first half of 1998, the number of visitor arrivals declined sharply by 21 percent as compared to the first half of 1997 (see Figure 4.8). Visitor arrivals from Japan, Southeast Asia and Europe sustained the largest drop.

As to Hong Kong's other goods and services which are non-competing with other countries either because they are non-tradeable or because of the unique location of Hong Kong with respect to China, the fall in their demand has also been sharp. Recession in several neighbouring Asian countries and the slowdown in the growth of China reduced profits and the prospect of profit of the business operations in Hong Kong. It is clear that Asia will no longer be the centre of growth for some years to come, as it has been in the last two decades. High profit becomes

*Figure 4.8*

## Growth Rate of Tourists, January–August 1998

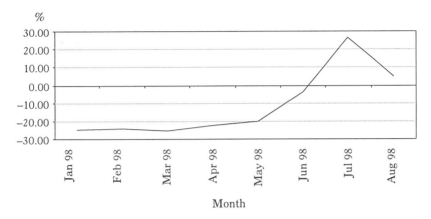

Month

***Source***: *Hong Kong Monthly Digest of Statistics*
1998 (January)–1998 (September)

something of the past. The high cost of operations in Hong Kong cannot be sustained. Examples of non-competing sectors are property and retail which cater mainly to local demand, and services for China operations.

The contraction in demand for goods and services is underpinned by a sharp rise in interest rate. The defence of the Hong Kong dollar link by HKMA caused interest rates to rise sharply every time there is a speculative attack on the currency. Interest rates fall after the attack recedes but stay at a higher level than before. The spread between the three-month Hong Kong interbank interest rate and the three-month US Treasury bill rate has widened from less than 1 percent of the pre-crisis level to 3–6 percent, reflecting the increase in risk premium in holding the Hong Kong dollar (Figure 4.9).

In a market as open, free and flexible as Hong Kong, the cost adjustment was swift. Asset price deflation was dramatic. Residential property prices fell by over 50 percent in 12 months since the last quarter of 1997. Commercial property prices fell even more sharply. From the peak of 16,673 in August 1997, the

Hang Seng index fell by 60 percent to a low of 6,600 points in August 1998. The swiftness of asset price deflation was no doubt abetted by the sharply rising and volatile interbank interest rate.

Cost deflation is also rather swift, following the pace of asset price deflation. Office and retail rentals fell dramatically. Not only new leases are signed at a much lower rent, existing leases are re-negotiated downward between the sitting tenants and the landlords. The labour market, however, is somewhat more sticky in adjustment. The initial cost adjustment is accomplished through layoffs. The unemployment rate rose from 2.5 percent in 4th quarter 1997 to 5 percent in 3rd quarter 1998. In recent months, price adjustment is picking up pace as wages for new hires fall substantially and existing wages of employees in hard-hit sectors like retail, restaurants and hotels, are slashed.

The deflation of the high cost structure brought on by the Asian financial crisis has been swift and the adjustment has been

*Figure 4.9*

**Spread of 3-month Interest Rates**
**January 1997 – September 1998**

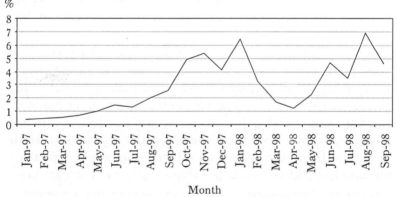

Month

*Source*: For Hong Kong Dollar Interbank Offered Rate
Hong Kong Monetary Authority: *Monthly Statistical Bulletin*
1997 (January)–1998 (October)

For US Treasury Bills
Federal Reserve Board of the United States
Website: http:/www.bog.frb.fed.us.

deep, causing enormous pain as jobs are lost and asset value evaporates. Were it not for the crisis, it was quite likely that the high cost structure would adjust downward anyway after July 1997 because the newly installed chief executive of the Hong Kong SAR government was determined to vastly increase the supply of land for residential property, a commitment which he emphasized in his inaugural speech as well as his first policy address of 8 October 1997. The bubble economy could be deflated slowly and a soft landing of the residential property market would be possible. Unfortunately only two weeks after the policy address, the Asian financial crisis swept into Hong Kong, and the property market collapsed.

There are several reasons why the economic adjustment of the economy of Hong Kong brought on by the Asian financial crisis is much sharper and steeper than that of Singapore. First, the Hong Kong dollar is linked to the US dollar. Unlike the Singapore dollar, the Hong Kong dollar has not depreciated. As a result, all adjustments have to work through prices and the real economy. Second, the Hong Kong capital market is more open than that of Singapore, making it an easier target for speculative attacks. Hence interest rates are more volatile, shooting up more whenever there is an attack. The currency defence mechanism adopted by the HKMA prior to September 1998 also induced higher interest rates than are necessary under a currency board arrangement. High interest rates and uncertainty caused sharp adjustments to the economy. Third, the property market bubble of Hong Kong was much bigger than that of Singapore at the onset of the Asian financial crisis. Deflation of Singapore's property market bubble started in mid-1996, one year before the crisis.

## Post-Crisis Challenges

When Hong Kong emerges from the Asian financial crisis, possibly one to two years from now, its high cost structure would have adjusted downwards. Hong Kong faces the challenges of another restructuring of its economy after the bubble economy is deflated by the crisis. Specifically, what are the driving forces for future economic growth? After wages have adjusted downwards substantially, what will sustain future wage growth?

In the last decade two factors have supported the full employment, high wage growth and rising standard of living in Hong Kong. They are the high value-added services associated with the opening up of China, such as the high re-export margin, and the high profit from the booming property sector which spills over to other related sectors. In the medium term, after Hong Kong emerges from the Asian financial crisis, it is questionable whether these two factors can continue to support full employment and high wage growth to the same extent as before.

The high value-added nature of the services Hong Kong provides for investment in China and her re-export trade is reflected in the large wage gap between Hong Kong and China. Wages in Hong Kong are often 10 times higher than corresponding wages in China. The reasons for the large wage gap are manifold. The openness of Hong Kong, access to international markets, free flow of information, the rule of law, the advanced physical infrastructure, and the efficient financial sector are comparative advantages of Hong Kong. They are the reasons why China relies on Hong Kong to source its materials, to merchandise, to market and to export its goods, and to finance its trade and investments. The high wages of Hong Kong are supported by these high valued-added activities. However, as China opens up further, gains freer access to information and international markets, develops its legal system and invests in infrastructure, Hong Kong's comparative advantages in these aspects will be eroded. Some of the services which Hong Kong provides will be replaced by cheaper services available in China. It is questionable that the huge wage gap between Hong Kong and China can persist.

Furthermore, the bursting of the bubble in the property market inflicted huge capital losses on many investors and homeowners, and caused painful adjustments of the economy. The Hong Kong SAR government is intent on managing land supply to avoid a repetition of a boom-bust property cycle. It is certainly sensitive to having another bubble in the property market. In the last several months, the Hong Kong SAR government has started to build up a land bank which will be used to moderate excessive property price movements in the future. The era of the bubble economy during which there are high profits from property development, investment and speculation is probably over. Another important driving force behind high wage growth and the rising standard of living of the past is gone.

To maintain the standard of living of Hong Kong which is among the highest in the world and to keep it rising, Hong Kong must find other high value-added economic activities which can generate employment and support high wage. Hereby lie the challenges for Hong Kong.

There are two areas of high value-added activities that Hong Kong may exploit. First, Hong Kong can develop into a truly first rate international financial centre, anchoring on the prospect of rapid economic growth of China which generates a growing demand for foreign funds in the next decade or two. Hong Kong is already a leading regional financial centre, but so far it is not in the same league as London and New York. As China continues to grow rapidly, more of its state enterprises will float in Hong Kong's stock market. It has been estimated that two to three decades from now, Hong Kong could become the largest stock market in the world in capitalization. Hong Kong can become the international financial centre of China while Shanghai develops as China's domestic financial centre. Hong Kong has the conditions to be an international financial centre: its financial markets are open; its banking sector is efficient and relatively transparent; and the supervisory framework is robust and the judicial system trustworthy.

However, to be an international financial centre has its costs. Openness makes one's currency an easy target for speculative attacks, particularly if there are structural weaknesses in the local economy or if the contagion effect of currency attacks spreads from neighbouring economies. Experience of the current Asian financial crisis shows that countries that have the most open financial markets are more vulnerable to speculative attacks, whereas countries which are shielded from the international capital markets like China, or countries which have some measures of capital control like Taiwan and Singapore, are less subject to attacks.

95

Another cost of being an international centre is the giving up of some monetary autonomy. International fund flows are measured in trillions of US dollars and are growing rapidly. It is difficult for a small country to operate a completely open international financial centre using its small volume of domestic currency as the instrument. Regular fund flows in and out of the financial centre will cause too many shocks to the domestic monetary system, let alone occasional speculative attacks. To immunize the domestic economy from the shock of currency conversion, more and more transactions of the international financial centre will have to be conducted in an international currency like the US dollar. For instance, not only syndicated loans will have to be denominated in US dollars, bonds and share market listings will also have to be in US dollar. As Hong Kong develops into an international financial market, market force will drive the economy towards more extensive use of the US dollar, and there will be progressive dollarization. The Hong Kong SAR government should allow the market to evolve and not prevent this from happening. In this regard, the successful defence of the Hong Kong dollar link at 7.8, and its continuation after the crisis will help to strengthen Hong Kong's development into an international financial centre.

A second area of high value-added activities which Hong Kong can exploit is innovation and technology. Studies by Young (1994, 1995), Kim and Lau (1994a, 1994b), and Lau (1997) show that technical progress and total factor productivity make negligible contribution towards the rapid growth of the Asian newly industrializing economies (NIEs). For an economy as advanced as Hong Kong, there is little room for fast growth on the basis of high savings and investment. Technical progress underpins the further growth of the US and European economies and that is the direction in which Hong Kong should be heading. In restructuring into a service economy, labour-intensive manufacturing operations have been relocated from Hong Kong into South China. Hong Kong has not invested much in technology in the past. However, there is a potential that Hong Kong can become a regional centre of innovation and technology. Hong Kong can capitalize on its synergy with South China, make use of the scientific and engineering personnel in the region, organize research and development (R&D)

and commercialize the product. Innovation and technology are not only confined to manufactured products. They can be applied to processes, such as design, and deployed to upgrade the service sector performance as well. They also have the benefit of diversifying the Hong Kong economy. An economy narrowly based on financial services is more vulnerable to external shocks as we are keenly aware in the current financial crisis.

In early 1998, the chief executive of the Hong Kong SAR appointed a Commission on Innovation and Technology. The recommendations of the interim report were accepted by the Chief Executive and incorporated into his recent policy address in October 1998. An Applied Science and Technology Research Institute will be established to do mid-stream research, filling in the gap between up-stream research done in the universities, and down-stream research of the corporations. An innovation and technology fund of HK$5 billion will be set up to support R&D. Greater co-operation between universities and industries will be promoted.

It will be some years before these efforts on innovation and technology will bear fruit. At the end of the day, innovation and technology are not likely to replace financial services as the major pillar of the Hong Kong economy. However, it could be a significant sector of the economy with an important spillover effect on the service sector, and it helps to diversify the economy. Innovation and technology will be a major challenge for Hong Kong in the next decade or two.

A key ingredient in developing Hong Kong into an international financial centre and a centre for innovation and technology is human capital. A first-rate international financial centre like New York does not rely on New York City solely to supply the skilled professionals. It draws talent from all over the US and, indeed, from all over the world. Similarly, leading R&D in major corporations in the US. such as Microsoft, IBM, and Intel, are supported not only by scientists who are US nationals but by researchers from all over the world. Indeed, the percentage of foreign-born scientists and engineers in the US is very high.

To become a first-rate international financial centre and a centre for innovation and technology, Hong Kong must draw on the global pool of talent. Herein lies a comparative advantage of

Hong Kong. While Hong Kong may offer limited attraction to Western professionals to come to work in Hong Kong, it is very attractive to professionals in the Mainland as well as mainland professionals residing overseas. This pool of talent is virtually unlimited, by virtue of the sheer size of China's population. Under the "one country, two systems" arrangement, it is possible to bring in talent from the Mainland to study, work and ultimately reside in Hong Kong. Before the changeover of sovereignty in 1997, this would not have been politically possible.

Large-scale admission of talent from China is essential to the development of Hong Kong into a first-rate international financial centre and a centre for innovation and technology. It could catapult Hong Kong into other areas of high value-added activities as well. It will help to sustain the economic growth of Hong Kong through productivity gain, maintain the large wage gap between Hong Kong and the Mainland, and keep Hong Kong's standard of living rising. Studies on immigration in the US and Hong Kong have shown that immigrants do not have a significant adverse impact on wages and employment of local people (Suen, 1994; Lam and Liu, 1998). Quite the contrary, immigration expands the productive capacity of the economy and creates employment for other people. The Hong Kong SAR government must muster political support to change its immigration policy to allow mainland talent to come to study, to work and to stay in Hong Kong.

# The Third Economic Restructuring

Since the Second World War, the economy of Hong Kong has gone through two major economic restructuring. In each instance, Hong Kong was able to exploit the economic opportunities which arose from a hardship situation, and was flexible in adjusting its economic structure. Each restructuring has propelled Hong Kong to higher levels of GDP and a higher standard of living.

The first major economic restructuring came during and after the Korean War. Before the Korean War, Hong Kong served as an entrepot for South China. The trade embargo imposed by the United Nations on China during the Korean War stifled the entrepot trade between China and the Western world. Hong Kong's livelihood was under threat. The people of Hong Kong were able to turn the crisis into opportunities by transforming its economy from being an entrepot into a manufacturing centre. Entrepreneurs from Shanghai who arrived in Hong Kong after 1949 brought with them capital, skills and experience. They took advantage of the availability of cheap labour from the vast pool of refugees who fled the Mainland after 1949, and started labour-intensive manufacturing in Hong Kong.

For two decades Hong Kong developed as a centre of labour-intensive manufacturing, becoming the world's largest producer of garments, toys and watches at one time or the other. The abolition of the "reached-base" immigration policy in 1980 closed off the possibility of a future large influx of cheap labour through illegal immigration. By the late 1970s, industrial wages had increased to such a level that labour-intensive manufacturing in Hong Kong was rapidly losing its competitiveness *vis-à-vis* other newly industrializing countries in Asia. Manufacturing industries in Hong Kong were in serious difficulties. Just around this time, China launched its economic reform and open-door policy in 1979. Again Hong Kong manufacturers seized the opportunity and relocated their factory operations in the Pearl River Delta to take advantage of the cheap land and labour. Hong Kong was transformed from a manufacturing economy into a service economy. This is the second major economic restructuring.

After Hong Kong emerges from the Asian financial crisis, Hong Kong could be facing its third major economic restructuring to transform itself into a first-rate international financial centre and a regional centre of innovation and technology. Unlike the previous two restructuring experiences, instead of capital in search of cheap labour, the third economic restructuring will be driven by a large scale inflow of human capital in the form of highly skilled professionals, scientists and engineers of Mainland origin from the Mainland and overseas. The changeover of sovereignty in 1997 and the "one country, two systems" arrangement make this flow of talent into Hong Kong politically possible. The Hong Kong SAR government must change its immigration policy to make this happen. As in the previous history of Hong Kong's economic restructuring, opportunities beckon. It is up to the people and the government of the Hong Kong SAR to take up the challenge.

## NOTES

1. See "Analysis of Hong Kong's Retained Imports, 1989–1994", *Hong Kong Monthly Digest of Statistics*, February 1996.

## REFERENCES

Business and Professionals Federation of Hong Kong (1993). *Hong Kong 21: A Ten Year Vision and Agenda For Hong Kong's Economy*. May.

Hong Kong Government (1996). "Analysis of Hong Kong's Retained Imports, 1989–1994". *Hong Kong Monthly Digest of Statistics*. February.

Kim, Jong-Il and Lawrence J. Lau (1994a). "The Sources of Economic Growth of the Newly Industrialized Countries on the Pacific Rim". In L.R. Klein & E.T. Yu (eds.), *The Economic Development of ROC and the Pacific Rim in the 1990s and Beyond* (Singapore: World Scientific Publishing Co.).

———— (1994b). "The Sources of Economic Growth of the East Asian Newly Industrialized Countries". *Journal of The Japanese and International Economies,* 8:235–71.

Kono, Shigemi (1996). "Relation between Women's Economic Activity and Child Care in Low-Fertility Countries". In United Nations, *Population and Women* (New York: United Nations.

Lam, Kit Chun and Liu, Pak Wai (1998). *Immigration and The Economy of Hong Kong*. (Hong Kong: City University of Hong Kong Press).

Lau, Lawrence J. (1997). "The Sources of and Prospects for East Asian Economic Growth". Mimeo. Stanford University. July.

Suen, Wing (1994). "Estimating the Effects of Immigration in One City". Discussion paper no. 159. School of Economics and Finance, The University of Hong Kong. April.

———— (1995). "Sectoral Shifts: Impact on Kong Kong Workers." *Journal of International Trade and Economic Development,* 4(July ):135–52.

Young, Alwyn (1994). "Lessons from the East Asian NICS: A Contrarian View". *European Economic Review,* 38:964–73.

———— (1995). "The Tyranny of Numbers: Confronting the Statistical Realities of the East Asian Growth Experience". *Quarterly Journal of Economics,* 110 (August):641–80.

CHAPTER 5

## CHANGING STRUCTURE OF HONG KONG'S ECONOMY

Tsang Shu-ki

## The Contagion Effect in Hong Kong

The East Asian financial turmoil began in Thailand, Malaysia and the Philippines in the summer of 1997. Each of these countries showed some kind of external imbalances, in terms of current account deficits or foreign exchange exposure. So had South Korea and Indonesia, which were affected shortly after. Several schools of thought in mainstream economics have attempted to explain the unprecedented crisis in East Asia (Tsang, 1998g), including Krugman's (1998) "crony capitalism", the "panic" theory of Radelet and Sachs (1998) and McKinnon's (1998) view on "exchange rate misalignment" between the Japanese yen and the US dollar. However, these theories could not explain clearly why the crisis spread to Singapore, Taiwan and Hong Kong — all relatively "healthy" economies. In 1996, for example, Hong Kong had a roughly balanced current account, while Singapore managed to have a *surplus* of 16 percent of GDP! Taiwan's surplus was less impressive, but the ratio still stood at about 5 percent of GDP. Moreover, all three economies had some of the largest foreign exchange reserves in the world.

The culprit is the so-called "contagion effect". How did it start? Fred Bergsten (1997), a former undersecretary of the US treasury and now Director of the Institute for International Economics, pointed the accusing finger at Taiwan. He criticized the Taiwanese authorities for "[choosing] to let its currency join the decline after a minimal defensive effort" and, therefore, spreading the crisis to the "strong center" economies of Hong Kong and Singapore. "On every measure, its [Taiwan's] competitive position remained very strong even after the depreciations in southeast Asia and Korea. Hence its action was totally unnecessary and violated every norm of international cooperative behaviour."

The Hong Kong Monetary Authority (HKMA) holds the same line of argument, albeit more diplomatically. In the *Report on Financial Market Review* released in April 1998, the Hong Kong government said, "On 20 October (1997), the New Taiwan dollar depreciated by 5.8%, as a result of the authorities' announcement of allowing the currency to float. This sparked off speculation on the resolve of Hong Kong authorities in maintaining the linked exchange rate with the US dollar" (FSB, 1998:7).

# The Unexpectedly Deep Recession in Hong Kong

The impact of the financial crisis on Hong Kong turned out to be deeper than most analysts anticipated. Even by May 1998, most economists and financial experts forecast either a pessimistic negative growth of between –0.5 percent and zero growth or a modest positive growth of 1 percent to 2 percent for the whole year. Then came the series of bad news: GDP growth was –2.8 percent in the first quarter of 1998, and –5 percent in the second; while the unemployment rate shot up to 5 percent in the months of May to July, the highest in 15 years. Now it seems likely that Hong Kong might witness a negative growth of –5.0 percent for the whole year of 1998 — the worst recession since reliable statistics became available in the early 1960s! The deterioration in the past few months has caught most commentators by surprise.

That would put Hong Kong much nearer to the category of the Asian disaster zone, than to Singapore and Taiwan, our real competitors. Economies with worse than –5 percent negative real growth in 1998 are expected to include only South Korea, Thailand and Indonesia. Taiwan should be able to register a positive growth of 4 percent to 5 percent, and Singapore may end up with 0.5 percent or 1 percent. All the economies in the region have been facing *the same external crisis*. But what were the conditions in Hong Kong that made it so vulnerable to the financial crisis? I shall argue that *three different sets of internal factors* have contributed to Hong Kong's predicament.

First, the structural imbalance that had built up in the Hong Kong economy before the crisis was more serious than that in Singapore and Taiwan. Second, since Hong Kong has stuck to the linked exchange rate in the face of *persistent* speculative attacks instead of letting the currency depreciate, the impact tends to be harder, particularly regarding high and volatile interest rates. Third, the government has not been decisive enough in handling the rapidly unfolding crisis, resulting in the loss of opportunities and a lamentable increase in economic costs.

Let me elaborate on each of these factors.

## *Structural Imbalance and the Economic Bubble*

The first internal factor contributing to the present crisis is the structural imbalance in the Hong Kong economy. Two major forces have been driving the imbalance since the early 1980s which now contribute to the present post-1997 problems. The first is the "China factor": Hong Kong's economic "integration" with Mainland China. The second is the escalating dominance of the property sector.

Both factors have pushed Hong Kong down the path of what I describe as "Manhattanization" (Tsang, 1994; 1998d). Between 1980 and 1996, contribution to GDP by the manufacturing sector dropped from 23.7 percent to 7.2 percent (see Table 5.1), while the number of workers in the manufacturing sector fell from over 900,000 in 1980 to less than 290,000 by the end of 1997. At the same time, employment in the major service sectors more than doubled. Hong Kong has developed rapidly as a monetary centre and resembles New York's financial hub (see Table 5.2). The speed of such a "structural transformation" of an economy is very rare in modern economic history.

*Table 5.1*

**Production-based GDP at current prices by economic activity (unit: %)**

|                                                                      | 1980  | 1990  | 1996  |
| -------------------------------------------------------------------- | ----- | ----- | ----- |
| Agriculture and fishing                                              | 0.8   | 0.3   | 0.1   |
| Mining and quarrying                                                 | 0.2   | 0.0   | 0.0   |
| Manufacturing                                                        | 23.7  | 17.6  | 7.2   |
| Electricity, gas and water                                           | 1.3   | 2.3   | 2.4   |
| Construction                                                         | 6.6   | 5.4   | 5.8   |
| Wholesale/retail, import/export trades, restaurants and hotels       | 21.4  | 25.2  | 25.4  |
| Transport, storage and communications                                | 7.4   | 9.5   | 10.2  |
| Financing, insurance, real estate & business services               | 23.0  | 20.2  | 24.9  |
| Community, social and personal services                              | 12.1  | 14.5  | 17.9  |
| Ownership of premises                                                | 8.9   | 10.6  | 13.9  |
| Adjustment for financial intermediation services indirectly measured | −5.4  | −5.5  | −7.9  |
|                                                                      | 100.0 | 100.0 | 100.0 |

*Table 5.2*

## Employment by Industry Group

(persons engaged at year-end)

| | 1980 | 1990 | 1997 |
|---|---|---|---|
| Manufacturing | 902,521 | 741,366 | 288,887 |
| | (46.5) | (30.1) | (12.6) |
| Wholesale/retail, import/export trades, restaurants and hotels | 441,892 | 805,411 | 1,003,072 |
| | (22.8) | (32.7) | (43.8) |
| Transport, storage and communications | 74,109 | 129,551 | 178,104 |
| | (3.8) | (5.2) | (7.8) |
| Financing, insurance, real estate and business services | 123,883 | 270,610 | 410,979 |
| | (6.4) | (11.0) | (17.9) |
| Other industrial sectors | 396,767 | 517,107 | 411,035 |
| | (20.5) | (21.0) | (17.9) |

*Note*: *Figures in parentheses represent percentage shares of the total.*

Such a process is, in my view, inconsistent with the framework of "one country, two systems", in which Hong Kong is not supposed to "dissolve" itself into the Chinese economy in a complete division of labour. The fact that Hong Kong's manufacturing base has actually become larger in the Pearl River Delta provides no comfort because employment is not created inside Hong Kong. It is just like an outflow of capital and a shift of industries offshore.

As stipulated by the Basic Law, Hong Kong has to take care of her own fiscal, monetary and manpower problems. Hong Kong will not be able to expediently "export" its difficulties (including unemployment or the lack of demand for its goods and services) to Mainland China, like what New York in the United States or London in the United Kingdom can do against the backdrop of a country of one unified economic system. As far as the exporting of unemployment is concerned, there are actually two major barriers:

(1) Legal barrier. Hong Kong citizens are not entitled to employment rights in the Mainland other than through the route of "foreign invested enterprises".

(2) Economic barrier. The wide gaps in wages and social infrastructure, such as housing, education and medicine between the two systems may constrain labour mobility.

Because of these two barriers, the Hong Kong economy needs to maintain some "coherence" in its own structure (Tsang, 1994; 1998d).

Unfortunately, these economic constraints of "one country, two systems" were not fully understood before 1997. Even worse, the Chinese and the British were engaging in hostile politics that had the side effect of paralyzing any significant initiatives in economic restructuring. The Patten Administration's failure to build a land bank and to provide an adequate supply of land to the market was one clear and disappointing example (Tsang, 1998d).

The dramatic "economic restructuring" of Hong Kong has led to voids that have been largely filled by real estate developments and their related businesses, as reflected in the huge increases in property prices and rentals. Take the example of residential property prices. As Table 5.3 shows, their average level rose by eightfold between 1985 and 1997, yielding an annual nominal growth rate of 19.0 percent, far above those of Hong Kong's GDP (13.5 percent) and per capita GDP (11.8 percent) growth. In many categories of property, Hong Kong was the most expensive in the world by 1997. Moreover, more than 40 percent of bank loans were extended to property-related activities, including property mortgages, building and construction, and property developments. A direct consequence of the surge in property prices and rentals was that it pushed up the profitability of the real estate sector and its affiliates, e.g.

legal services and finance, while squeezing that of other services (e.g. retail outlets and restaurants), not to mention the manufacturing industries.

## Worrying Developments in the 1990s

Worrying trends emerged in the Hong Kong economy in the 1990s. The average annual real growth rate of the economy slowed to 5.3 percent in 1991–97, compared with 6.5 percent in the 1980s. Some put the blame on the slowing expansion of Hong Kong's workforce. While the local labour force grew at an annual rate of 4.2 percent in the 1970s, providing a large pool of cheap labour, its annual expansion rate fell to 1.7 percent in the 1980s. However, it actually revived and grew at a rate of 2.3 percent per annum in

*Table 5.3*

**Annual average indexes of stock prices, residential property prices and nominal per capita GDP**

| Year | Hang Seng Index | Private residential property price index | Nominal per capita GDP index |
|------|------|------|------|
| 1984 | 100.0 | 100.0 | 100.0 |
| 1985 | 155.4 | 109.7 | 104.8 |
| 1986 | 195.2 | 121.4 | 119.1 |
| 1987 | 286.0 | 148.9 | 145.0 |
| 1988 | 253.5 | 181.6 | 170.2 |
| 1989 | 275.8 | 229.1 | 193.9 |
| 1990 | 300.2 | 254.9 | 214.9 |
| 1991 | 379.7 | 350.5 | 244.6 |
| 1992 | 549.9 | 492.6 | 282.8 |
| 1993 | 763.1 | 543.5 | 320.1 |
| 1994 | 937.3 | 670.7 | 352.5 |
| 1995 | 902.1 | 623.7 | 368.2 |
| 1996 | 1,154.8 | 683.3 | 397.6 |
| 1997 | 1,406.5 | 958.4 | 424.2 |

1990–96 as a result of local demographics, returned migrants and increased intakes from Mainland China. Theoretically, this should have resulted in greater growth momentum. However, in reality this has not occurred. Real per capita GDP growth in Hong Kong dropped from an annual average of 5.2 percent in the 1980s to 3.5 percent in 1990–96; and per worker GDP fell from 4.7 percent to 3.3 percent. It appears that the Hong Kong economy had "matured" very quickly.

Kwong, Lau and Lin (1997) find that the "total factor productivity" (TFP) in the manufacturing sector had declined from 1984–93. They use total output instead of value-added in measurement, and attempt "to capture the input of Chinese (cheap) labour into Hong Kong manufacturing output by taking into account the intermediate inputs injected into the local manufacturing sector". Their conclusion is that "[g]iven the same amount of inputs, the manufacturing sector could produce in 1993 only 87 percent of the output in 1984". It seems that access to much cheaper labour in the Pearl River Delta, with its consequential windfall profit, has weakened the pressure for the local industrialists to climb the technological ladder. The China factor has led to a relative decline in Hong Kong's manufacturing productivity.

There has not been any rigorous study on productivity in the service sectors in Hong Kong. One key issue is to define service efficiency itself, with all the well-known problems of measurements, such as the standards of services. Many employees who have moved from the manufacturing sector to the lower-end service sectors (such as retail sales and restaurants) in massive scales are not noted for their graceful manners. At higher levels, influential employers have lamented the lack of general knowledge and the falling standard of English among university graduates.

Another emerging trend is that of widening income inequality (e.g. Tsang, 1993). Table 5.4 shows the worrying trend in the past two and a half decades. The share of the poorest 10 percent of households had fallen persistently from 2.3 percent in 1971 to 1.1 percent in 1996, while the share of the richest 10 percent of households rose from 34.6 percent to

*Table 5.4*

## Changes in household income distribution in Hong Kong

| Income group | Share in total household income (%) | | | | | |
|---|---|---|---|---|---|---|
| | 1971 | 1976 | 1981 | 1986 | 1991 | 1996 |
| Lowest decile (10%) | 2.3 | 1.9 | 1.4 | 1.6 | 1.3 | 1.1 |
| 2nd decile | 3.9 | 3.5 | 3.2 | 3.4 | 3.0 | 2.6 |
| 3rd decile | 5.1 | 4.6 | 4.4 | 4.4 | 4.0 | 3.6 |
| 4th decile | 5.1 | 5.5 | 5.4 | 5.4 | 5.0 | 4.6 |
| 5th decile | 7.0 | 6.8 | 6.5 | 6.4 | 6.1 | 5.7 |
| 6th decile | 7.3 | 8.1 | 7.8 | 7.6 | 7.4 | 7.0 |
| 7th decile | 9.0 | 8.8 | 9.4 | 9.1 | 9.0 | 8.5 |
| 8th decile | 11.0 | 11.3 | 11.5 | 11.4 | 11.4 | 10.6 |
| 9th decile | 14.7 | 15.9 | 15.2 | 15.2 | 15.5 | 14.5 |
| Highest decile | 34.6 | 33.6 | 35.2 | 35.5 | 37.3 | 41.8 |
| **Total** | **100.0** | **100.0** | **100.0** | **100.0** | **100.0** | **100.0** |
| **Gini Coefficient** | **0.43** | **0.43** | **0.451** | **0.453** | **0.476** | **0.518** |

41.8 percent. In 1996, the Gini coefficient rose above 0.5 for the first time since reliable statistical records became available. A widening income gap would affect local consumption, particularly in view of the structural disequilibrium created by persistently high property prices and rentals. People just would not have much purchasing power left after paying for the very high mortgage payments or rentals for their flats.

## Bubble in the Run-up to the 1997 Transition

A tired economy is vulnerable to speculation. The narrowing of the range of profitable activities would force money into the already shrinking "funnel". In a way, it is like a scenario of "too much money chasing too few profitable opportunities". Ironically, by design or by default, the China factor also contributed directly

*Figure 5.1*

## Hong Kong's Stock Market Indexes

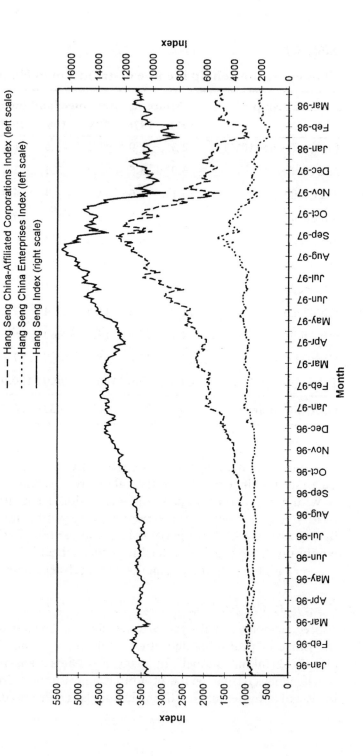

to the latest financial bubble in Hong Kong. Since October 1996, Chinese capital reportedly poured into the property and stock markets in the territory.

Fed by rumours and observable transactions, property prices went on a dramatic upswing in the last few months of 1996. The average price index of residential property units rose by 40 percent to 60 percent in the following 12 months. In the stock market, prices of China-related stock shares listed in Hong Kong also soared. From the beginning of June 1997 to late August 1997, the H-shares index (the China Enterprises Index) rocketed 60 percent, while the red-chips index (the China-Affiliated Corporations Index) surged 40 percent, compared with the 7 percent rise in the Hang Seng Index composed of an elite basket of stocks. Their fall from the peak, which actually began before the October 1997 speculative attack on the Hong Kong dollar, was equally breathtaking: the H-shares index plunged by 50 percent between late August and mid-October 1997, as the red-chips index took a 38-percent battering. The Hang Seng Index meanwhile fell by about 18 percent.

In other words, just before the East Asian financial crisis, a huge economic bubble was building up in Hong Kong. It was larger than anything that could be observed in either Singapore (where the private residential property sector was much smaller than that in Hong Kong) or Taiwan (where there was no pre-1997 rally). Hence the economic adjustment in Hong Kong has been much more pronounced.

## The Hong Kong Linked Exchange Rate System: Anchor or Curse?

The second factor aggravating Hong Kong's economic agony is the dilemma created by the linked exchange rate system, under which the Hong Kong dollar has been pegged to the US dollar at the rate of 7.80 since October 1983. It was a product of politics, in fact a rescue measure to save the dollar in the heat of Sino-British conflicts over the future of Hong Kong. Hence, unlike the implicit nominal and real pegs practised by many East Asian economies, or the "crawling peg" in the case of the Singapore dollar (pegged to a basket of currencies including the US dollar), the Hong Kong dollar link is explicit, officially announced and defended with the utmost effort. Moreover, it carries with it a political meaning, which sometimes becomes almost sacred.

Before the 1997 transition, nobody dared to propose any changes to this exchange rate system. It was seen as the most important anchor in a turbulent time, keeping "ill-intended speculators" away. But in the post-1997 era, "quiet re-floating" could always be an option.[1]

Unfortunately, just as the Hong Kong people thought that they could feel relief after the political transition, the speculative attack on the Hong Kong dollar occurred. There are actually only two time points when a fixed exchange rate system can *optimally* change under attack: (1) immediately when the attack takes place; and (2) after the storm is over and when everything calms down again.

The first option is "wise" in the sense that the speculators lose a "target" (notwithstanding what was said previously about Taiwan's action on 20 October 1997). Nevertheless, Hong Kong missed that opportunity. On 23 October, the HKMA defended the link vigorously, and overnight interbank interest rates shot up to 280 percent briefly. Since then, interest rates had remained at very high levels and shown huge volatility. That phenomenon proved to be the most depressing factor in the Hong Kong economy, leading to a "credit crunch" in the banking system that strangled normal economic activity and added to our economic blues (Tsang, 1998d).

Now, after several more rounds of speculative attacks on the "target", abandoning the link might produce a disaster. It could result in a massive loss of confidence in the government and a scale of capital flight that would be difficult to imagine. Hence the second choice of soldiering on seems to be the only optimal choice left, unless the world enters a great depression like the 1930s and "competitive devaluation" prevails again. Even in that doomsday scenario, when the economic pain becomes unbearable, the Hong Kong dollar should not be floated, but be re-pegged at a lower level, say HK$10 or HK$12 to US$1 (Tsang, 1998h). The devaluation would, of course, undermine the confidence in the sanctity of the currency board system and should, therefore, be used only as a last resort.

# The HKSAR Government's Handling of the Crisis

The third factor that has probably aggravated the recession in Hong Kong is the SAR government's management of the unfolding crisis. As a "currency board system", the Hong Kong linked exchange rate system was flawed in that there was no effective arbitrage mechanism that really fixed the spot exchange rate (Tsang, 1996a; 1996b; 1998a; 1998c). The Hong Kong Monetary Authority (HKMA) had to resort to the manipulation of interbank liquidity and interest rates, as well as outright intervention in the foreign exchange market (Tsang, 1998a). These were inconsistent with the basic principles of market-driven fixed rate systems, including the gold standard and currency board arrangements (CBAs).

In 1996, the Hong Kong Policy Research Institute (HKPRI) conducted research on ways to strengthen the link. A report by this author was completed in October 1996 and disseminated to top officials in the government. In the report, two proposals were made to improve the link: (1) incorporating cash in the settlement system; and (2) adopting the AEL model of Argentina, Estonia and Lithuania, under which the central bank guarantees the convertibility at the fixed exchange rate of the whole monetary base (instead of just the cash base as in the classical currency board). Under the AEL model, an effective electronic arbitrage mechanism would be in place, whereby banks could arbitrage against each other without the movement of cash. No banks would dare to quote a spot exchange rate that deviates from the official rate. The spot rate would, therefore, be firmly "locked" and the central bank need not intervene (Tsang, 1996a; 1996b; 1997). After the speculative attack in October 1997, the government reviewed the AEL model again but did not adopt the proposals in its April 1998 Report (FSB, 1998; Tsang, 1998a).

Then the government made a historical move in August 1998 by intervening in the stock and futures markets, citing the danger of "double market play" (Yam, 1998). This means that speculators had been attacking the Hong Kong dollar, pushing up local interest rates, so that their short positions in the stock and futures markets would yield handsome profits. The Hong Kong government refused to accept such activities and wanted to restore order in the financial markets through direct intervention. The action touched off a huge controversy, including an open criticism by Alan Greenspan, the chairman of the US Federal Reserve System (US Fed), which seemed out of place given the fact that the Fed itself had to intervene and bail out the hedge fund Long-term Capital Management (LTCM) later.

On 5 September 1998, the HKMA belatedly implemented "seven technical measures" to reform Hong Kong's currency board system (CBA). The measures could be categorized into two major moves, the first and the most important one being the partial adoption of the AEL model (Tsang, 1998c; 1998e; Sung, 1998; *Hong Kong Economic Journal*, 1998; Dow Jones Newswires, 1998). The HKMA now undertakes to buy Hong Kong dollars in the clearing accounts of licensed banks at the fixed rate of HK$7.75/US$1. This simply means that convertibility is extended to the whole monetary base: following the core spirit of the AEL model. Problems still remain to be sorted out, including how to shift the rate of convertibility from 7.75 to 7.80, which is an unpalatable legacy of the past failure to institute an effective arbitrage mechanism for Hong Kong's CBA (Tsang, 1998e). All the other six technical measures, on the other hand, constituted the establishment of a discount window with the intention of dampening interest rate volatility.

If the government had adopted the AEL model in late 1997, or in April 1998, Hong Kong's economic crisis would have been less severe. The government might not even have had to intervene in the stock and futures markets. The "seven technical measures" announced on 5 September 1998 could have been implemented

*Table 5.5*

**Interest Differential between 3-month HIBOR and LIBOR (daily average)** (unit: %)

|  | 3-month HIBOR | 3-month LIBOR | Difference |
|---|---|---|---|
| 2/1/96–22/10/97 | 5.92 | 5.60 | 0.32 |
| 23/10/97–4/9/98 | 9.68 | 5.72 | 3.96 |
| 7/9/98–12/10/98 | 8.74 | 5.43 | 3.31 |
| 12/10/98 | 6.75 | 5.31 | 1.44 |

earlier, as there had been few technical difficulties to surmount (Tsang, 1998e).

Table 5.5 shows that on average, three-month HIBOR (Hong Kong interbank offered rate) was only 0.32 percent above three-month LIBOR (London interbank offered rate) in the 22 months before the currency attack in late October 1997. Since then and up to the time when the seven technical measures were announced, the differential rose dramatically to nearly 4 percent. The local inflation rate was in the range of 4–5 percent, which means that Hong Kong faced a real interest rate of 5–6 percent! It was the very real high interest rates that pushed the Hong Kong economy into a deep recession.

The move by the HKMA to adopt the electronic arbitrage mechanism of the AEL model was certainly welcome, but the inevitable question remains: why did it take the HKMA so long to come to this decision? This was a point conceded even by the HKMA advisor, Charles Goodhart of the London School of Economics, who disapproved of the AEL model as well as the other recommendations made by the academics in the government's consultation exercise in December 1997 (FSB, 1998, Annex 3.6). His objection was clearly cited in the *Report on Financial Market Review* (FSB, 1998) when the Hong Kong SAR government rejected various proposals (e.g. paras. 3.49 and 3.65). In a recent interview by an international news service, Goodhart admitted, "Clearly, if you think it was right now, why was it not right earlier?" (Dow Jones Newswires, 1998).

This question, however, belongs to the realm of political economy rather than monetary economics. The AEL model, as a modern version of the currency board system, is more of an interpretation, and *certainly not* an invention (Tsang, 1998e). How can one invent something that already exists? One has also to be fully aware that these three countries (Argentina, Estonia and Lithuania) may "interpret" their own system differently. Living in a regime where the spot exchange rate is firmly fixed and observing no actual arbitrage (because arbitrage efficiency is "perfect"), must make people in these three countries wonder at the fuss that Hong Kong officials and economists are creating. They probably do not know that their breakthrough lesson in currency board economics could have saved Hong Kong tens of billions of dollars, if it had been learnt earlier.

# The East Asian Crisis Getting in the Way

Some say that the worst is over for the East Asian currency crisis. Others predict that the worst is yet to come. There may even be a worldwide meltdown, given the instability in the US and Japan. The situation is still uncertain and we can only work on probabilities.

The East Asian currency crisis is a typical case of international market failure and the lack of effective global coordination and governance as a public good. In such a messy situation, any nation or territory must act with extra caution. Ronald McKinnon's (1998) suggestion of a monetary anchor in terms of a stable exchange rate between the US dollar and the Japanese yen would be a useful starting point though how this is going to be realized is another matter.

Hong Kong is supposed to be a "strong economy" in the "core" of the East Asian region (Bergsten, 1997), along with Singapore and Taiwan. Few could have imagined such a deep recession. On hindsight, China's resumption of sovereignty over Hong Kong in 1997 did not launch the Hong Kong economy into a brand new future. Rather, it facilitated an overdue scrutiny of the anomalies built up in the pre-1997 years. Hence the chief executive of the Hong Kong SAR government, Tung Chee-hwa, vowed to deal with the issues of housing, education, elderly poverty and the development of high "value-added" sectors (both in manufacturing and service) in his first policy address on 8 October 1997. Such emphases were not edifying for a "new era". They looked more like rectifying measures.

Immediately after Tung's inaugural policy address, however, the Hong Kong economy faced a huge shock when the stock market bubble burst, aggravated by the attack on the Hong Kong dollar in late October 1997. A severe process of asset deflation set in. By the middle of 1998, property and stock prices had fallen by over 50 percent from their peaks in 1997. The banking system was also affected and it started to tighten credit. The total amount of outstanding Hong Kong dollar loans extended by licensed banks peaked at HK$1,609.013 billion in September 1997, and fell 3.7 percent by February 1998. By July 1998, the outstanding amount was HK$1,545.889 billion, down 3.9 percent.

To arrest the downward spiral of asset deflation and to avert the credit crunch, some fiscal initiatives to increase public expenditure and reduce taxes were obviously needed. The Hong Kong government launched a package of seven measures in April, focusing on the relaxation of restrictions on property futures. That did not generate any observable impact on the decline of property prices. Hence on 22 June 1998, a further nine measures were announced, including some cuts in taxes. The key initiative was the suspension of land sales for nine months (until March 1999), which was intended to shore up the collateral value of the banking system. That represented a major departure from the policy initiatives announced in Tung's 1997 policy address. However, it still did not seem to be good enough. The government was "forced" to intervene in the stock and futures markets in August 1998.

With a cumulative fiscal reserve that represents nearly two years of government expenditure and a foreign exchange reserve that is the third largest in the world, even after the stock market intervention, the Hong Kong SAR should be in a strong position to handle the aftermath of the East Asian crisis and the bursting of its own economic bubble. Nevertheless, managing the structural reforms required to lead the economy on a more balanced development path, consistent with the "one country, two systems" framework, is a very different matter. If not carefully handled, short-term rescue measures could seriously undermine long-term strategies.

A clear example is the moratorium of nine months imposed on land sales which was announced on 22 June 1998. The suspension would take 39,000 units out from supply and might derail the SAR government's plan of supplying 85,000 residential units per year to the market (Donald Tsang, 1998). It also had the undesirable consequence of shutting out medium- and small-sized property developers from acquiring lands exactly when they became cheaper. There were highly vocal complaints and a journalist strongly criticized the government for playing unwittingly into the hands of the tycoons (van der Kamp, 1998).

Given the important role of the real estate sector in Hong Kong's high-density metropolis, and the time lag involved in the production of usable property, sales of land by the government should better be "cycle-neutral", instead of "pro-cyclical" or "anti-cyclical", and need to be backed by a suitable buffer, i.e. a land bank. It is advisable for the government to keep to a supply rule that matches long-term demand and to let the market adjust to it, rather than for the government to react to market conditions in a knee-jerk manner. To add some flexibility to the rule, the Consumer Council in Hong Kong actually recommended in 1996 that the government should publish a "rolling" five-year plan of land disposal (Consumer Council, 1996:chapter 7, recommendation 2). The idea is to introduce transparency and predictability in land supply.

When the SAR government finally realized the wisdom of such a land supply rule, its strategy was severely constrained by the need to carry out a counter-cyclical policy to alleviate the recession. Hence the moratorium of land sales. It is important for the government to map out the trajectory to a transparent and predictable supply regime after the suspension, if the credibility of its longer-term structural reform strategy is not to be seriously compromised. At stake would also be another property boom-and-bust cycle a few years down the road.

Adding to the gloom about the Hong Kong economy are worries and doubts such as: What are the forces that would drive the economy after this crisis? How would the SAR remain or become more competitive? What kind of economic structure should be developed after the storm? In the previous two crises that Hong Kong experienced, namely the 1974–75 oil crisis and the 1982–85 political crisis, what eventually pulled the economy out of recession was exports. Real export growth was 28.8 percent in 1976 and 33.5 percent in 1987. Can we nurture the same hope for Hong Kong in 1999 and 2000? What would serve as the "locomotive"?

In a speech marking the first anniversary of the establishment of the Hong Kong SAR on 1 July 1998, Tung Chee-hwa said that he was well aware of the contradictions between the long-term need to help the Hong Kong economy move on to a more viable developmental path and the necessity for short-term rescue measures.

> The SAR government has drawn up long-term plans to enhance Hong Kong's competitiveness and maintain its economic vitality. The Asian financial turmoil has exposed the weaknesses of our rather narrow economic structure. Therefore, while we are committed to the strengthening and reinforcing of major economic pillars, such as finance, property development, tourism, shipping and trade, we have to promote actively the growth of our economy by strengthening and developing further our cooperation with the mainland, .... developing high value-added and high technology industries; and developing such new and integrated industries as information technology, telecommunication, filming and television.
>
> ... The biggest challenge we have now is how to integrate the development for our bright future with our efforts in relieving the people's hardship (Tung, 1998a).

# The Second Policy Address

In his second policy address delivered on 7 October 1998, Tung had little to say about short-term counter-cyclical policies. He did not give a clear indication on future housing strategies and said that a decision on the land sale moratorium would be made in early 1999 (Tung, 1998b). Tung's response to the crisis in his address created popular discontent as the man in the street saw little that could help him out of his difficulties. Moreover, he got the impression, rightly or wrongly, that Tung was more concerned about the fortune of the property tycoons and the bankers.

Tung chose not to draw any lessons from the SAR government's handling of the economic crisis, perhaps so as not to undermine the morale of the civil service at a critical time. Whilst experts and scholars found this understandable, most citizens saw this as a sign of being unrepentant. There must have been a more tactful way of addressing policy "mistakes". On the other hand, quite a few counter-cyclical measures have been implemented to "save" the economy from plunging into the abyss, not least the nine measures announced on 22 June 1998 (which included the land sale moratorium) as well as the unprecedented stock market intervention in August 1998 (that represented a very bold "fiscal" measure). Unfortunately, Tung failed to highlight them and to link the measures to the well-being of the populace, e.g. a deeper economic crisis might mean even high unemployment and sharper wage adjustments.

Instead, Tung focused on a more detailed description of his future plans to launch the Hong Kong economy onto a high-tech and high value-added developmental path. He pointed out important growth sectors, such as information technology, broadcasting and telecommunications, the film industry and Chinese medicine, which could be promoted through a better employment of technology and an emphasis on innovation. At the same time, he also proposed various measures to strengthen existing sectors, including financial services, tourism, small- and medium-sized enterprises, and manufacturing. Tung seemed to rely on the provision of hardware and software, as well as fiscal stimulus, to strengthen the sectors in both categories.

While the government has an important role to play in the Hong Kong economy's search for a more balanced and dynamic developmental path, a few immediate observations are appropriate.

(1) Hong Kong remains a "high cost" economy, even after so much battering in the financial storm. An obvious way of maintaining existing or generating new growth momentum is to nurture "high value-added" sectors. In general, innovation and technology should be a significant source of value-added in a developed or mature economy.

(2) However, Tung's latest initiatives on innovation and technology, no matter how well intended, have apparently not been based on a thorough soul searching in the Hong Kong community. Given the territory's past preoccupation with the ideology of *laissez-faire*, it is not clear that the majority of the citizens agree with such a strategy and the proposed role of the government in it. This could spell trouble in the actual implementation of Tung's policies. What he needs is a kind of social consensus and commitment, and that can only be attained through skilful political leadership and much wider consultation. Moreover, greater details have to be worked out before one can assess whether the overall strategy is viable. After all, Hong Kong now is a "latecomer" in the high-tech scene. It is not easy to identify its comparative advantages in the field, if there is any at all.

(3) Tung seems to be relying on a "sectoral approach": directly picking winners and avoiding losers among economic sectors. This should be augmented by an "activity approach", e.g. providing fiscal and other incentives for research and development (R&D) activities in all sectors, and letting the market select the winners. The justification is, of course, that R&D is typically high-risk in nature and, if successful, may generate positive externalities for the rest of the economy.

(4) There is a problem that has been neglected in the agenda. The fast increasing labour supply in Hong Kong needs to be properly absorbed. Largely because of the inflow from the Mainland and returned migrants, the local population is growing at about 2 percent per annum, roughly doubling the past average annual rate. How to create sufficient jobs for the expanding labour force is an issue that should be carefully addressed. High-tech industries and services by nature have relatively limited employment-generating capabilities. The small- and medium-sized enterprises, which employ about two-thirds of the workforce, constitute a key to job creation and should therefore be given further help.

In the end, a "dual economy" may emerge and consolidate in Hong Kong. Working within that scenario, there will be a "high-tech, high value-added" layer providing the key momentum to growth, and it will co-exist with a "low-tech, high employment" sector that takes up the task of supplying the laymen with jobs and decent incomes. How to bring about that dual structure smoothly is not easy. Nor is the effort to manage the interaction between the two sectors (Tsang, 1998i).

## Concluding Remarks

In the pre-1997 era, serious problems accumulated in the Hong Kong economy which the new and seemingly not well prepared SAR leadership had to tackle after the political transition. A lopsided economic structure, in the form of "Manhattanization", and the imbalance in the property sector posed as the major challenges. Both factors had undermined Hong Kong's competitiveness and upset its socioeconomic equilibrium by significantly pushing up the cost of business operations and the cost of living for the average citizen. Unfortunately, pre-transition politics had prevented an earlier response to these problems.

The chief executive of the SAR, Tung Chee-hwa, unveiled a policy package in October 1997, which partially addressed the dilemma confronting Hong Kong. However, the government had to confront immediately the double shocks of having the local economic bubble burst and coping with the East Asian financial crisis. While the turmoil might facilitate a quicker adjustment in the real economy, it has also led to severe difficulties that have threatened the short-term prospects of the local economy. The long-term health of the economy could be jeopardized by knee-jerk responses of the government — reactions without careful planning of upcoming scenarios.

In any case, Tung seems to be insistent on a high-tech, high value-added economic future for Hong Kong. Whether his colleagues in the government and the community at large share his vision remains to be seen. How effective he will be to put it into concrete action and to achieve the intended results is also an open question. In any case, the issue of the rapid expansion of the local labour supply, mainly as a result of population inflow from the north, should be addressed. It seems likely that Hong Kong has to tackle the difficulties of a "dual economy" in the 21st century.

The key short-term uncertainty hanging over Hong Kong hinges on the direction the world economy will take. The East Asian turmoil has put Japan in a very difficult position in which the country's unstable government has not responded effectively. The US economy is also showing signs of fatigue under the impact of the emerging problems in the financial system, including the difficulties for major investment funds and banks that have financed them. If the world plunges into a depression like that in the 1930s, Hong Kong's currency board system will be severely tested.

Another scenario is that the developed economies led by the US finally wake up and engineer packages that will relieve the emerging worldwide credit crunch. This includes lowering interest rates and implementing fiscal stimuli, setting the international anchorage (the exchange rate between the yen and the dollar) at a sustainable level, and restoring stability in the international monetary order. With the softening of the US dollar in the international foreign exchange market, the pressure on Hong Kong and the other East Asian economies would be alleviated. There is a chance that their recession would bottom out sooner rather than later. The light at the end of the long and dark tunnel could finally be glimpsed. For Hong Kong then, the longer-term agenda of economic restructuring may again become very important.

## Notes

1. After the dust had settled, the HKMA could, for example, choose a hot and boring Friday afternoon in mid-summer, when most fund managers and top government officials have gone on vacation, and announce the floating of the Hong Kong dollar. Few would notice the move. Two weeks later, the SAR government could disclaim any responsibility, whichever way the exchange rate moves.

## References

Bergsten, C. Fred (1997). "The Asian Monetary Crisis: Proposed Remedies". Statement before the Committee on Banking and Financial Services, US House of Representatives, 13 November.

Consumer Council (1996). *How Competitive is the Private Residential Property Market?* Hong Kong, July.

Dow Jones Newswires (1998). "HKMA Adviser Sees Lending Window as Key Change in System". By James T. Arredy. Report placed on Hong Kong Baptist University's web site: www. hkbu.edu.hk/~econ/web9811.html. 25 September.

Financial Services Bureau (FSB) (1998). *Report on Financial Market Review.* Hong Kong Government.

*Hong Kong Economic Journal* (1998). "Improving the Mechanism, Improving the Manner". (In Chinese). Editorial. 7 September.

Krugman, P. (1998), "What Happened to Asia?". Paper on Krugman's web site (web.mit.edu/krugman/www). January.

Kwong, Kai-sun, Lawrence J. Lau and Lin Tzong-Biau (1997). "The Impact of Relocation on Total Factor Productivity of Hong Kong Manufacturing". Mimeo. August.

McKinnon, Ronald I. (1998). "Exchange Rate Coordination for Surmounting the East Asian Currency Crisis". Keynote speech at the 6th Convention of the East Asian Economic Association. Kitakyushu, Japan. 4–5 September.

Radelet, S. and J. Sachs (1998). "The Onset of the East Asian Financial Crisis". Harvard Institute for International Development. Mimeo. 30 March.

Sung, Yun-wing (1998). "Academic Opinion is the Best Prescription for Reforming the Link". (In Chinese). *Ming Pao.* Hong Kong. 7 September.

Tsang, Donald (1998). "Speech by Financial Secretary". The Hong Kong Government Information Office, 22 June.

Tsang, Shu-ki (1993). "Income Distribution". *The Other Hong Kong Report 1993*. Hong Kong: The Chinese University Press. pp. 361–68.

———— (1994). "The Economy". *The Other Hong Kong Report 1994*. Hong Kong: The Chinese University Press. pp.125–48.

———— (1996a). *A Study of the Linked Exchange Rate System and Policy Options for Hong Kong*. A report commissioned by the Hong Kong Policy Research Institute. October.

———— (1996b). "The Linked Rate System: Through 1997 and into the 21st Century". In Ngaw Mee-kau and Li Si-ming (eds.), *The Other Hong Kong Report 1996*. Hong Kong: The Chinese University Press Institute. Chapter 11.

———— (1997). "Currency Board the Answer to Rate Stability". *Hong Kong Standard*. 31 October.

———— (1998a). "The Hong Kong Government's Financial Market Review Report: An Interpretation and a Response". Article placed on Hong Kong Baptist University's web site: www. hkbu.edu.hk/~econ/web985.html.

———— (1998b). "Is a Currency Board System Optimal for Hong Kong?" Article placed on Hong Kong Baptist University's web site: www.hkbu.edu.hk/~econ/web986.html.

———— (1998c). "The Case for Adopting the Convertible Reserves System in Hong Kong". *Pacific Economic Review*, vol. 3, no. 3. pp. 265–75.

———— (1998d). "Handling Credit Crunch under Hong Kong's Currency Board System". Article placed on Hong Kong Baptist University's web site: www.hkbu.edu.hk/~econ/web987.html.

———— (1998e). "Welcome on Board the AEL Model, Hong Kong, but ...". Article placed on web page: www.hkbu.edu.hk/~econ/web989.html.

———— (1998f). "The Hong Kong Economy: Opportunities out of the Crisis?" *Journal of Contemporary China*. Forthcoming.

———— (1998g). "The Hong Kong Economy in the Midst of the Financial Crisis". Opening speech at the Regional Conference on the Financial Crisis. Organized by the Hong Kong Journalists Association. 26 September. Article placed on web page: www.hkbu.edu.hk/~econ/web9810.html.

———— (1998h). "Why is the Recession in Hong Kong So Serious?" (In Chinese). *Hong Kong Letter*. Radio Hong Kong. 3 October.

———— (1998i). "The Dual Economy: Hong Kong's Future Challenge". (In Chinese). *Ming Pao*, 13 October.

Tung Chee Hwa (1997). *Building Hong Kong for a New Era*. Policy address at the Provisional Legislative Council, 8 October.

———— (1998a). "Speech at the ceremony marking the first anniversary of the establishment of the Hong Kong SAR". *Daily Information Bulletin*. Government Information Centre, Hong Kong SAR Government. 1 July.

———— (1998b). *From Adversity to Opportunity*. Policy address at the Legislative Council. 7 October.

van der Kamp, Jake (1998). "Land premium game takes inevitable course". *Business Post*, p. 16; *South China Morning Post*, Hong Kong. 11 July.

Yam, Joseph (1998). "Why We Intervened". *The Asian Wall Street Journal*. 20 August.

CHAPTER 6

# THE FINANCIAL SECTOR IN THE WAKE OF THE RECENT ASIAN ECONOMIC CRISIS

Y.C. Jao

## Introduction

As an extremely open economy and a major international financial centre, Hong Kong cannot avoid being buffeted by the Asian financial turmoil (AFT) which broke out and spread with astonishing speed on 2 July 1997.[1] In this paper, I will examine the impact of the AFT on Hong Kong's financial sector in four areas, namely, its currency, its banking system, its securities markets, and its position as an international financial centre (IFC). Owing to space constraint, I will only briefly mention the effect on the real economy, especially as the other chapters will deal with it in fuller detail.

While it is impossible, within the parameters of this paper, to analyse the origins and causes of the AFT, it would nevertheless be desirable to delineate the proximate causes of this calamitous event. Scholars and experts are still divided on this matter, and an analytic literature is already growing (see *inter alia* Krugman,

1998; Radelet and Sachs, 1998a; 1998b; Moreno, Pasadilla and Remolona, 1998; Kaminski and Reinhart, 1998; and Miller, 1998). I personally subscribe to what I would like to call the "financial imprudence view". This can be conveniently summarized in Figure 6.1, a schema of the financial crisis.

According to this view, reckless borrowing by both public sector and private sector entities, matched by equally reckless lending by the banks, without adequate risk management and prudential supervision, will quickly result in illiquidity or even insolvency when a sudden shift in market conditions or sentiments occurs. Runs on depository institutions will be accompanied or followed by runs on the currency. To attract an inflow of capital and to protect the exchange rate, high interest rates become inevitable, which cause a sharp downturn in economic activity. This, in turn, aggravates illiquidity or insolvency of firms and banks. This schema applies particularly well to Thailand, Indonesia and South Korea, and to a lesser extent, to other Asian countries in distress.

Figure 6.1 does not apply, however, to Hong Kong. The banks are well regulated, and there is no banking crisis. There is no evidence of reckless and excessive borrowing. The Hong Kong government has no external debt. Even more important, as Hong Kong has steadfastly refused to join in the game of competitive devaluation, it cannot be accused of transmitting financial disturbances abroad. In short, Hong Kong is basically a victim, and not an originator, of the AFT. Figure 6.2, therefore, is much more relevant to Hong Kong.

## Impact on the Currency

Since July 1997, several waves of speculative attacks on the Hong Kong dollar's link to the US dollar have been launched, but all of them have been repulsed by the Hong Kong Monetary Authority (HKMA). The link has held steady between 7.73 and 7.76, below the official rate of US$1=HK$7.8.

As shown in Table 6.1, the Hong Kong dollar and the Chinese renminbi are the only two major currencies in Asia that have not depreciated against the US dollar. Moreover, since the renminbi

*Figure 6.1*

**A Schema of Financial Crisis**

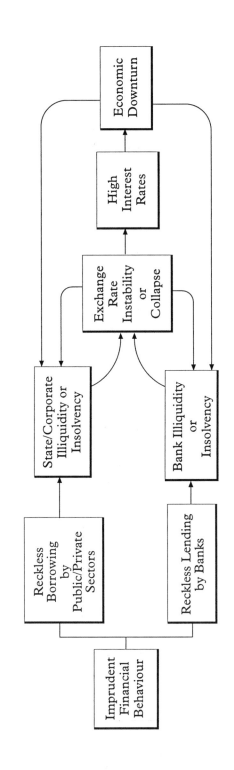

*Figure 6.2*

**The Financial Crisis Contagion**

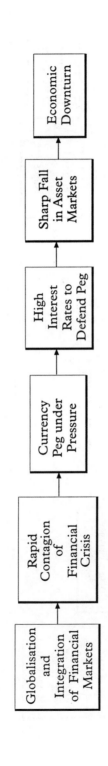

*Table 6.1*

## Exchange Rates of Major Asian Currencies vs. US dollar

| Currencies | 1 July 1997 | 5 November 1998 | Appreciation (+) Depreciation (-) |
|---|---|---|---|
| Chinese renminbi | 8.29 | 8.2778 | ⋆ |
| Hong Kong dollar | 7.7452 | 7.7432 | ⋆ |
| Indian rupee | 35.8 | 42.36 | −15.4% |
| Indonesia rupiah | 2,432.63 | 8,800.00 | −72.5% |
| Japanese yen | 114.96 | 117.80 | −2.4% |
| Korean won | 887.8 | 1,313.80 | −32.4% |
| Malaysian ringgit | 2.5247 | 3.7998 | −33.5% |
| Philippine peso | 26.36 | 39.52 | −33.3% |
| Singapore dollar | 1.4305 | 1.6226 | −11.8% |
| New Taiwan dollar | 27.8 | 32.47 | −14.4% |
| Thai baht | 24.7 | 36.40 | −31.4% |

*Note*: ⋆Changes less than 0.5%

*Source*: Underlying data from Standard Chartered Bank

is not a convertible currency, the Hong Kong dollar is the only convertible currency that has not depreciated.

Several major reasons may be cited for the stability of the Hong Kong dollar. One obvious reason is Hong Kong's strong foreign exchange reserves. Table 6.2 shows that at the end of September 1998, Hong Kong's total foreign exchange reserves amounted to US$88.4 billion. This could cover 3.6 times the enlarged monetary base, now defined as the sum of legal tender currency, the banking system's clearing balance with HKMA, and Exchange Fund bills. Because of the intervention in the equity market in August 1998, there was a net loss of US$8.1 billion

*Table 6.2*

**Hong Kong's Foreign Exchange Reserves (billion US$)**

| Year | End of Month | Excluding Foreign Assets in Land Fund | Including Foreign Assets in Land Fund |
|------|--------------|---------------------------------------|---------------------------------------|
| 1997 | July | 66.1 | 81.7 |
| | August | 69.5 | 85.3 |
| | September | 71.4 | 88.1 |
| | October | 74.4 | 91.8 |
| | November | 79.5 | 96.9 |
| | December | 75.3 | 92.8 |
| 1998 | January | 80.3 | 98.1 |
| | February | 78.6 | 96.7 |
| | March | 78.5 | 96.8 |
| | April | 77.6 | 96.1 |
| | May | 77.9 | 96.4 |
| | June | 77.9 | 96.5 |
| | July | 77.8 | 96.5 |
| | August | 73.4 | 92.1 |
| | September | 69.3 | 88.4 |

*Source:* HKMA

compared to July, but it was smaller than the US$15 billion believed by the market. Moreover, Hong Kong still had the third largest foreign reserves in the world, as shown in Table 6.3.

Second, Hong Kong not only does not have any fiscal deficit, but actually has an accumulated fiscal reserve, estimated at about HK$400 billion. Although this is expected to fall during the current economic recession, it is still an important cushion for both the monetary system and the economy. Third, Hong Kong has no sovereign debt, another extreme rarity.

China has also been most helpful both before and after the handover, and this is undoubtedly another factor

*Table 6.3*

## World Rankings of Foreign Exchange Reserves (billion US$)

| Countries/Territories | US$ billion | As at end of |
|---|---|---|
| 1. Japan | 209.3 | August 1998 |
| 2. China | 140.6 | July 1998 |
| 3. Hong Kong | 88.4 | September 1998 |
| 4. Taiwan | 83.6 | July 1998 |
| 5. Germany | 83.5 | July 1998 |
| 6. USA | 72.9 | July 1998 |
| 7. Brazil | 71.5 | May 1998 |
| 8. Singapore | 69.3 | July 1998 |
| 9. Spain | 68.7 | July 1998 |
| 10. Italy | 45.6 | July 1998 |

*Source:* HKMA, IMF, Reuters

responsible for Hong Kong's monetary and financial stability. On 1 July 1997, the day of the reunification, China punctually transferred, as promised, the Land Fund worth some HK$197 billion (of which US$15.8 billion was in foreign currency assets) to the government of the Hong Kong Special Administrative Region (SAR).[2] Overnight, Hong Kong's forex and fiscal reserves were boosted by 23% and 41% respectively, strengthening enormously both domestic and international confidence in the Hong Kong dollar. Moreover, China's leaders, from President Jiang Zemin and Prime Minister Zhu Rongji downwards, have repeatedly declared publicly that China strongly supports Hong Kong's linked exchange rate system, and will come to the aid of Hong Kong if requested, and that China will not devalue its yuan despite the competitive devaluations of other Asian countries. These declarations have also an important positive psychological effect on Hong Kong. Thus, the sensational conjectures and assertions, some even by respected scholars, that China would take over Hong Kong's foreign reserves and abolish the Hong Kong dollar after the handover, can now be seen as totally groundless.

Hong Kong's financial strength by itself will not, however, impress critics and sceptics, of whom there are many, especially abroad. One of their favourite refrains is that no fixed exchange rate regime can last forever in the face of sustained speculative attacks. The fallacy of this argument lies in the confusion between Currency Board and non-Currency Board fixed exchange rate regimes.

The Currency Board was established during the period of the British colonies and the protectorates in the 19th century, and because sterling was the predominant anchor currency at that time, the system was also called Sterling Exchange Standard. In its evolution during the past 150 years, the system gradually got rid of its colonial trappings, so that the currency chosen as the anchor need not be the currency of a colonial power. The International Monetary Fund (IMF) now uses the terminology Currency Board Arrangement (CBA) to denote the various forms of the monetary system where the domestic currency is either wholly or predominantly backed by an international reserve currency, and to which the former is linked at a fixed rate of exchange.

Hong Kong's linked exchange rate regime since 17 October 1983 is a form of CBA, under which the legal tender currency must be backed in advance by US dollars at the rate of US\$1=HK\$7.8. In fact, Hong Kong's present forex reserve can cover 3.6 times the enlarged monetary base.[3] Hong Kong's currency, however, is not issued by a formal currency board, but by three commercial banks. The Exchange Fund, the sole repository of forex and fiscal reserves, and the counterpart of the prototype currency board, is now managed by HKMA, which performs certain quasi-central banking functions (Jao, 1998a; 1998b).

Under this system, there are two automatic adjustment mechanisms which are broadly similar to those that operated under the classical gold standard. One is the specie flow mechanism, or the Cantillon-Hume mechanism. In Hong Kong, it works as follows. After an outflow of capital, or a speculative attack, the forex reserve will initially fall. The note-issuing banks, having lost foreign assets, cannot issue more notes. They may even have to surrender their Certificates of Indebtedness to the Exchange Fund to redeem their US dollars. Also, the banks' clearing balances with the HKMA will be automatically debited when HKMA sells US dollars. Hence, the monetary base must shrink, and with it the money supply will contract as well. Domestic prices, therefore, will fall and interest rates will rise, all of which will stabilize the exchange rate. The other mechanism, called "arbitrage and competition", works in a similar way as the "gold points". Briefly, the market rate cannot diverge from the official rate of 7.8 by more than the transaction costs between the US dollar and the Hong Kong dollar (in cash), otherwise the note-issuing banks will engage in arbitrage with the Exchange Fund, resulting in the convergence of the market rate towards the official rate again. This mechanism, however, is secondary to the first one. For a more detailed exposition of the Cantillon-Hume mechanism, see appendix.

By contrast, under the non-CBA central banking regimes, there is no prior foreign exchange constraint, hence there is no automatic adjustment mechanism of any kind. The central bank may sell foreign exchange to stabilize the exchange rate for a time, but there is nothing to prevent the central bank from issuing more notes or creating more money again. Under such a regime, it is indeed true that no amount of foreign exchange reserve can withstand repeated speculative attacks indefinitely, because the domestic money supply will not automatically contract.

The classical adjustment mechanism entails interest rate adjustment which can be quite painful. Thus, on 23 October 1997, when speculation reached its height, the Hong Kong interbank offered rate (HIBOR) reached an unprecedented 280%, even though for only a few hours. Moreover, under the Real Time Gross Settlement (RTGS) system installed in December 1996, all licensed banks are required to maintain positive clearing balance with the HKMA, for which overdraft is not allowed. When the HKMA debits the banks' clearing accounts as it sells US dollars, there can be overshooting of HIBOR.

A number of measures have, therefore, been implemented by the HKMA. In June 1998, it installed a system to predict the aggregate clearing balance for the next two days. This has the merit of alerting the banks to manage their liquidity, thus avoiding undue volatility in the interbank rates. On 5 September 1998, the HKMA announced a package of seven technical measures to further strengthen the currency board arrangements and make them less susceptible to manipulation by speculators to produce extreme conditions in the interbank market and interest rates.

(1)   The HKMA provides a clear undertaking to all licensed banks in Hong Kong to convert Hong Kong dollars in their clearing accounts into US dollars at the fixed exchange rate of HK$7.75 to US$1. This explicit Convertibility Undertaking is a clear demonstration of the government's commitment to the linked exchange rate system.

(2)   The bid rate of the Liquidity Adjustment Facility (LAF) is abolished. This will prevent some banks from deliberately placing funds with the HKMA in the last business hour rather than lending them to the interbank market.

(3)   A Discount Window replaces the LAF with the Base Rate (formerly known as the LAF Offer Rate) to be determined from time to time by the HKMA. In determining the Base Rate, the HKMA will ensure that interest rates are adequately responsive to capital flows while allowing excessive and destabilizing interest rate volatility to be dampened.

(4)   The HKMA removes the restriction on repeated borrowing in respect of the provision of overnight Hong Kong dollar liquidity through repo transactions using Exchange Fund Bills and Notes. Allowing for freer access to day end liquidity through the use of Exchange Fund paper, which is fully backed by foreign currency reserves, will make Hong Kong's monetary system less susceptible to manipulation and dampen excessive interest rate volatility without departing from the discipline of the Currency Board arrangement.

(5)   New Exchange Fund paper will be issued only when there is an inflow of funds. This will ensure that all new Exchange Fund paper will be fully backed by foreign currency reserves.

(6)   A schedule of discount rates is applicable for different percentage thresholds of holdings of Exchange Fund paper

by the licensed banks for the purpose of accessing the Discount Window. This will ensure that the interest rate adjustment mechanism is fully kicked in when the Hong Kong dollar is under significant pressure.

(7) The restriction on repeated borrowing in respect of repo transactions involving debt securities other than Exchange Fund paper is retained. No new issues of paper other than Exchange Fund paper will be accepted at the Discount Window. This will prevent significant liquidity from being provided to licensed banks against paper not backed by foreign currency reserves.

Reactions from the public and the markets to these measures have been generally favourable. Interest rate volatility has been dampened, and the whole term structure has eased across the board. One reliable and sensitive indicator of confidence in the Hong Kong dollar is the yield differential between the 2-year Hong Kong Exchange Fund note and US Treasury note. This fell from 566.5 basis points on 31 August to 262.4 basis points on 3 November, or a fall of 304.1 points in barely two months.

# Impact on the Banking System

During the period 1983–86, Hong Kong was hit by a banking crisis, hard on the heel of the currency crisis of 1982–83, in the midst of a general confidence crisis on the 1997 handover issue. The government had to bail out several "problem banks".

Thanks to the overhaul of the prudent framework of the banking sector since the banking crisis of the 1980s, including the installation of such measures as the extensive amendment of the Banking Ordinance, the imposition of "fit and proper" criteria for bank management, the implementation of the capital adequacy ratio (CAR), the revision of the liquidity ratio and the tightening of the bank examination, the impact of the Asian turmoil on Hong Kong's banking sector has been under control. The average capital adequacy ratio remained high at 17.5% at the end of 1997, more than twice the Basle Committee's recommended minimum of 8%. However, as most banks had prudently made large provisions for non-performing loans, their profitability in the first half of 1998 had declined by 15–30%.

On 10–11 November 1997, the International Bank of Asia, a locally incorporated licensed bank, suffered runs as a result of unfounded rumours on its solvency. The runs, however, petered out after the HKMA put out a strong statement in support of the bank, which was declared sound and well-managed. Since then, no other bank has experienced any similar difficulty. Several financial institutions which failed in 1998 were securities investment and brokerage firms, and not depository institutions under the three-tier banking structure.

Nevertheless, the slump in the property market has caused considerable concern about the liquidity of the banking sector. Property prices had already fallen by 50% from their peaks. Although the HKMA had long ago issued a guideline advising the banks to keep their property-related loans below 40% of their total loan portfolio, some banks were known to have exceeded this ceiling. Over-exposure to the property market was one of the key causes of the banking crises of the 1960s and 1980s, .

Since January 1998, high government officials, including the Chief Executive, have begun to stress the importance of stabilizing the property market by "flexibly" managing land sales and implementing the target of supplying 85,000 residential units per annum. In the 1998–99 budget, mortgage interest became tax-deductible for home-owners for the first time in Hong Kong's history. In June, land sales were suspended until March 1999. The government's intention was clear: while moderate price correction in the property market was deemed desirable, the total collapse of the market was seen as threatening to the banking sector and the Hong Kong dollar itself and must, therefore, be prevented by all available means without, however, compromising Hong Kong's traditional financial probity.

On the positive side, the Hong Kong Mortgage Corporation (HKMC), which began operations in October 1997, could not have come at a more appropriate time. Modelled after the US Federal National Mortgage Association ("Fannie Mae"), the HKMC purchases mortgage loans from the banks, and repackages and resells them as marketable securities to investors. As such, it can enhance the liquidity and correct "maturity mismatch" in the banking sector, encourage securitization, and promote the development of capital markets. It plans to issue bonds of about HK$20 billion to fund its operations.

Since early 1998, the authorities have been pushing for "fixed rate mortgages" in order to insulate homebuyers from the volatility of interest rates. The main idea is to encourage banks to grant "fixed-rate mortgage loans" to homebuyers. These mortgages will then be sold to the HKMC, which in turn securitizes them for sale to the bond market and the cash-rich Hong Kong Housing Society.

On 18 March 1998, two licensed banks, Chase Manhattan and Dao Heng, signed a pilot scheme with the HKMC, under which the HKMC would buy HK$250 million worth of mortgages each from the two banks, carrying a fixed interest rate of 10.5% for the first three years. At the end of the three-year period, the borrower can either re-fix the rate for another three-year term, or convert the fixed rate to a floating rate at the best lending rate plus 1.5%. The maximum mortgage loan allowed is HK$4 million. Since its inception, the HKMC had, by 18 March 1998, bought HK$3 billion in floating-rate mortgages.

Another stabilizing factor is the fact that the banks have observed since 1991, the HKMA guideline that mortgage loans can only be granted up to a maximum of 70% of the value of the property, which in turn has been conservatively evaluated. As a consequence, the delinquency rate of mortgages in Hong Kong is among the lowest in the world. According to the latest HKMA survey of local banks, only 0.34% of all mortgage payments were overdue for more than three months (Carse, 1998; Guyot and Wong, 1998). The correspondent rate in the US in the downturn of 1994–95 was 3.71%.

Finally, demographic, economic and social forces all seem to be working for the long-term stability of the property market, despite the current downturn: such as increased immigration quotas for people from Mainland China, the decline of the extended family and the rise of the nuclear family, the return of emigrants and the desire to upgrade the quality of housing. Thus the situation in some countries like Japan and Thailand, where the banking sector is crippled because of the high vacancy rates in both commercial and residential buildings, will be most unlikely to happen in Hong Kong. Indeed, since the policy address of the chief executive on 7 October 1998, and a moderate cut of interest rates by 0.25% nine days later, a partial recovery of the property market has been under way.

Since 1981, a three-tier structure of deposit-taking financial institutions, officially called "authorized institutions", has been in force. This banking structure, as revised in 1990, consists of three classes of depository institutions. The first tier is called licensed banks. They must have a minimum paid-up capital of HK$150 million. They can take all types of deposit, without any restriction on their minimum denomination and original term to maturity. The second tier is called restricted licenced banks (formerly licensed deposit-taking companies), which must have a minimum paid-up capital of HK$100 million. They can only take time deposits of not less than HK$500,000, without restriction, however, on their original term to maturity. The third tier is deposit-taking companies, which must have a minimum paid-up capital of HK$25 million. They can only take time deposits of not less than HK$100,000, with an original term to maturity of not less than three months. All three types of depository institutions must observe a liquidity ratio, defined as the ratio of assets convertible into cash within seven days, to the total amount of deposits, of 25%, and a capital adequacy ratio (CAR), defined as the ratio of the sum of paid-up capital, reserves and undistributed profits to the total amount of risk assets, of 8%. The HKMA, however, has the power to ask a licensed bank to raise its capital adequacy ratio to 12%, and a restricted licensed bank or a deposit-taking company to raise its capital adequacy ratio to 16%. The HKMA has recently proposed that the minimum CAR be raised to 12% across the board.

During the period 1990–97, the primary objective of the regulatory authorities was to strengthen the prudent supervision of the banking sector in preparation for the transition to the postcolonial era. Now that the handover has taken place much more smoothly than expected, a more long-term and strategic planning for the whole banking industry becomes necessary, in view of the prevailing trends in worldwide banking and finance, namely, the globalization of financial markets, proliferation of new banking and financial products, rapid progress in information technology, and growing competition from other banking or financial centres. The AFT has, in its turn, underlined the urgency of this review.

Accordingly, the HKMA in March 1998 commissioned a consultancy firm to conduct an in-depth review of Hong Kong's banking sector for the next five years. The study will consist of two phases. Phase 1 will be devoted to a strategic review of the banking sector, including such issues as the three-tier structure, the one-branch policy for new foreign banks, the remaining interest rate rules, and other global and local trends that impinge on the profitability, competitiveness and soundness of the banking industry. Phase II will be concerned with an evaluation of the current organizational structure of the supervisory function of the HKMA, and its capability to deal with the challenges ahead. The report of this review will not be published, however, until the end of 1998.

Finally, Hong Kong was among the earliest to recognize the implications of the "millennium bug" for the banking system. Thanks to the HKMA's timely supervision, most banks would have solved this problem by the end of 1998.

## Impact on the Securities Markets

While the currency and the banking system have fared relatively well in the course of the AFT, the stock and futures market have been severely battered. The need to raise interest rates to defend the currency peg was enough to deal a heavy blow to the securities markets, which are highly interest-sensitive. The best lending rates were raised twice by 0.75% in October 1997 and January 1998 to 10.25%, but was only slightly lowered to 10% at the end of March 1998. The situation has been aggravated by economic downturn and lower corporate profitability.

After reaching an all-time high of 16,673 on 7 August 1997, the Hang Seng Index of stock prices began a long downtrend, occasionally interrupted by weak rallies, and by 13 August 1998, it had reached a low of 6,660, or 60% off its peak. At this point, the government decided to intervene. According to Joseph Yam, chief executive of the HKMA, international speculators were engaged in a massive "double market play" (Yam, 1998). The typical tactic of the speculator-manipulator can be roughly described as follows. He will buy US dollars aggressively forward (or sell HK$ forward, generally for six months). By the covered interest rate parity mechanism, the current interest rate, especially the highly sensitive HIBOR, must rise. If the forward premium rises further, the speculator can immediately resell his futures at a profit to another party, who may be another speculator, or a hedger or an arbitrageur. At the same time, he will also sell Hang Seng Index futures aggressively. Because the higher interest rates will hit the cash market index, he can reap a huge profit by such "double market play" which can be very damaging to the whole financial system. During the month of August, international speculators, notably several hedge funds of US origin, made unscrupulous use of unfavourable news, such as floods in China and weakening economies in Japan and Hong Kong, to spread all sorts of lies and rumours about the impending devaluation of both the renminbi and the Hong Kong dollar. Clearly, such direct assault on Hong Kong's financial integrity must be stopped. The government's strategy was to buy in both the cash and futures markets, in order to force speculators to liquidate their short positions at higher prices. On 6 November 1998, the Hang Seng Index closed at 10,140, or up by 52.2% compared to the low of 13 August. Thus the government could claim considerable success against the speculators-manipulators.

The government's counter-attack has given rise to considerable controversy. While a substantial body of public opinion supported the government in its bid to safeguard the peg and the financial system, certain sections of the financial community and the media, in particular the media abroad, have strongly condemned the government's moves as a significant departure from Hong Kong's traditional "non-interventionist" policy and philosophy, despite the government's repeated assurances that its intervention was aimed at speculators-manipulators, and not at genuine investors, and that its aim was to restore financial order, not to prop up prices at any pre-destined level. The critics' views were in any case rather one-sided, since they typically ignored the vulture-like behaviour of the speculators-manipulators, who have played havoc with so many emerging markets and economies.[4] Criticizing Hong Kong's "interventions" is like criticizing a victim of an act of robbery (or an even worse crime) for trying to defend herself/himself.

A more reasonable concern is whether such interventions might result in a loss of taxpayers' money and, therefore, endanger our reserves. The government's response is that it has bought only the highest quality blue chips, which now sell at single-digit P/E ratios, and are highly liquid both locally and internationally. When the market conditions become more stable and favourable, some holdings will be disposed of in an orderly manner, but being income-yielding assets, they may be held as long-term investments if necessary. What has happened is a reshuffle of the portfolios in the Exchange Fund and the Land Fund, and there is no question of losing taxpayers' money. Related to this, one may recall that, during the banking crisis of the 1980s, when the government took over several problem banks, it was also roundly condemned for wasteful interventions. However, the problem banks, after being restructured under government control, were eventually sold at a profit to other stronger banks, without any loss to the taxpayers (Jao, 1987). Anyhow, on 26 October, the government announced the formation of an independent company called Exchange Fund Investment Co. Ltd. and revealed that it had acquired equities at a cost of HK$118 billion, with an unrealized profit of about HK$30 billion.

On 7 September, the government unveiled a 30-point package designed to tighten regulations of the futures and stock markets, including criminalizing unreported short selling, and increasing penalties for illegal short selling from a maximum fine of HK$10,000 and six months' jail to a HK$100,000 fine and two years' jail. Another part of the package concerns more coordination between the exchanges and regulatory agencies, and more transparency of the exchanges.

Predictably, this package was also attacked by speculators and their friends as well as by those who have vested interests, such as brokerage houses, for violating "free market principles". Again, such self-interested arguments cannot be taken seriously. Short selling by itself is not illegal, provided it observes the rule that stocks must be borrowed in advance. However, during the recent episode, many "naked short-sellers" did not even bother to abide by this rule, which was glaringly illegal. Another loophole was that the T+2 rule (delivery two days after transaction) was not observed. The Hong Kong Clearing was found to have given big speculators the escape route of T+5, frustrating the government's plan to squeeze them. Fortunately, the government and Hong Kong Clearing have now reached an agreement to strictly enforce T+2. One controversial measure that has arisen in the process is that the government is studying whether to grant the chief executive of the Hong Kong Special Administrative Region (HKSAR) the power to "give direction to the Exchange and Clearing houses to ensure that the Government can react quickly whenever public interests are under threat". However, even if this measure is adopted, it will only be exercised under exceptional circumstances.

The 30-point package is designed to deal with the asymmetry problem — the classic "asymmetric information" — a fundamental issue which even serious economists have missed. The government is expected to be more and more transparent in its operations, and over the past decade it has been doing just that. However, hedge funds and other major players in the futures and stock markets are not under such constraints.

Table 6.4 shows changes in Asia's leading stock indexes from 2 July 1997 to 4 November 1998. Hong Kong ranked 7th in terms of market decline. Note that in October 1998, there was a general rally of stock prices in Asia, except in India and Taiwan. At its worst, the fall in stock prices was much deeper and more pervasive.

# Impact on Status as an International Financial Centre (IFC)

Prior to Hong Kong's return to China, there was acute concern whether Hong Kong's status as an international financial centre (IFC) could survive the transition to Chinese sovereignty. One scenario projected was that if China conscientiously observed its commitments and promises to Hong Kong, then the much feared exodus of capital, talent, and foreign banks and corporations would not happen. It also proposed that if Hong Kong could preserve its traditional advantages as a free port and a financial and business

*Table 6.4*

## Changes in Leading Stock Price Indexes

| Country/<br>Territory | 2 July<br>1997 | 4 November<br>1998 | Change (%) |
| --- | --- | --- | --- |
| China (Shanghai) | 1,253.0 | 1,313.3 | +4.8 |
| Hong Kong | 15,196.8 | 10,508.3 | -31.9 |
| India (Mumbai) | 4,333.9 | 2,812.1 | -35.1 |
| Indonesia (Jakarta) | 730.2 | 330.5 | -54.7 |
| Malaysia<br>(Kuala Lumpur) | 1,084.9 | 431.7 | -60.2 |
| Philippines<br>(Manila) | 2,764.9 | 1,714.1 | -38.0 |
| Singapore | 1,968.9 | 1,301.1 | -33.9 |
| South Korea (Seoul) | 777.3 | 413.5 | -46.8 |
| Taiwan (Taipei) | 8,996.7 | 6,905.3 | -23.2 |
| Thailand (Bangkok) | 568.8 | 354.1 | -37.7 |
| Japan (Tokyo) | 20,196.4 | 14,527.8 | -28.1 |

*Source*: Underlying data from *The Economist*, London

hub, then it would have nothing to fear in the postcolonial era (Jao, 1997; Sheng, 1998).

China has indeed shown much integrity with respect to Hong Kong. One specific act, already mentioned, was the punctual transfer of the huge Land Fund to Hong Kong, underpinning the territory's financial soundness and status as an IFC. China's scrupulous respect for Hong Kong's autonomy in economic and financial affairs is also an indisputable fact.

Ironically, the threat to Hong Kong as an IFC has not come from China, but from a pernicious contagion called the AFT. The AFT has affected Hong Kong's position as an IFC in three major ways. First, many international banks, especially the Japanese ones, have reduced their lending and other related activities, even though they have not actually withdrawn totally from Hong Kong. Second, the fall in asset prices in general, and the fall of share prices in particular, has adversely affected Hong Kong's role as a capital-raising centre, particularly for China. Third, the sharp fall in the profitability of the banks and other non-bank financial intermediaries has also had a negative effect on the dynamism of the whole financial sector.

While these effects are true and serious enough, it can be reasonably argued that they are not confined to Hong Kong. Hong Kong's main rivals in the Asia-Pacific region, Tokyo and Singapore, have also been affected adversely by the AFT. Japan has been affected even more because of its crippling and protracted banking crisis. Tokyo, at any rate, is much less open and internationalized than Hong Kong and Singapore. It is regarded as a global financial centre mainly because of the enormous size of Japan's domestic financial sector, its huge savings pool, and its capacity as a capital-exporter to the world.

Numerous quantitative indicators rank Hong Kong as an IFC in both the Asia-Pacific region and the world (Jao, 1997). Some indicators, such as the foreign exchange and derivative markets, are based on triennial surveys conducted under the auspices of the Bank for International Settlements (BIS), the latest results of which are still pending. As a synopsis, we may note that, despite the AFT, Hong Kong remains:

- the third largest IFC in the world in terms of the number of foreign banks and other non-bank financial intermediaries;
- the second largest IFC in the Asia-Pacific region and one of the seven largest IFCs in the world;
- the fifth largest banking centre in the world;
- the seventh largest forex centre in the world;
- the seventh largest stock market in the world in terms of total value traded;
- the fourth largest source of foreign direct investment (FDI) in the world.

An IFC cannot exist in a vacuum. It is no mere coincidence that all the great IFCs in the world are also great international centres of business and commerce. Hong Kong is no exception. According to a government survey, in 1997, 935 overseas parent companies had their Asian or Asia-Pacific regional headquarters, and 1,611 overseas parent companies had their regional offices, in Hong Kong (Hong Kong Industry Department, 1997).[5]

Another survey (Hong Kong Trade Development Council, 1998) indicates that Hong Kong is a major centre for offshore trade and manufacturing investment, with offshore trade totalling HK$1,052 billion in 1997. Official statistics, however, were unable to capture this fully. The *Economist* of London has also reported Hong Kong as a major source of FDI, which controls manufacturing activities offshore.[6] For six consecutive years, Hong Kong has been the busiest container port of the world, handling some 14.6 million 20-foot equivalent units (TEUs) in 1997. Despite its small size, Hong Kong ranked 9th among the world's leading exporters in 1996.

Two other aspiring financial centres, Shanghai and Taipei, are most unlikely to replace Hong Kong in the foreseeable future. Being unable or unwilling to remove capital controls, and to offer full national treatment in financial services, both cities are domestic financial centres rather than IFCs. The AFT will make them even more cautious in the liberalization of their financial sectors and internationalization.

Only Singapore is pressing ahead with liberalization and internationalization, despite the AFT. Indeed, the efforts by the Singapore International Monetary Exchange (Simex) to re-launch the Hang Seng index futures is widely seen in Hong Kong as an act of invasion. Thus Singapore poses a greater challenge to Hong Kong as an IFC. While Hong Kong still has an edge over Singapore, "it is so small that Singapore can easily overtake Hong Kong, especially if the 1997 transition is not managed well" (Jao, 1997). Hong Kong and Singapore have been, however, rivals as IFCs for 30 years that one wonders whether their "competition" has not been sometimes overblown. The fact is that the two centres also highly complement each other, both geographically and functionally. Like any catastrophe, the AFT will pass one day.

Once Asia resumes its vibrant growth path, there will surely be enough room for two prospering IFCs, each with its own niche and comparative advantage.

## Concluding Remarks

In his immortal classic, *Les Misérables*, Victor Hugo characterized the outcome of the Battle of Waterloo as *"quid obscurum, quid divinum"*.[7] Has Asia, which has been lavishly praised for its "economic miracle" until very recently, finally met its Waterloo? At the time of revising this paper (early November 1998), the outlook is, to say the least, still murky, even though there is a glimmer of hope that the worst may be over. Thus, Hugo's Latin expression is still highly apposite.

The purpose of this paper is, however, much more modest. Its aim is to examine the challenges to Hong Kong's financial sector in the wake of the AFT. Our findings are that, while Hong Kong's currency, banking system, and position as an IFC have fared relatively well, its asset markets and its real economy, expected to shrink by 4% in real terms in 1998, have been savagely battered.

Hong Kong takes the view that, as long as monetary and banking stability is maintained, then the real economy, after a period of adjustments, will eventually recover. While such adjustments, as shown by falling asset prices as well as general prices, costs and wages, have been very painful, they are inherent to the working of a CBA, of which Hong Kong's linked exchange rate regime is a special form. But this is not the first time that Hong Kong has experienced severe economic difficulties and challenges. The "1997 ordeal" during 1982–97 is only the most recent case in point. Hong Kong can draw comfort from, as well as pin its hopes on, its proven track record of flexibility, resourcefulness and resilience.

## NOTES

1. The extreme openness of Hong Kong can be illustrated by the fact that, in 1997, total external trade was 213.6% of GDP, one of the highest in the world.

2. The Land Fund was created in August 1986, in accordance with Annex III of the 1984 Sino-British Joint Declaration, under which half of the net sales

of land up to 30 June 1997 would be paid into the Land Fund and reserved for the SAR. Until the handover, the fund was managed by China.

3. The monetary base used to be defined as the sum of legal tender currency and banks' clearing balances with the HKMA. Since 5 September 1998, it has been enlarged to include Exchange Fund bills and notes.

4. A notable exception was the world-renowned economist, Paul Krugman of MIT, who supported the Hong Kong government's intervention. He said that if international hedge funds were deliberately manipulating the markets, the HKMA had no alternative but to intervene. The practices of hedge funds alleged by the HKMA would "constitute criminal activity in the United States if spotted by the Securities and Exchange Commission". See *South China Morning Post Business Post*, 27 August 1998.

5. "Regional headquarters" are defined as organizations which have control over the operation of one or more other offices or subsidiaries in the region without the need to make frequent referrals to, or consult with, the overseas parent companies or headquarters. "Regional offices" are companies which are responsible for general business activities in other countries in the region for the overseas parent companies. "Overseas parent companies" are companies which have final control over the operations of one or more other offices or subsidiaries in any region.

6. See "The ever-spreading tentacles of Hong Kong", in *Manufacturing Survey, The Economist*, 20–26 June 1998.

7. See *Les Misérables*, tome 1, p. 323. New edition by Librairie Générale Française, Paris, 1985. The Latin phrase means "something obscure, something divine".

## REFERENCES

Carse, D. (1998). "The impact of the Asian Crisis on the Hong Kong banking sector". *HKMA Quarterly Bulletin*, no. 16, August. pp. 76–79.

Guyot, E. and Y. Wong (1998). "Home loans insulate banks in Hong Kong from crisis". *Asian Wall Street Journal*, 12 March.

Hong Kong Industry Department (1997). *Survey of Regional Representation by Overseas Companies in Hong Kong* (Hong Kong: Government Printing Department).

Hong Kong Trade Development Council (1998). *The Rise in Offshore Trade and Offshore Investment* (Hong Kong: Research Department, Hong Kong TDC).

Jao, Y.C. (1987). "A comparative analysis of banking crises in Hong Kong and Taiwan". *Journal of Economics and International Relations*, vol. 1, no. 4. pp. 301–22.

————— (1997). *Hong Kong as an International Financial Centre: Evolution, Prospects and Policies* (Hong Kong: City University Press).

———— (1998a). *Money and Finance in Hong Kong: Retrospect and Prospect* (Singapore: World Scientific and Singapore University Press).

———— (1998b). "The working of the currency board: the experience of Hong Kong, 1935–1997". *Pacific Economic Review*, vol. 3, no. 3, October. pp. 203–18.

Jao, Y.C. and A. Sheng (1998). "The impact of higher interest rates on Hong Kong: A graphical analysis". *HKMA Quarterly Bulletin*, no. 14, February. pp. 10–14.

Kaminski, G.L. and C.M. Reinhart (1998). "Financial crises in Asia and Latin America: Then and now". AEA Papers and Proceedings. *American Economic Review*, May. pp. 444–48.

Krugman, P. (1998). "Will Asia bounce back?" Paper presented to Credit Suisse First Boston Asian Investment Conference in Hong Kong. March.

Miller, V. (1998). "The double drain with a cross-border twist: More on the relationships between banking and currency crises". AEA Papers and Proceedings. *American Economic Review*, May. pp. 439–43.

Moreno, R., G. Pasadilla and E. Remolona (1998). "Asia's financial crisis: Lessons and policy responses". Working paper no. PB98–02. Center for Pacific Basin Monetary and Economic Studies, Federal Reserve Bank of San Francisco.

Radelet, S. and J. Sachs (1998a). "The onset of the East Asian financial crisis". Harvard Institute for International Development. 30 March.

———— (1998b). "The East Asian financial crisis: Diagnosis, remedies, prospects". Harvard Institute for International Development. 20 April.

Sheng, A. (1998). "Hong Kong as an international financial centre to 2010". *HKMA Quarterly Bulletin*, no. 15. pp. 83–88.

Yam, J. (1998) "Why we intervened", *Asian Wall Street Journal*, 20 August.

# A Note on the Cantillon-Hume Mechanism

The price-specie-flow mechanism, or the automatic adjustment mechanism under the gold standard, has been widely attributed to David Hume (1711–76), the renowned Scottish philosopher and economist. Careful research though now establishes that Hume was anticipated by many other writers, notably Richard Cantillon (1680–1734), an Irish economist and banker. His masterpiece, *Essai sur la nature du commerce en général*, was written and published in French. This perhaps explains why he was better known and more influential in France than in English-speaking countries.

Cantillon was "rediscovered" by the eminent English economist, W.S. Jevons (1881), who thought his treatment of currency, foreign exchange and bank credit, judged against the work of the time, "almost beyond praise" (p. 342). Schumpeter (1954) considered Cantillon's analysis of banks, bank credit and coinage a "brilliant performance, which in most respects stood unsurpassed for about a century" (p. 223). He further said that although many economists had described and discussed the automatic adjustment mechanism, the most eminent were "Cantillon and Hume" (p. 366).

Hong Kong's linked exchange rate regime is a variant of the Currency Board Arrangement which, in turn, works more or less like the Gold Standard, except that the anchor currency (US dollar in Hong Kong's case) now replaces gold. Since there is no specie flow involved, it seems more appropriate to call the automatic adjustment mechanism the Cantillon-Hume mechanism.

Cantillon and Hume wrote at a time when money consisted almost entirely of currency. Their automatic mechanism was one where gold inflow and outflow matched one for one changes in currency. The modern version of the Cantillon-Hume mechanism takes into account a much more sophisticated banking system, and a key concept called monetary base. It says that changes in foreign reserves lead to proportional changes in monetary base, and hence money supply, in the same direction.

The easiest way to present this modern version is to use the well-known model of money supply determination developed by Friedman and Schwartz (1963) and modify it for our purposes.

The Friedman-Schwartz framework can be described as follows: Let

M = money supply (The various definitions of money can be ignored because they will not affect the substance of the model).

C = legal tender currency

D = total bank deposits (again the various forms of deposits can be ignored).

H = high-powered money, or monetary base

R = banks' reserves with the Central Bank or monetary authorities

Then, by definition,

$$M = C + D \qquad (1)$$
$$H = C + R \qquad (2)$$

Dividing (1) by (2), and further dividing through by C and multiplying through by D/R,

$$\frac{M}{H} = \frac{C+D}{C+R} = \frac{D/R(+D/C)}{C/R+D/C} \qquad (3)$$

Let b = D/R, p = D/C, and by substituting and rearranging,

$$M = H \cdot b(1+p)/(b+p) \qquad (4)$$

It will be noted that b is the reciprocal of the reserve ratio, the banks' behavioural parameter, while p is the reciprocal of the currency ratio, the non-bank public's behavioural parameter. Taking logs of (4)

$$\log M = \log H + \log b + \log (1+p) - \log (b+p) \qquad (5)$$

Differentiating (5) with respect to time, t, and collecting terms,

$$\frac{\dot{M}}{M} = \frac{\dot{H}}{H} + \frac{P}{b(b+p)}\frac{db}{dt} = \frac{(b-1)}{(1+p)(b+p)}\frac{db}{dt} \tag{6}$$

where a dot over a variable means its time derivative, i.e.,

$$\dot{M} = \frac{dM}{dt} \text{ etc.}$$

Friedman and Schwartz assume that .

$$\frac{p}{b(b+P)} \simeq \frac{1}{b}, \frac{(b-1)}{(1+p)(b+P)} \simeq \frac{1}{p}$$

Substituting into (6),

$$\frac{\dot{M}}{M} \simeq \frac{\dot{H}}{H} + \frac{\dot{b}}{b} + \frac{\dot{p}}{p} \tag{7}$$

They further assume that b, p, the two behavioural parameters, are stable and can be taken as constants in the short run. Hence,

$$\frac{\dot{M}}{M} \simeq \frac{\dot{H}}{H} \tag{8}$$

This framework can be modified for the Currency Board Arrangement (CBA) case.
Let F = foreign reserves. Then CBA requires that

$$H = \alpha eF \tag{9}$$

where e is the exchange rate, $\alpha$ is the ratio of H to F. Note that in Hong Kong, there is no Central Bank, and the Hong Kong Monetary Authority does not require the banks to keep reserves with it against their deposit liabilities. However, it does require them to keep positive clearing balances with it after the implementation of the Real Time Gross Settlement in December 1996. Hence R in (2) should denote aggregate clearing balance of the banking system.

Second, e in Hong Kong means of course the peg at US$1=HK$7.8. Third, the prototype CBA requires that $\alpha = 1$. But in Hong Kong, even the enlarged monetary base is 3.6 times backed by foreign reserves, hence $\alpha < 1$.

Substituting (9) back into (4), and working through the same algebraic manipulation, while assuming that $\alpha$ is constant,

$$\frac{\dot{M}}{M} \simeq \frac{\dot{F}}{F} \tag{10}$$

From (8), we finally get

$$\frac{\dot{M}}{M} \simeq \frac{\dot{F}}{F} \simeq \frac{\dot{H}}{H} \tag{11}$$

In words, the proportional rate of change in foreign reserves is matched by approximately the same rates of change in monetary base and money supply in the same direction. This is the essence of the modern Cantillon-Hume mechanism.

By contrast, under the non-CBA conventional fixed exchange rate regime, the monetary base has no full foreign reserve cover. The loss of foreign reserves will not lead to a contraction in monetary base or money supply. Hence the inability of this regime to withstand speculative attacks.

One caveat is that, while the assumption that b, p are constants, while probably valid in normal times, may not hold in extreme circumstances, e.g. a severe banking crisis. The monetary authorities, in performing their lender-of-last-resort duties, may depart temporarily from the monetary rule in (11), even under a CBA.

## REFERENCES

Cantillon, Richard (1775). *Essai sur la nature du commerce en général*. Edited with English translation by H. Higgs (London: Macmillan, 1931).

Friedman, M. and A.J. Schwartz (1963). *A Monetary History of the United States* (Princeton: Princeton University Press).

Hume, David (1752). *Political Discourses* (Edinburgh: Kincaid and Donaldson).

Jevons, W.S. (1881). "Richard Cantillon and the Nationality of Political Economy". *Contemporary Review*, January.

Schumpeter, J.A. (1954). *History of Economic Analysis*. (New York: Oxford University Press).

Yam, Joseph. (1998) "Why We Intervened". *The Asian Wall Street Journal*. 20 August.

CHAPTER 7

# ECONOMIC INTEGRATION WITH THE MAINLAND: BEYOND GUANGDONG

Sung Yun-wing

Since the inauguration of China's open policy in 1979, Hong Kong and the Mainland have rapidly become each other's foremost partner in investment and trade. The opening of China coincided with the emergence of labour shortage in Hong Kong. The labour-intensive export-oriented industries of Hong Kong have rapidly relocated to the Mainland. This movement has led to intense flows of trade and investment between Hong Kong and the Mainland. The main destination of Hong Kong manufacturing firms has been Guangdong province due to geographic and cultural proximity.

Hong Kong's investment in Guangdong transformed both economies. Hong Kong's manufacturing firms reportedly employ four million workers in Guangdong, while the manufacturing labour force in Hong Kong fell from a record of 905,000 in 1984 to 288,887 by the end of 1997. The expansion of exports from processing operations in Guangdong also increased the demand for Hong Kong's service industries, including entrepot trade, shipping, insurance, business services and financial services. The Hong Kong economy became increasingly service-oriented. In short, Hong Kong has become the economic capital of an industrialized Guangdong.

The economic integration of Hong Kong and Guangdong has been highly beneficial for both parties. The Tiananmen incident of 1989 had led to an outflow of skills and capital from Hong Kong. However, the prosperity brought about by the successful economic integration of Hong Kong and Guangdong quickly overshadowed the gloom of the Tiananmen incident. The net emigration of permanent Hong Kong residents reached a peak of 48,100 in 1990 but declined to 38,900 and 24,100 respectively in 1991 and 1992.

Guangdong's successful economic development also strengthened the reforms in China. Deng Xiaoping toured Guangdong early in 1992 and designated Guangdong as the "dragon head" of China's economic reforms. Deng's tour led to a quantum leap in foreign direct investments (FDI) into China. Hong Kong's contracted FDI in China jumped from US$7 billion in 1991 to US$40 billion in 1992 and again to US$74 billion in 1993. Hong Kong's net emigration of permanent Hong Kong residents also turned abruptly into a net immigration of 1,100 in 1993, rising rapidly to 63,900 in 1996 and 127,000 in 1997.

Hong Kong's investment in China is very large. By the end of 1996, the stock of Hong Kong FDI in China was US$99.2 billion. This was 88 percent of Hong Kong's stock of outward FDI, and 57 percent of China's stock of inward FDI. Since 1993, China has become the second largest recipient of FDI in the world after the United States, and Hong Kong has become the world's fourth largest source of FDI after the United States, the United Kingdom and Germany, but ahead of France and Japan.

China's investment in Hong Kong is smaller in comparison but still substantial. By the end of 1996, the stock of China's FDI in Hong Kong was US$14.8 billion. This was 82 percent of China's stock of outward FDI, and 18.7 percent of Hong Kong's inward FDI. In 1996, China was the fifth largest source of FDI among developing countries. Since 1993, China has been the second investor in Hong Kong after the UK.

The large share of Hong Kong in the Mainland's inward FDI conceals Hong Kong's important middleman role as what is regarded as investment from Hong Kong includes the investment of subsidiaries of multinationals incorporated in Hong Kong. Many multinationals like to test the Chinese investment environment through investments from their Hong Kong subsidiaries because of the agglomeration of the required expertise in Hong Kong. Though not all the capital involved originates in Hong Kong, there is no doubt that Hong Kong is a very large mediator of investment for the Mainland.

Hong Kong's investments in outward processing on the Mainland (especially in Guangdong) have generated huge trade flows. In outward processing, the mainland partners of Hong Kong firms process raw materials and semi-manufactured goods produced in Hong Kong or purchased by the Hong Kong parent in the world market, and the processed output is sold via the parent to the world market. Outward processing thus increases both the domestic exports (i.e. exports made locally) of semi-manufactured goods from Hong Kong to the Mainland and also Hong Kong's Mainland-related entrepot trade.

Since the opening of China in 1979, exports produced in enterprises involving foreign investment have increased rapidly. By 1997, 54 percent of China's exports were produced in enterprises involving foreign investment.[1] As Hong Kong accounts for the bulk of foreign investment on the Mainland, it is no exaggeration to say that Hong Kong's investments have been the backbone of China's spectacular export drive. China rose from the 32nd place in world trade in 1978, to the 11th in 1992, and to the 10th in 1997.

While the Mainland's exports have long surpassed those of Singapore, Taiwan and South Korea, they are still less than Hong Kong's because Hong Kong re-exports Mainland products to third places and third-party products to the Mainland. Hong Kong's domestic exports were only a fraction of those of the Mainland. Due to Mainland-related re-exports, Hong Kong's rank in the world as an exporter rose from the 18th in 1979 to the 9th in 1997. In 1997, the Mainland accounted for 70 percent of Hong Kong's trade and Hong Kong accounted for 43 percent of Mainland's trade. The Mainland's share in Hong Kong's trade is large partly because goods re-exported via Hong Kong appear twice in Hong Kong's trade statistics: they appear both as imports and re-exports.

Among developing economies, Guangdong is a large exporter. In 1997, Guangdong's exports of US$76 billion (42 percent of Mainland's total) vastly surpassed Thailand's exports of US$57 billion. Guangdong accounts for the bulk of Hong Kong–Mainland trade and is also the foremost destination of Hong Kong's FDI in the Mainland. At the end of 1997, Guangdong accounted for 40 percent of Hong Kong's cumulative FDI in the Mainland and 22 percent of all cumulative FDI in the Mainland.

Though the Hong Kong–Guangdong economic nexus is thriving, Hong Kong's investments and links are spreading beyond Guangdong. This chapter will focus on the links beyond Guangdong. Unfortunately, statistics on Hong Kong's trade and investment with Guangdong are more complete than those with other provinces, hence, Hong Kong's links beyond Guangdong are often inferred as a residual by taking the Guangdong figure out of the national total. The chapter will discuss the recent trends in the Chinese economy that led to links developing beyond Guangdong. It will then analyse the impact of Hong Kong's reversion to China and the Asian financial crisis on Hong Kong's integration with the Mainland.

# Recent Trends in the Chinese Economy

The main reason for Hong Kong's links spreading beyond Guangdong are due to the emergence of new opportunities elsewhere rather than to rising costs in Guangdong. As the migration of unskilled workers is quite free between Guangdong and the rest of China, Guangdong enjoys a vast supply of labour and labour-intensive industries in Guangdong are still profitable. The new opportunities beyond Guangdong are associated with four recent trends in the Chinese economy:

1. The shift of the focus of China's developmental effort from Guangdong to Shanghai, evidenced by the opening of Pudong in 1990.

2.  The spread of export-oriented industrialization northward to Fujian, Zhejiang, Jiangsu and Shangdong.
3.  The movement to reform State Owned Enterprises (SOEs).
4.  The liberalization of foreign investment in service sectors since 1992.

## Shift of China's Developmental Focus to Shanghai

Since Deng Xiaoping's 1992 southern tour, Hong Kong's investment in Shanghai has grown rapidly. Tables 1 and 2 show respectively Hong Kong's utilized and contracted FDI in the Mainland by area. Guangdong and Shanghai has respectively 40.6 percent and 6.2 percent of Hong Kong's cumulative utilized direct investment in the Mainland from 1979 to 1997. The corresponding figures for Hong Kong's cumulative contracted direct investment were 40.2 percent and 7.3 percent. Guangdong is clearly the prime destination of Hong Kong's investment, though close to 60 percent of Hong Kong's direct investment in the Mainland is outside Guangdong. Both tables show that Guangdong's share of Hong Kong's investment was usually high when the investment environment in the Mainland was not so good, and its share usually declines with improvements in the Chinese investment environment, as investors spread out from Guangdong to other provinces.

Guangdong's shares were high in the early years of China's opening, from 1979–85, when the Chinese investment environment was not mature. Guangdong's shares were also high during the years of the Tiananmen crisis from 1989 to 1991, when Chinese investments suffered heavily, and Guangdong was less affected by the conservative policies than the North. However, Deng's 1992 southern tour led to a dramatic improvement in the investment environment throughout China, especially in Shanghai, and Guangdong's share of Hong Kong's direct investment declined somewhat from 1991 to 1992. Guangdong's share of Hong Kong's utilized investment was quite stable (around 40 percent) since 1992, but Guangdong's share of Hong Kong's contracted investment fell from 44.3 percent in 1995 to 21.6

159

percent in 1997. This is significant as contracted investment indicates future trends.

Shanghai's shares of Hong Kong's direct investment were small before 1992. However, Hong Kong's investment in Shanghai rose rapidly after Deng's tour of 1992. In 1996, Shanghai has respectively 9 percent and 12.6 percent of Hong Kong's utilized and contracted direct investment in the Mainland. Since 1992, Hong Kong accounted for roughly half of the FDI in Shanghai. However, Hong Kong's investment in Shanghai fell markedly in 1997. This is related to the crash of the real estate market in Shanghai due to overbuilding.

Despite the recent rise in Shanghai's share, Guangdong is still the prime destination of Hong Kong's investment. This is because Guangdong's growth continues to be very robust despite the shift of China's focus to Shanghai. Table 3 compares the shares of Guangdong and Shanghai in China's GDP, industrial output, value-added of the tertiary sector, and exports. In 1978, Shanghai's share of China's GDP, industrial output, and exports were 7.5 percent, 12.1 percent and 29.7 percent respectively, which were the highest among the provinces/sub-central cities. However, Guangdong grew much faster than Shanghai, and surpassed Shanghai in GDP in 1983, in exports in 1986, and in industrial output in 1989. Guangdong has been China's top province in inward foreign investment since 1979, in exports since 1986, in GDP since 1989, and in industrial output since 1995.

Despite the opening of Pudong in 1990, the gaps between Guangdong and Shanghai in GDP, industrial output and exports widened even more, and the gap in value-added services remains quite large. In a nutshell, Guangdong is still the premier region in China.

## The Spread of Industrialization Northward

After Deng's 1992 southern tour, other coastal provinces emulated Guangdong's early success in export-oriented industrialization, and provinces such as Fujian, Zhejiang, Jiangsu and Shangdong have grown rapidly to become significant exporters. Fujian has special ties with Taiwan and Shangdong has special ties with South Korea due to geographic and cultural proximity.

Unfortunately, data on Hong Kong's investment in outward processing in the above provinces have not been published. However, statistics on processed exports for China and Guangdong are available. Guangdong's share of the Mainland's processed exports declined from 64 percent in 1992 to 55 percent in 1997, showing the spread of export-oriented industrialization northward. Despite this decline, the bulk of Hong Kong's investments in outward processing in the Mainland should still be in Guangdong simply because Guangdong has over half of the Mainland's processed exports. Moreover, Hong Kong's share of investments in processed exports in Guangdong should be higher than that outside Guangdong. For Hong Kong, Guangdong has the advantage of linguistic and geographic proximity. It is easier for Hong Kong to exploit vertical complementarity in Guangdong by using trucks to carry semi-manufactures to its subsidiaries across the border.

Though Hong Kong's investments in processing operations outside Guangdong should be increasing, it appears that the inputs and outputs of these operations are often not re-exported through Hong Kong for geographical reasons. From surveys conducted on Hong Kong traders/manufacturers (Hong Kong Trade Development Council, 1996), Hong Kong firms rely increasingly on offshore trade instead of re-exporting through Hong Kong. Off-shore trade refers to trade that is handled by Hong Kong traders but do not touch Hong Kong at all in transportation. The rise in offshore trade is consistent with the diversification beyond Guangdong of Hong Kong's investment in outward processing.

The inputs/outputs of Hong Kong's outward-processing operations in Guangdong are still mostly re-exported via Hong Kong for geographical reasons. As a result, Guangdong continues to dominate Hong Kong's trade with the Mainland.

Figures on Hong Kong's imports from the Mainland and from Guangdong involving outward processing are available from surveys of the Hong Kong government. Table 7.4 shows that outward processing has accounted for a rising share of Hong Kong's imports from the Mainland, from 58 percent in 1989 to 81 percent in 1997. Moreover, Guangdong has accounted for a very high and stable share (over 93 percent) of Hong Kong's imports from the Mainland related to outward processing.

Hong Kong's trade with the Mainland is largely dominated by Hong Kong's outward processing activities in Guangdong. Outward processing has accounted for an increasing share of Hong Kong's trade with the Mainland, from 56.5 percent in 1989 to 67.5 percent in 1997. This implies that Guangdong's share of Hong Kong's commodity trade is rising and the corresponding shares of the other provinces are declining.[2]

## The Movement to Reform the SOEs

China has recently speeded up its reform of the SOEs. The large SOEs will be restructured and corporatized whereas the small ones will be hived off. Foreign investors can take over the operation of small- and medium-sized SOEs through acquisition, leasing, or subcontracting. The reform of the SOEs will raise the Mainland's demand for financial and professional services which can be supplied by Hong Kong. This leads to Hong Kong links with areas beyond Guangdong. Unlike Shanghai, the Beijing–Tianjin area and the Northeast, Guangdong has few SOEs.

In 1992, China approved the public listing of selective SOEs in the Hong Kong stock market and their shares were popularly called H-shares. Besides tapping external funds, listing in Hong Kong also speeds up China's enterprise reforms, since listed firms have to follow international accounting standards. Since the listing of the first SOE (Tsingtao Brewery) in July 1993, the number of listings rose rapidly to 39 by the end of October 1997, and rose further to 41 by the end of December 1998. The rise from October 1997 to December 1998 was slow due to the Asian financial crisis. Among the 41 listed SOEs, only four are Guangdong enterprises.

Hong Kong is a major centre for financing the Mainland's economic development. Besides FDI and H-shares listed in Hong Kong, around 90 percent of the syndicated loans extended to the Mainland was arranged through Hong Kong (Hong Kong Trade Development Council, 1998). Unlike outward processing, which is largely in Guangdong due to the dependence on the transportation of raw materials and products, the role of Hong Kong as a financier goes largely beyond Guangdong.

While Hong Kong is strong in financing, providing SOEs with management and technology is a different matter. For historical reasons, the majority of SOEs are engaged in import-substituting and capital-intensive industries. Hong Kong has little expertise in such industries. Hong Kong's industrial links with the mainland are thus largely confined to Guangdong.

## The Liberalization of Foreign Investment in Service Sectors

Since Deng's 1992 southern tour, China has gradually allowed foreign investment in non-manufacturing sectors, such as real estate, banking, retail trade, infrastructure and import/export trade. Such liberalization has an impact on Hong Kong's economic links with the Mainland by region, and the regional impacts have to be analysed sector by sector as services are highly heterogeneous. Unfortunately, the data on Hong Kong's investment in the Mainland by industry has not been published, not to speak of Hong Kong's investment in the provinces by industry. The following discussion is thus based largely on anecdotal evidence.

The shares of industry and real estate in cumulative FDI in the Mainland from 1979–96 were 53 percent and 24.9 percent respectively. The shares of other sectors were quite small. For Hong Kong's utilized FDI in Guangdong from 1979–95, the shares of industry and real estate were 72.5 percent and 17.9 percent respectively (Zheng, Wang and Chen, 1997:Table 6), and the shares of the other sectors were again small. In both cases, industry and real estate are the sectors that receive the most FDI.

The sectoral distribution of Hong Kong's investment in Guangdong is not too different from the sectoral distribution of all inward FDI in China, except that the share of industry was higher and the share of real estate was lower. This is expected as Guangdong is the prime site for the relocation of Hong Kong's industries due to geographic and linguistic proximity. From anecdotal evidence, Hong Kong's investment in real estate in the Mainland is very substantial. The educated guess is that Hong Kong's investment beyond Guangdong comprises a smaller share in industry and larger shares in other sectors, including the real estate sector, when compared with Hong Kong's investments within Guangdong.

Hong Kong's investment in banking in the Mainland obviously goes beyond Guangdong for the simple reason that Shanghai is the domestic financial centre of China. As for infrastructure, it is well known that Hong Kong has invested considerably in infrastructure both within and beyond Guangdong. For instance, Hutchison–Whampoa has invested in container terminals and port facilities in Guangdong's ports (e.g. Yantian, Gaolan, Jiuzhou) as well as in Shanghai.

# Impacts of the Asian Financial Crisis and Hong Kong's Reversion to China

The Asian financial crisis occurred simultaneously with Hong Kong's reversion to China, and both events have significant impacts on Hong Kong's trade and investment with Guangdong and beyond.

Hong Kong's reversion does not change the framework of Hong Kong–Mainland economic relations, which has long been laid down in the Sino-British Declaration of 1984 and also the Basic Law. For all practical purposes, Hong Kong is a separate economic entity. It is a separate customs territory with its own border and immigration controls. It has a currency of its own which is linked to the US dollar and it runs its own monetary and fiscal policies. It does not pay any tax to the central government.

Despite Hong Kong's reversion to China, there is very little hope that Hong Kong and the Mainland can form some kind of trade bloc, such as a Free Trade Area, a Customs Union, or a Common Market. A Customs Union is out of the question and it requires that Hong Kong and the Mainland levy the same external tariff, which is zero as Hong Kong is a free port. A Common Market is even more problematic as it requires free migration within the bloc and this runs against Hong Kong's very strict immigration controls against the Mainland. Even a Free Trade Area (FTA), which is the trade bloc with the lowest degree of formal economic integration, is impractical because the Mainland would lose tariff revenue and there would be no offsetting gains in Mainland exports as Hong Kong is already a free port.

Though a formal Hong Kong–Mainland trade bloc is out of the question, reversion has facilitated policy coordination between Hong Kong and the Mainland, leading to tighter economic integration. The scope of coordination involves border issues with Guangdong and also national policies beyond Guangdong, namely, quotas for Mainland tourists visiting Hong Kong, a policy on technology and exchange-rate policies. The Asian financial crisis has strengthened the need for policy coordination in many areas, especially coordination to stabilize the exchange rate.

# Policy Coordination on the National Level beyond Guangdong

The main areas of coordination involve tourism, a policy on technology, and coordination to stabilize the exchange rate.

## Tourism

Hong Kong's tourist industry has been severely hit by the Asian financial crisis because the Hong Kong dollar did not depreciate. Tourist arrivals dropped by 11 percent in 1997 and fell by another 21 percent in the first half of 1998 (over the first half of 1997). Boosting tourism is thus high on the government's agenda.

At the end of May 1998, the government announced a package of seven measures to stimulate the sagging economy. One of these involved a 30-percent increase in the quota allocated to mainlanders joining the Group Tour Scheme to visit Hong Kong (such tours were started in the early 1980s and the quota was instituted to avoid illegal immigration). Another measure was to simplify visa formalities for Taiwanese tourists who tour Hong Kong on their way to the Mainland. Such measures brought an upturn in tourist arrivals. From July to November of 1998, visitors arrivals from the Mainland and Taiwan rose by 37 percent and 1.8 percent over the same period in 1997. This led to a growth in total tourist arrivals by 6.7 percent. The Group Tour Scheme is not new to Guangdong as it began in the early 1980s. The increase in quota thus involved mainly areas beyond Guangdong.

## Technology Policy

Despite Hong Kong's lagging technical capacity in comparison with Singapore, Taiwan and South Korea, Hong Kong is uniquely positioned to utilize the research and engineering capability of the Mainland. Moreover, in comparison with its rivals, Hong Kong has the advantage of close links with the Mainland's vast internal market. The government is taking important steps to promote technology. In his policy address in October 1998, the chief executive of Hong Kong, Tung Chee-hwa, announced that, on top of existing policies to construct the first science park and funds to support applied research and industrial technology, the government would create an Innovation and Technology Fund of HK$5 billion and also establish an applied science and technology research institute to turn basic research into commercial applications. The government would also consider measures which would enable employers to recruit the best professionals from the Mainland and other countries.

Though the details of the policy on technology has yet to be worked out, it will largely involve links beyond Guangdong because Guangdong lags way behind Shanghai and Beijing–Tianjin in technology.

## Coordination to Stabilize the Exchange Rate

Unlike other East Asian economies, the Mainland and Hong Kong have stood firm and they have thus far maintained their exchange rates against the US dollar. Both governments have reiterated their determination to keep their exchange rates stable. Coordination in exchange rate policies between the Mainland and Hong Kong have contributed to financial stability in East Asia.

The financial turmoil generated by the rapid depreciation of the Japanese yen in mid-June 1998 highlighted the importance of Mainland–Hong Kong policy coordination. Mainland officials repeatedly called upon the US, Japan and also the G-7 nations to stabilize the yen from 9 June to 17 June 1998. Tung Chee-Hwa was then visiting Australia and New Zealand and he echoed such calls. On 15 June 1998, the Hong Kong Monetary Authority stated that it would use its reserves to buy the yen if the G-7 nations would do the same. On 17 June 1998, the Vice-Minister of China's

Ministry of Foreign Trade and Economic Cooperation (MOFTEC) hinted that China might renege on its pledge not to devalue if the yen should continue to depreciate. The hint was widely perceived to be a threat to the US and Japan to take action. On the same day, the US and Japan intervened decisively in the New York market, and the exchange rate of the yen to the US dollar rose from around 144 to 138. It was widely believed that the pressure from China played an important part in US intervention. The weaknesses of the Japanese economy has enhanced China's role in the international economic arena. President Bill Clinton has acknowledged the importance of the economic roles of the Mainland and Hong Kong in the Asian financial crisis in his visit to China and Hong Kong in late June and early July 1998.

## Policy Coordination between Hong Kong and Guangdong

Besides the increase in policy coordination at the national level, coordination on border issues with Guangdong is also important. This involves border checkpoints and cross-border infrastructure, border tourism, and environmental protection. On 25 September 1998, Hong Kong and Guangdong reached a formal agreement on these issues.

### Border Checkpoints and Infrastructure

Congestion of border checkpoints has long been a source of complaint. Truck crossings are heavily congested, and the Hong Kong General Chamber of Commerce estimated in 1992 that Hong Kong's losses from congestion amounted to HK$3 billion a year. Passenger crossings often take an hour or more, and large number of commuters suffer as a result. There have long been proposals to allow 24-hour operation of the major checkpoints, but the agreement reached in late September after long negotiations is disappointing as the opening hours of the four land crossings will be extended by only one to two hours from 15 October 1998 or from 1 April 1999. Even after the opening hours of the checkpoints are extended, no checkpoint will be open from 11.30 p.m. to 6.30 a.m.

There has been opposition to a 24-hour operation of checkpoints in Hong Kong. Since the onset of the Asian financial crisis, real estate prices in Hong Kong have halved, and the Hong Kong government fears that the proposal will depress prices further in the northern New Territories. Moreover, retail sales in Hong Kong have plummeted and Hong Kong shoppers have swarmed to Shenzhen. The proposal is likely to aggravate retail sales even more.

## Cross-border Tourism

As mentioned earlier, the tourist industry in Hong Kong was fighting for survival as a result of the Asian financial crisis. Hong Kong and Guangdong reached an agreement on five measures to boost tourism. First, visa-free access for overseas visitors from Hong Kong will be extended to Zhuhai, and these visitors will also be allowed to visit six other cities in Guangdong. Second, more Hong Kong registered travel agencies (in addition to those operated by Mainland capital) will be allowed to organize visa-free access package tours to Guangdong. Third, non-Guangdong mainlanders in Shenzhen will be allowed to join the Group Tour Scheme to visit Hong Kong. Fourth, Hong Kong and Guangdong agencies will be allowed to organize overseas tours for Guangdong residents. Fifth, quotas for tourist coaches carrying overseas visitors into and out of Shenzhen will be relaxed.

Besides facilitating mainlanders visiting Hong Kong, the measures will also increase the attraction of Hong Kong to overseas visitors as they can visit more places in Guangdong without a visa. Moreover, Hong Kong tourist agencies can share in part of the tourist business involving overseas tourists visiting Guangdong and also Guangdong tourists visiting Hong Kong or elsewhere. Of course, Guangdong will also benefit from the increase in overseas tourists. The impacts of these measures are yet unknown because they have to be first approved by Beijing before implementation.

## Environmental Protection

To protect the environment, both Hong Kong and Guangdong agreed to subject all large-scale public works in the border areas to environmental evaluation and mutual consultation. The two sides will undertake a joint study of air quality in the Pearl River Delta in 1999. Pollutants in the Pearl River Delta have led to a substantial deterioration in air quality in Hong Kong.

## Impact of the Asian Financial Crisis

Hong Kong has been severely hit by the Asian financial crisis, and its GDP has been forecasted officially to decline by 5 percent in 1998. The Mainland is less affected because its economy is large and is relatively less dependent on foreign trade and investment. Moreover, speculators cannot easily attack the renminbi due to China's stringent foreign exchange control. The crisis, nevertheless, has adverse impacts on the Mainland's exports and inward FDI. China used expansionary fiscal and monetary policies to maintain its growth rate and China's 1998 growth rate was 7.8 percent, which was only slightly less than the official target of 8 percent. The Mainland will still be among the fastest growing economies of the world.

As growth in the Mainland is still robust, Hong Kong is turning increasingly to the Mainland. The net effect of the crisis has thus strengthened economic integration between Hong Kong and the Mainland.

## Hong Kong–Mainland Commodity Trade

The Mainland's export growth has slowed down markedly. The rate of growth of the Mainland's trade was 12.1 percent in 1997, but the rates of growth in the first, second and third quarters of 1998 fell to 8.9 percent, 2.2 percent, and –2 percent respectively. The rates of growth in October and November 1998 were –17 percent and –9 percent respectively.

Until 1997, Hong Kong's Mainland-related trade has grown rapidly in absolute terms (though it has declined relative to Mainland's trade since 1993 because the latter has grown even faster). The Asian financial crisis brought about the first negative growth in Hong Kong's Mainland-related trade in the open-door era. In the first half of 1998, Hong Kong's trade with the Mainland fell by 0.9 percent (compared with the first half of 1997), but Hong

Kong's total trade fell even more (–4.0 percent). This implies that the Mainland's share of Hong Kong's trade has risen (from 69.8 percent in 1997 to 70.8 percent in the first half of 1998) while Hong Kong's share of the Mainland's trade has declined (from 43.3 percent in 1997 to 42.6 percent in the first half of 1998).

## Hong Kong–Mainland Investment Links

The crisis also brought about a reversal in Hong Kong's investment in the Mainland. In the first half of 1998, Hong Kong's utilized FDI and contracted FDI in the Mainland fell by 11 percent and 18 percent respectively. This has a substantial impact on the Mainland as Hong Kong is the foremost investor. The rate of growth of utilized FDI in the Mainland dropped markedly from 14.1 percent in the first quarter of 1998 to –0.5 percent in the second quarter of 1998. From 1997 to the first half of 1998, the share of Hong Kong in Mainland's contracted FDI fell from 36 percent to 30 percent.

The depressed state of Hong Kong's stock market also has an adverse impact on the listing of China's state enterprises in Hong Kong. The Mainland's investment in Hong Kong also suffered, though precise figures are lacking. China tightened capital control in September 1997 due to capital flight induced by the Asian crisis. Such controls hamper the Mainland's investments in Hong Kong. Mainland enterprises, which hitherto were allowed to keep part of the earnings in foreign exchange in Hong Kong, have to hand over such earnings to the People's Bank.

## Hong Kong–Mainland Tourist Trade

Despite the reversal in Hong Kong's Mainland-related trade and investment, Hong Kong's Mainland-related tourism continues to grow. As mentioned above, mainland tourists visiting Hong Kong have grown rapidly since June 1998 due to the increase in the quota of the Group Tour Scheme.

Hong Kong residents visiting the Mainland also been increasing rapidly, rising by 17 percent in 1997 and by 18 percent in the first half of 1998 (compared to the first half of 1997). The strength of the Hong Kong dollar has stimulated outward tourism in general. Though the official rate of the renminbi has remained quite stable, its exchange rate in the offshore Hong Kong market has depreciated slightly, and this might account for part of the increase in departures to the Mainland. However, two other factors probably play a more important role. The first is the continuing integration between Hong Kong and the Mainland. The number of Hong Kong residents working in the Mainland has increased rapidly, and there are also more Hong Kong residents who live in Shenzhen and commute to Hong Kong. The other factor is that, for Hong Kong residents, Shenzhen is an increasingly popular place for the shopping of low-end consumer goods. As recession sets in, consumers try to economize, and there is a surge of Hong Kong shoppers to Shenzhen.

## Guangdong and Beyond

The crisis has significant impacts on Hong Kong's trade and investment with Guangdong and also beyond Guangdong. Three factors suggest that Hong Kong links with Guangdong may suffer less than those beyond Guangdong, but three other factors operate in the opposite direction. The three positive factors are covered first.

First, in bad times, Hong Kong firms tend to concentrate on their traditional business (those in Guangdong) and curtail their new business (those outside Guangdong). Second, as mentioned earlier, there has been a surge of Hong Kong tourists in Shenzhen. Third, Hong Kong's role as the Mainland's financier has suffered heavily in this financial crisis, and the financing function of Hong Kong is nationwide rather than confined to Guangdong. From the end of October 1997 (when the Hong Kong dollar was attacked savagely and the stock market collapsed) to December 1998, only two mainland SOEs listed their shares in Hong Kong. The share of the market capitalization of all H-shares in the Hong Kong stock market fell from 2.01 percent on 31 October 1997 to 1.03 percent on 31 August 1998. These shares involved mostly SOEs beyond Guangdong.

The other three factors that work against Guangdong may be more powerful. First, Asean's exports are very competitive after depreciation, and such exports compete with the labour-intensive exports of Guangdong. Before mid-1998, ASEAN exporters have difficulties in obtaining bank loans to finance exports, and some orders were diverted to Guangdong. In the first half of 1998, Guangdong's export growth at 10.5 percent was appreciably faster than that of the nation at 7.6 percent. However, since July 1998, ASEAN exports seem to have a significant adverse impact on Guangdong. In the third quarter of 1998, Guangdong's exports fell by 3.6 percent while the Mainland's exports outside Guangdong fell by only 0.8 percent. Present signs indicate that Guangdong's exports will face a very hard time. This will slow down Hong Kong's recovery from the Asian financial crisis and also adversely affect Hong Kong's investment in Guangdong's outward processing operations.

Second, as mentioned earlier, in reaction to capital flight induced by the Asian financial crisis, China has tightened foreign exchange controls. China has also cracked down hard on smuggling since September 1998 to protect its import-substituting industries. While enterprises and local authorities in many coastal provinces are involved in the evasion of foreign exchange controls and smuggling, such activities are particularly prevalent in Guangdong due to its extensive Hong Kong links. While the tightening of these controls are good for growth in the long run, they have adverse short-run impacts on the Hong Kong–Guangdong economic nexus.

Third, Guangdong suffers more than other provinces from the collapse of the stock and real estate markets in Hong Kong because of its extensive Hong Kong links. The closure of the Guangdong International Trade and Investment Corporation (GITIC), the second largest corporation owned by Guangdong, in early October 1998, highlighted the plight of Guangdong enterprises. GITIC owns two publicly listed companies in Hong Kong and it made losses of over 10 billion renminbi from overseas investments. Banks and investors are expected to tighten credit to mainland enterprises due to the closure of GITIC.

Overall, it appears that other provinces have suffered less than Guangdong. Hong Kong links may increasingly go beyond Guangdong. Presently, Hong Kong's growth is forecasted to stagnate in 1999 and this is expected to have a continuing adverse effect on Guangdong's trade and investment.

## Conclusion

Hong Kong's increasing links beyond Guangdong can be accounted for by the emergence of opportunities in places outside Guangdong. Since 1990, the focus of national development has shifted from Guangdong to Shanghai. Deng's 1992 southern tour deepened the reform process in China and the coastal provinces beyond Guangdong successfully followed Guangdong's example of export-oriented industrialization. Moreover, China has gradually liberalized investment in services since 1992. Unlike manufacturing, which is more dependent on geographic proximity due to the need to transport semi-manufactures and products, the opportunities in services spread beyond Guangdong.

Simultaneous with the emergence of rich opportunities beyond Guangdong, Guangdong's economic growth has continued to be robust and the Hong Kong–Guangdong economic nexus continues to thrive. Guangdong continues to be the prime destination of Hong Kong investment and the Hong Kong–Guangdong trade continues to dominate Hong Kong's trade with the Mainland.

The Asian financial crisis, however, has adverse impacts on China, especially on the Hong Kong–Guangdong economic nexus. The crisis has strengthened the demand for policy coordination, and Hong Kong's reversion to China has facilitated such coordination. Coordination has started on many fronts, from nationwide issues such as exchange-rate stability to border issues between Hong Kong and Guangdong. Policy coordination has softened the adverse impacts of the crisis.

Since Deng's 1992 tour, the process of economic integration has expanded beyond manufacturing to service industries. However, barriers to services trade are usually much higher than those in commodity trade because services are performed on people and require people-to-people contacts. Hong Kong's severe controls on migration from the Mainland is one barrier. As most services cannot be exported and are sold in the domestic market, China's foreign exchange controls is another barrier. Lastly, China's heavy regulation of many service industries (e.g. telecommunication, media, transportation, banking and insurance) represent additional barriers. In this context, policy coordination is crucial for the integration of services as many service industries are dependent on the regulatory framework.

Recently, coordination to stabilize the exchange rate has required that officials on the Mainland and Hong Kong be in close contact, especially officials who are responsible for monetary affairs. The process has built up rapport between officials on both sides and may facilitate coordination in other areas in future.

## REFERENCES

Hong Kong Trade Development Council (1996). "Hong Kong's trade and trade supporting services" (Hong Kong). April.

Zheng, Bojian, Wang, Liwen and Chen, Shengho (1997). "The development and prospect of Hong Kong-funded enterprises in Guangdong". In *The Ninth Five-Year-Plan, the Long-term Target for the Year 2010, and the Hong Kong Economy*, vol. I (Hong Kong: The Better Hong Kong Foundation and One Country Two Systems Economic Research Institute). pp. 95–124.

# Appendix

*Table 7.1*

## Hong Kong's Utilized FDI in the Mainland by Area
(US$mn)

| | | Guangdong | Shanghai | Elsewhere | Total | National Total |
|---|---|---|---|---|---|---|
| | | | Hong Kong's FDI in | | | |
| 1979 B | | 3,413 | 108.7 | 4,269 | 7,791 | 12,105 |
| 1988 | (i) | (43.8) | (1.4) | (54.8) | (100) | (100) |
| | (ii) | (28.2) | (0.9) | (35.3) | (64.4) | (100) |
| | (iii) | (83.6) | (15.5) | (58.3) | (64.4) | 3392 |
| 1989 | | 953 | 171 | 913 | 2,037 | 3,392 |
| | (i) | (46.8) | (8.4) | (44.8) | (100) | – |
| | (ii) | (28.1) | (5.0) | (26.9) | (60.0) | (100) |
| | (iii) | (82.4) | (38.7) | (50.9) | (60.0) | (100) |
| 1990 | | 996 | 39.0 | 845 | 1,880 | 3,487 |
| | | (53.0) | (2.1) | (44.9) | (100) | – |
| | | (28.6) | (1.1) | (24.2) | (53.9) | (100) |
| 1991 | | 1,356 | 39.2 | 1,010 | 2,405 | 4,366 |
| | (i) | (56.4) | (1.6) | (42.0) | (100) | – |
| | (ii) | (31.1) | (0.9) | (23.1) | (55.1) | (100) |
| | (iii) | (74.4) | (27.1) | (42.1) | (55.1) | (100) |
| 1992 | | 3,069 | 206 | 4,232 | 7,507 | 11,008 |
| | (i) | (40.9) | (2.7) | (56.4) | (100) | – |
| | (ii) | (27.9) | (1.9) | (38.4) | (68.2) | (100) |
| | (iii) | (86.4) | (42.8) | (60.7) | (68.2) | (100) |
| 1993 | | 6,530 | 925 | 9,820 | 17,275 | 27,515 |
| | (i) | (37.8) | (5.4) | (56.8) | (100) | – |
| | (ii) | (23.7) | (3.4) | (35.7) | (62.8) | (100) |
| | (iii) | (87.1) | (29.3) | (58.3) | (62.8) | (100) |

*continued next page*

| | | Hong Kong's FDI in | | | |
|---|---|---|---|---|---|
| | | **Guangdong** | **Shanghai** | **Elsewhere** | **Total** | **National Total** |
| **1994** | | **7,768** | **1,276** | **10,621** | **19,665** | **33,767** |
| | (i) | (39.5) | (6.5) | (54.0) | (100) | – |
| | (ii) | (23.0) | (3.8) | (31.4) | (58.2) | (100) |
| | (iii) | (82.7) | (51.6) | (48.7) | (58.2) | (100) |
| **1995** | | **7,973** | **1,854** | **10,233** | **20,060** | **37,521** |
| | (i) | (39.7) | (9.2) | (51.0) | (100) | – |
| | (ii) | (21.2) | (4.9) | (27.4) | (53.5) | (100) |
| | (iii) | (78.3) | (64.1) | (41.9) | (53.5) | (100) |
| **1996** | | **8,387** | **1,865** | **10,425** | **20,677** | **41,726** |
| | (i) | (40.6) | (9.0) | (50.4) | (100) | – |
| | (ii) | (20.1) | (4.5) | (25.0) | (49.6) | (100) |
| | (iii) | (72.2) | (47.3) | (39.8) | (49.6) | (100) |
| **1997** | | **8,262** | **887** | **11,481** | **20,630** | **45,257** |
| | (i) | (40.1) | (4.3) | (55.6) | (100) | – |
| | (ii) | (18.3) | (2.0) | (25.4) | (45.6) | (100) |
| | (iii) | (70.6) | (18.4) | (40.0) | (45.6) | (100) |
| **1979–** | | **48,707** | **7,370** | **63,849** | **119,927** | **220,142** |
| **1997** | (i) | (40.6) | (6.2) | (53.2) | (100) | – |
| | (ii) | (22.1) | (3.4) | (29.0) | (54.5) | (100) |
| | (iii) | (78.1) | (35.0) | (46.7) | (54.5) | (100) |

*Note*:   (i)   Percentage share of Hong Kong's FDI in the Mainland

        (ii)  Percentage share of inward FDI in the Mainland

        (iii) Percentage share of inward FDI in respective areas

*Source*: Mainland data:   *China Statistical Yearbook*;

        Guangdong data: *Guangdong Statistical Yearbook*;

        Shanghai data:   *Shanghai Statistical Yearbook*.

*Table 7.2*

# Hong Kong's Contracted FDI in the Mainland by Area (US$mn)

| | | Hong Kong's contracted FDI in | | | | |
|---|---|---|---|---|---|---|
| | | Guangdong | Shanghai | Elsewhere | Mainland | National Total |
| **1979–** | | | | | | |
| **1988** | | **10,361** | **597.1** | **6,682.9** | **17,641** | **28,165** |
| | (i) | (58.7) | (3.4) | (37.9) | (100) | – |
| | (ii) | (36.8) | (2.1) | (23.7) | (62.6) | (100) |
| | (iii) | (82.6) | (26.5) | (50.0) | (62.6) | (100) |
| **1989** | | **1,800** | **111** | **1,249** | **3,160** | **5,600** |
| | (i) | (57.0) | (3.5) | (39.5) | (100) | – |
| | (ii) | (32.1) | (2.0) | (22.3) | (56.4) | (100) |
| | (iii) | (73.8) | (30.8) | (44.6) | (56.4) | (100) |
| **1990** | | **2,109** | **111** | **1,613** | **3,833** | **6,596** |
| | (i) | (55.0) | (2.9) | (42.1) | (100) | – |
| | (ii) | (32.0) | (1.7) | (24.5) | (58.2) | (100) |
| | (iii) | (78.4) | (29.6) | (45.7) | (58.2) | (100) |
| **1991** | | **3,926** | **122** | **3,167** | **7,215** | **11,977** |
| | (i) | (54.4) | (1.7) | (43.9) | (100) | – |
| | (ii) | (32.8) | (1.1) | (26.4) | (60.3) | (100) |
| | (iii) | (80.1) | (28.4) | (47.7) | (60.3) | (100) |
| **1992** | | **15,992** | **1,526** | **22,526** | **40,044** | **58,124** |
| | (i) | (39.9) | (3.8) | (56.3) | (100) | – |
| | (ii) | (27.5) | (2.6) | (38.8) | (68.9) | (100) |
| | (iii) | (84.8) | (52.6) | (62.0) | (68.9) | (100) |
| **1993** | | **27,927** | **4,321** | **41,691** | **73,939** | **11,1436** |
| | (i) | (37.8) | (5.8) | (56.4) | (100) | – |
| | (ii) | (25.1) | (3.9) | (37.4) | (66.4) | (100) |
| | (iii) | (84.3) | (61.8) | (58.5) | (66.4) | (100) |

*continued next page*

*continued* **Table 7.2**

| | | Hong Kong's contracted FDI in | | | |
|---|---|---|---|---|---|
| | | Guangdong | Shanghai | Elsewhere | Mainland | National Total |
| **1994** | | **18,740** | **5,842** | **22,389** | **46,971** | **82,680** |
| | (i) | (39.9) | (12.4) | (47.7) | (100) | – |
| | (ii) | (22.7) | (7.1) | (27.1) | (56.9) | (100) |
| | (iii) | (78.7) | (62.9) | (45.1) | (56.9) | (100) |
| **1995** | | **18,156** | **3,638** | **19,202** | **40,996** | **91,282** |
| | (i) | (44.3) | (8.9) | (46.8) | (100) | – |
| | (ii) | (19.9) | (4.0) | (21.1) | (45.0) | (100) |
| | (iii) | (73.1) | (35.3) | (34.2) | (45.0) | (100) |
| **1996** | | **9,592** | **3,513** | **14,897** | **28,002** | **73,276** |
| | (i) | (34.3) | (12.6) | (53.1) | (100) | – |
| | (ii) | (13.1) | (4.8) | (20.3) | (38.2) | (100) |
| | (iii) | (61.6) | (34.9) | (31.3) | (38.2) | (100) |
| **1997** | | **3,936** | **561** | **13,723** | **18,220** | **51,004** |
| | (i) | (21.6) | (3.1) | (75.3) | (100) | – |
| | (ii) | (7.7) | (1.1) | (26.9) | (35.7) | (100) |
| | (iii) | (51.2) | (10.6) | (36.1) | (35.7) | (100) |
| **1979–** | | **11,2539** | **20,342** | **135,141** | **280,022** | **520,140** |
| **1997** | (i) | (40.2) | (7.3) | (52.5) | (100) | – |
| | (ii) | (21.6) | (3.9) | (26.0) | (53.8) | (100) |
| | (iii) | (76.8) | (70.0) | (39.2) | (53.8) | (100) |

*Note*:  (i)  Percentage share of Hong Kong's FDI in the Mainland

(ii)  Percentage share of inward FDI in the Mainland

(iii)  Percentage share of inward FDI in respective areas

*Source*: Mainland data:  *China Statistical Yearbook*;

Guangdong data: *Guangdong Statistical Yearbook*

Shanghai data:  *Shanghai Statistical Yearbook*.

*Table 7.3*

## Share of Shanghai & Guangdong in China's GDP, Industrial Output, and Exports (percent)

| | Share of Shanghai in China's | | | | Share of Guangdong in China's | | | |
|---|---|---|---|---|---|---|---|---|
| | GDP | industrial output | Value-added of tertiary sector | Exports | GDP | industrial output | Value-added of tertiary sector | Exports |
| 1978 | 7.5 | 12.1 | 5.9 | 29.7 | 5.1 | 4.7 | 5.1 | 14.2 |
| 1979 | 6.7 | 11.9 | 6.2 | 26.9 | 5.0 | 4.6 | 5.8 | 12.5 |
| 1980 | 6.9 | 11.6 | 6.8 | 23.3 | 5.4 | 4.3 | 6.4 | 12.0 |
| 1981 | 6.7 | 11.5 | 6.7 | 18.2 | 5.9 | 5.0 | 6.8 | 11.4 |
| 1982 | 6.4 | 10.9 | 6.5 | 16.5 | 6.3 | 5.1 | 7.0 | 10.3 |
| 1983 | 6.0 | 10.3 | 6.3 | 16.4 | 6.1 | 5.1 | 6.5 | 10.7 |
| 1984 | 5.4 | 9.6 | 5.6 | 14.7 | 6.1 | 5.3 | 6.4 | 10.2 |
| 1985 | 5.2 | 8.9 | 4.8 | 13.0 | 6.2 | 5.5 | 6.1 | 11.4 |
| 1986 | 4.8 | 8.5 | 4.6 | 13.3 | 6.3 | 5.6 | 6.8 | 15.7 |
| 1987 | 4.6 | 7.8 | 4.6 | 12.0 | 6.8 | 6.4 | 7.3 | 25.7 |
| 1988 | 4.3 | 7.2 | 4.2 | 11.3 | 7.4 | 7.2 | 7.7 | 31.2 |
| 1989 | 4.1 | 6.9 | 3.7 | 11.6 | 7.8 | 7.5 | 8.0 | 34.5 |
| 1990 | 4.1 | 6.9 | 4.2 | 10.2 | 7.9 | 8.0 | 8.6 | 35.8 |
| 1991 | 4.1 | 6.9 | 4.3 | 9.4 | 8.2 | 8.9 | 8.5 | 37.7 |
| 1992 | 4.2 | 6.6 | 4.4 | 8.6 | 8.6 | 9.4 | 8.5 | 39.4 |
| 1993 | 4.4 | 6.3 | 5.1 | 8.3 | 9.4 | 9.9 | 9.3 | 41.0 |
| 1994 | 4.4 | 5.5 | 5.5 | 8.2 | 9.4 | 9.4 | 9.8 | 44.0 |
| 1995 | 4.3 | 5.2 | 5.5 | 8.8 | 9.4 | 9.5 | 9.9 | 39.7 |
| 1996 | 4.3 | 5.1 | 5.9 | 8.7 | 9.6 | 9.3 | 10.9 | 39.7 |
| 1997 | 4.5 | 5.0 | 6.4 | 8.1 | 9.8 | 9.7 | 11.0 | 41.6 |

China Customs Statistics have been used for Shanghai and Guangdong since 1993 and 1987 respectively (earliest available data) while MOFERT (Ministry of Foreign Economic Relations and Trade) statistics, which are less accurate, are used for previous years. MOFERT statistics greatly understates the exports of Guangdong due to the importance of processing exports in Guangdong (Sung, Liu, Wong and Lau 1997:71–74). The problem does not exist for Shanghai as processing exports are insignificant there.

*Source*: Exports since 1993: *China Customs Statistics*, Economic Information & Agency, Hong Kong; Guangdong's Exports from 1987–92: *The Statistics of the External Economy, Trade and Tourism of the Guangdong Province*; Guangdong Statistical Bureau (internal document), 1990, 1991, 1992; other statistics are obtained from the Shanghai, Guangdong and China *Statistics Yearbooks* of China Statistical Publishing House.

*Table 7.4*

## Hong Kong's Imports from the Mainland
## Involving Outward Processing (US$mn)

| | | Imports from the Mainland Involving Outward Processing | |
| | | US$mn | Share from Guangdong (%) |
|---|---|---|---|
| 1989 | | 14,562 | 93.4 |
| | (i) | (58.1) | |
| 1990 | | 18,629 | 94.4 |
| | (i) | (61.8) | |
| | (ii) | (29.3) | |
| 1991 | | 25,400 | 94.5 |
| | (i) | (67.6) | |
| | (ii) | (36.4) | |
| 1992 | | 32,566 | 93.1 |
| | (i) | (72.1) | |
| | (ii) | (28.2) | |
| 1993 | | 38,160 | 93.3 |
| | (i) | (73.8) | |
| | (ii) | (17.2) | |
| 1994 | | 45,925 | 94.4 |
| | (i) | (75.9) | |
| | (ii) | (20.4) | |
| 1995 | | 51,650 | 95.0 |
| | (i) | (74.4) | |
| | (ii) | (12.5) | |
| 1996 | | 58,558 | 95.2 |
| | (i) | (79.90) | |
| | (ii) | (13.4) | |
| 1997 | | 63,439 | 94.4 |
| | (i) | (81.2) | |
| | (ii) | (8.3) | |

*Note*:   (i)  Proportion of outward-processing trade in total (%)

       (ii)  Growth rate (%) over previous year.

*Source*: Hong Kong External Trade Census and Statistics Department, Hong Kong, various issues.

# CHAPTER 8

# CHANGING HONG KONG IDENTITIES

Wong Siu-lun

The year 1997 is a year of great significance for Hong Kong.[1] The long anticipated rite of passage is over. With the change of flag at the handover ceremony on 1 July of that year, Hong Kong ceased to be a British colony. It acquired the new status of a Special Administrative Region [SAR] of China. At the same time, the formal identities of its inhabitants were transformed. Most of them were no longer British subjects or stateless Chinese. They became Chinese nationals or permanent residents of the Hong Kong SAR, with a new set of rights and obligations as stipulated in the Basic Law, the mini-constitution that came into effect after the handover. They were given a new SAR passport, an emblem of their new identity.

These are the formal and objective aspects of the change in collective identity in Hong Kong. They occur rather smoothly, without much controversy. Yet beneath the calm surface, at the subjective level of hearts and minds, things are far less settled. Many Hong Kong people are troubled by doubts and uncertainties. The ringing cry of Jackie Chan's movie, *Who Am I?*, released during the first Chinese New Year holiday after the handover, is probably meant to articulate the sense of unease in the community. And it is

Anson Chan, Chief Secretary for Administration of the Hong Kong SAR, who put the matter into sharp focus. In a speech to the Asia Society in Washington, she described the personal journey she had travelled in the 11 months since the handover. "I am Chinese", she declared. Then she went on to ask, "Am I becoming an apologist for China? No. Am I beginning to turn my back on Britain's legacy? No." Her emphatic answers highlighted the difficulties and dilemma faced by many people in Hong Kong. They would probably agree with her that "[the] real transition has been much more complex, subtle and profound ... That is because the real transition is about identity and not sovereignty."[2]

What is this real transition? What has changed as far as subjective identities are concerned? What are the forces shaping such changes in the perceptions of self, whether by others or by the individuals involved? In this paper, I shall explore these questions through the vantage point of emigration or the outward movement of the Hong Kong people. The phenomenon of emigration would serve to throw into relief the importance of family strategies, personal networks and conceptions of home in moulding collective identities in the territory.

## Family Strategies and Identity

In Hong Kong, the desire to emigrate is linked with an individual's sense of identity. But that identity is not simply a product of personal preferences, it is rooted in family experiences and strategies. The family is the key factor which shapes an individual's decision on whether to leave or to stay. As the key decision-making unit and the carrier of the entrepreneurial spirit, the Hong Kong Chinese family typically seeks to maximize its autonomy and avoid submission to state domination. Such an orientation produces the special style of overseas Chinese capitalism that is not dependent on any particular political order (Hamilton, 1996).

### *Ambivalent Identities*

In our 1991 emigration survey, we discovered that our respondents, who were all ethnic Chinese, tended to embrace a mixed and ambivalent sense of identity. They were torn between regarding themselves primarily as "Chinese" or "Hongkongese". They had two choices. About 48.4 percent of the sample opted to be identified as a Hong Kong person, while some 45.9 percent regarded themselves as first of all Chinese. Their professed identities affected their attitude towards emigration. Those who upheld a Hong Kong identity were actually more likely to consider leaving the territory. Respondents who declared that they would stay were more inclined to regard themselves primarily as Chinese. Therefore, it seems that the Hong Kong identity is a mobile one, not fixed to a locality (S.L. Wong, 1995a).

More than a year after the handover, the sense of ambivalence remains undiminished. The Hong Kong identity is just as strong and it has not been eclipsed by the Chinese identity. In a survey conducted by the Social Sciences Research Centre of the University of Hong Kong in October 1998, it was found that 40 percent of the respondents preferred to call themselves "Hong Kong people", and another 22.9 percent chose to be known as "Hong Kong people in China". Only 20.6 percent called themselves "Chinese", and 15.5 percent "Chinese in Hong Kong".[3]

Besides being mobile and fraught with ambivalence, the identities as upheld by the Hong Kong inhabitants have several additional characteristics. First, they are tinged with a strong sense of pragmatism. The Hong Kong migrants tend to approach issues of passports and nationalities largely with an instrumental attitude. They would refer to the acquisition of foreign passports as the purchase of "insurance policies" to guard against political risks. In our 1991 survey, we asked our respondents the question, "As 1997 approaches, some people in Hong Kong are emigrating to foreign countries. Do you think their action is morally right or wrong?" The majority of the sample, about 55.6 percent, could not be drawn to give a response. They suspended judgement, maintaining that it was neither right nor wrong. For the rest, around 22.5 percent actually approved of the act and only 11.3 percent felt it was wrong (S.L. Wong, 1994a:381).

Second, the identities tend to be multiple and pluralistic. Hong Kong migrants have a keen eye on opportunities. In order to maximize options and security, they are seldom content to stick to just one "insurance policy". For instance, the Yip family that we have interviewed as part of our emigration project is quite typical. In the aftermath of the 1989 Tiananmen incident, the Yips rushed to apply for emigrant visas to Australia, New Zealand, Canada, the United States and Singapore. They were accepted by all these countries. Then the Yips gradually gave up the visas one by one when they were required to land. They held on to the Singapore offer of citizenship because they did not have to make a final decision until several years after 1997.

Third, a change of identity is often a very costly affair. Many Hong Kong migrants have to give up their careers or part with their savings in exchange for new sets of passport and identity. In our 1991 survey, we asked our respondents who were already working, whether they expected their income to increase or decrease if they were to emigrate. Over half of them, some 51.9 percent, anticipated a reduction. Only 29.4 percent believed that they would earn more after relocation (Lam, Fan and Skeldon 1995:130). In other words, most of them were not economic migrants looking for quick improvements in their livelihood overseas. If they leave, they have to pay quite dearly for their decisions. They have either to accept a lower income, or to invest considerable sums in business immigration programmes with little hope of profits or even getting their money back (see Smart, 1994).

Fourth, the identities are flexible and situational in nature. Migrants from the China coast have perfected the art of managing multiple identities which is the source of their cosmopolitan charm. Let me just cite the example of the Shanghainese cotton spinners in Hong Kong whom I interviewed in the late 1970s as an illustration (S.L. Wong, 1988:111–12):

> According to the situation, a Shanghainese can activate regional ties of various scope ... Like insects with a protective colouration, his identity can undergo subtle, and if need be, rapid changes to suit the context of interaction. In international forums such as textile negotiations, the cotton spinners usually present themselves as industrialists from Hong Kong, a vulnerable free port of the developing region of Asia. *Vis-à-vis* their foreign buyers or the senior British officials of the colony, they are Chinese. Meeting in regional associations, they are people from Ningpo or Shanghai city

who enjoy their local cuisine and theatrical entertainment. When they participate in the activities of their trade association, they are modern, Westernized businessmen.

Then lastly, these identities are effective shields to ward off state domination. Hong Kong migrants tend to use them as bargaining chips to negotiate with political authorities to gain autonomy of action. Modern governments, in their effort at nation-building, are often keen to demand an exclusive sense of allegiance from their nationals and to impose rigid classifications of citizenship. But in the case of Hong Kong, the large number of its people who are holding foreign passports of all sorts have forced the Chinese government to relax its nationality law and to adopt a flexible definition as to who would qualify as Chinese nationals in Hong Kong after 1997. In effect, the Chinese government is trying to turn a blind eye on the issue of dual nationality in the territory. It has announced that all ethnic Chinese in Hong Kong shall be regarded as Chinese nationals after the handover as long as they do not declare formally to the Hong Kong Special Administrative Region (SAR) government that they are holding foreign passports.[4] However, this is a problematic issue. According to the Chinese Nationality Law, there are two conditions by which Chinese nationality would be lost. One of them is the acquisition of a foreign citizenship through naturalization or some other voluntary act. In this way, the Chinese nationality of a person is lost automatically after he or she has acquired a foreign nationality. So the retention or loss of the Chinese nationality does not depend on whether the person has or has not declared the possession of a foreign passport. It is doubtful whether these foreign passport holders could legally secure Chinese citizenship, even when they do not make the declaration to the HKSAR (Ghai, 1996; Ng et al., 1997; Leung et al., 1998).

## Patterns of Identification

So far, I have been discussing the question of identities mainly at the level of individual attitudes as revealed in survey findings. In our research project, we try to supplement the survey method with longitudinal in-depth interviews with 30 families selected according to their emigration propensities and socioeconomic background. We interviewed them yearly from 1991 to 1997. Our interviews with them marked a number of significant changes. We began when Hong Kong was still reeling from the 1989 Tiananmen incident. By the mid-1990s, an unexpected and prolonged economic boom had created enough prosperity that even the working class invested heavily in stocks and real estates. Our final round of interviews with a quarter of these families took place in December 1997, six months after the Asian financial turmoil rocked the territory. That gave us insights into the more pessimistic views of the families about the local situation.

Through these interviews, we come to realize that the diverse identities held by our respondents are rooted in their social experiences, particularly those transmitted through their families. We discern four patterns of these identities and family experiences. We call them respectively the loyalists, the locals, the waverers, and the cosmopolitans (Salaff and Wong, 1997).

## Loyalists

The loyalists welcome reversion to China which they see as good for their families. They are not well-to-do. Economic concerns dominate their views. The past means hard times to them. The closing of the border in the early 1950s between Hong Kong and the Mainland divided some of these working class families. Others later fled rural poverty and entered Hong Kong illegally. They are now grateful that the turn towards privatization in China has improved the position of those family members whom they have left behind. They expect that after the reunification with Hong Kong, China will continue its economic progress. Most loyalists were born in China and lived their formative years there. Because they emigrated to Hong Kong late in their lifetime, their ties to their Chinese kin are ongoing and strong. They cross the border to see their Chinese kin often, and hope they can have closer contact after reunification. With few kins living abroad, the loyalists have no plans to leave Hong Kong. Their attention is drawn to China.

## Locals

The locals expect China to continue to progress economically and politically, but they have few personal connections with the Chinese mainland. Nor do they express an affinity with the British. They are firmly attached to Hong Kong, and they accept the changeover without fanfare. The majority of them were born to working and lower middle-class families, who were not subject to political movements on the Mainland. Most are fairly young. Brought up in Hong Kong, they are politically neutral. They are closely attached to the local cultural lifestyle, which includes wide-ranging personal freedoms and expressions. Trepidation about reversion to China centres around the fear of loss of this Hong Kong way of life. These locals have most of their important kin in Hong Kong. They no longer have close bonds with China. Few have kin abroad whom they wish to join. Thus they are not torn in different geographical directions. Their focus is Hong Kong.

## Waverers

We call waverers those families that want to emigrate but have been turned down by foreign countries. Over the course of our interviews, many changed their views from critical anxiety to a "wait and see" attitude, and some even went on to accept the reversion to China. Waverers are mostly working class. Their lack of resources make it hard for them to emigrate. Once rejected, they do not have the resources to reapply to other countries. They have not merely given up, however. They modify their attitudes. Cynical and negative about China when we first met them, they are now more optimistic. They expect no immediate change in Hong Kong, and they do not expect their children to suffer. But they distrust the Chinese system, and prefer what the British have done in the colony to what they see in China. Although most were born in Hong Kong, many of their kin live abroad, and others have applied to emigrate. They recognize few kin across the border on the Mainland. That their circle include those who think of going abroad, or who have already gone overseas, colours their attitudes towards the changeover. However, the bitter choice of the waverers is sweetened by Hong Kong's prosperity. They end up reasoning that while they cannot leave, at least they will be economically better off in Hong Kong.

## Cosmopolitans

The cosmopolitans are opposed to reunification with China and prefer life as it was. They are mostly from families of political refugees who fled China. They were once regarded by China as its class enemies. They generally have upper middle-class backgrounds. They have deep misgivings about the Chinese political system. Many have close family members who suffered persecution under Chinese communism. The collective memory of having lost family properties in the Mainland fuels their anxiety about the changeover. However, their response is not panic and exit. Instead, they plan their move carefully for years. They organize for emigration well in advance of 1997. Others within this group have not experienced class-based discrimination in China. Yet, their experiences as businessmen or professionals in China shake their trust in China's ability to handle the delicately balanced Hong Kong economy. Most of the cosmopolitans were born in Hong Kong. Some were born in China of well-to-do parents and fled after land reform. They lack ongoing contact with their kin on the Mainland because of this politically caused rupture. Most have kin living in the West. They have close friends and classmates abroad as well, with whom they keep in contact. They are part of a stratum that spans the seas.

## Linkages among the Patterns

Our thematic analysis of in-depth interviews with 30 families in Hong Kong describes their wide scope of identities. We group these into four sets of views, based on their attitudes towards their Chinese roots, the political and economic system, and cultural identification with the Hong Kong way of life. Loyalists and Locals are inclined to believe that China would respect Hong Kong's distinct institutions. Waverers and Cosmopolitans tend to suspect that China would impose their political will on Hong Kong.

Seeking the roots of these identities, our analysis suggests how family experiences contribute to political values and identity formation. First, experiences in the hands of the

Mainland Chinese were crucial. Those who fled China's politics, who were most likely to have had upper middle-class backgrounds, were least eager to live under communist rule. Those who fled China's poor economy, who were most likely to have had working and lower middle-class backgrounds with only labour to sell, tend to accept reversion to China. Next, where the husband and wife grew up and the age at which the respondents came to Hong Kong were also decisive. The longer our respondents lived in Hong Kong, the more they were used to local lifestyles and to feel that they would not be able to adjust to life on the Mainland under communist rule. Moreover, networks shape attitudes, and the location and interaction of their kin figured in their identities. This ranged from those for whom China was the home of their kin whom they often visited to those without personal links to the Mainland, and to those cosmopolitans whose kin lived mainly in the West.

Just as responses to reversion to China are complex, the desire to migrate abroad is more than a simple response to an external shock. We found that the locations of their kin shape these folks' desire to migrate abroad. Having a history of family migration and having close kin abroad is associated with making greater efforts to forge a dramatic move. In such ways, both the formation of identities and factors shaping emigration are rooted in family histories and experiences. It is thus not surprising that we found remarkable persistence over time. The passing of nearly a decade and many drastic changes did not greatly reshape popular views. We traced them through early pessimism to optimism and on to the early stage of economic downturn of Hong Kong and the wider region. Those we revisited in the short period after reversion maintain their views although they are more pessimistic about the economy than before. Identities are clearly dynamic and changeable. Yet, at the same time, they are deeply grounded in lived experiences, in structured socio-economies, and in networks.

## Networks and Identities[5]

In our research, we discovered three salient features in the use of personal networks for emigration purposes in Hong Kong. First, there is a quantitative variation in terms of occupational class. On the whole, the higher the class position of the family, the larger the number of social ties which can be mobilized for emigration. Options increase as one moves up the social ladder. Second, there is a qualitative variation too in the type of networks used by members of different occupational classes. Working class emigrants tend to depend heavily on family and kinship ties, while affluent emigrants are more inclined to activate diverse bonds of friendship. Third, members of the lower middle class, whose livelihood hinges on bureaucratic careers and wages, have the lowest emigration propensity. It seems that the assets they possess are the least mobile and transferable.

These findings suggest that it may be fruitful to regard networks as a form of capital. This idea is akin to the concept of social capital as proposed by scholars such as Pierre Bourdieu (1986) and James Coleman (1988). By putting forth the notion of network capital, we are trying to elaborate on Bourdieu's idea and relate *guanxi* (networking) and connections directly to the question of social inequality and class formation. When network capital is put on par with other forms of capital, such as economic and cultural capital, we may come to a better appreciation of the diversity and fluidity in the class and identity structure of Chinese communities such as Hong Kong. It would also lead us to demarcate at least three analytically distinct class segments which correspond to the three forms of capital, namely, the entrepreneurs with networks as assets, the capitalists with economic means of production as properties, and the professionals with knowledge and skill as resources. These class segments are, of course, only abstract theoretical constructions or ideal types. In reality, they would overlap and seldom exist in the pure form.

## *Institutionalization*

In comparison with economic and cultural capital, network capital is the least institutionalized form of assets. On the whole, economic capital is institutionalized in the form of property rights, and cultural capital in the form of educational qualifications (Bourdieu, 1986:243). Both forms depend heavily on the reliability of social institutions or system trust. Network capital, on the other hand, is basically a diffused asset. It may sometimes take the institutional form of associations of various kinds, but it is generally lodged in reciprocal relations that may or may not be upheld by the parties concerned. In order to reduce uncertainty and to reinforce mutual obligations, personal trust plays a more prominent role as a cementing force in the accumulation of network capital. Therefore, relatively speaking, network capital is less dependent on system trust though it can never be completely free of this form of trust as resources, such as classmate networks, are derived from reliable educational institutions. (On the distinction between personal and system trust, see Luhmann, 1979; S.L. Wong, 1991).

Because of the different degrees of institutionalization, the three forms of capital tend to have distinctive patterns of geographical mobility and would be drawn to different destinations. The movement of economic capital would typically follow the logic of comparative advantage. In the case of Hong Kong, for example, industrialists in the cotton spinning sector had a tendency to diversify their investments into Southeast Asia, Latin America and parts of Africa where labour costs were relatively low and textile quotas were available (S.L. Wong, 1988:39).

The movement of cultural capital is affected by the recognition of credentials and the compatibility in educational systems in host countries. Consequently, as revealed in our study, the most popular destinations for the present wave of educated migrants from Hong Kong are English-speaking countries, such as Canada, the United States and Australia.

Network capital, being less dependent on system trust, has a greater scope for diffusion and a better ability to transcend boundaries. It tends to spread with the Chinese diaspora through personal connections. It can venture into territories with shaky institutional frameworks for business operations, such as the People's Republic of China and Vietnam, and still manage to flourish (see Smart and Smart, 1991; S.L. Wong, 1995b).

## Network Capacity

After contrasting network capital with other forms of capital, it is necessary to examine the heterogeneous nature of networks and its implications more closely. Different types of networks exist, with various capacities in facilitating mobility and economic competition. There are kin and non-kin ties, and there are strong and weak linkages (Granovetter, 1982). In our study, we have found that reliance on kin ties and strong linkages are more characteristic of the working class. Members of the affluent class are actually disinclined to make use of such ties and often refuse help from family members and relatives. They tend to draw on diverse weak ties of friendship instead.

We can say that there exist both a restricted and elaborate style of network construction among our respondents. Dependence on kin relations and strong ties is the hallmark of the restricted network style, while flexible use of non-kin relations and weak ties is the key feature of the elaborate network style. An elaborate network style is useful in economic competition because it generates greater access to sources of information and provides more autonomy for action. It can create networks rich in "structural holes", that is, networks with relationships of low redundancy. Ronald Burt (1992:21) asserts that such "optimized" networks have two design principles. The first is efficiency, achieved by concentrating on the primary contact and allowing the relationship with others in the cluster to weaken into indirect relations. The second is effectiveness, attained through differentiating primary from secondary contacts in order to focus resources to preserve the former.

## Moral Economy

The "design" principles as set out by Burt alert us to what may be called the moral economy of network capital. In the attempt to optimize benefits, individuals would have to be calculative and manipulate relations in their favour. Granovetter seems to be conscious of this moral ambivalence inherent in network construction when he states wryly, "Lest readers of SWT [Strength of Weak Ties] and this chapter ditch all their close friends and set out to construct large networks of acquaintances, I had better say that strong ties can also have some value" (1982:113; see also Burt, 1992:262).

This defensive statement reveals the basic reason why those who are skilled at networking, such as entrepreneurs, tend to incur popular hostility and resentment in a society (see Yang, 1994:51–64; Chu and Ju, 1993:133–34; 150–53). They would appear to be too cunning and pragmatic. They spurn the sacredness of personal relations, turning ends into means. Thus they are open to charges of undermining social solidarity and eroding group allegiance. These are the dark sides of network capital.

## Conversion and Reproduction

Another source of hostility towards network construction can be traced to the sites of tension with other forms of capital, especially with cultural capital. In Hong Kong society, studies have shown that people tend to seek advancement through two major channels of mobility: the entrepreneurial route of starting one's own business, and the credential route of acquiring professional qualifications (T.W.P. Wong, 1991:164–65). Both network capital and cultural capital are apparently valued and sought after. Yet other studies have revealed a strong anti-capitalist sentiment and deep distrust of entrepreneurs among the educated and professional elites (S.L. Wong, 1994b:230–32). Evidently friction and rivalry exist between carriers of network and cultural capital.

Such a tension draws our attention to the problem of conversion and reproduction of various forms of capital. The conversion of cultural capital into network capital in the process of migration is relatively well documented by now. Research on small factory owners in Hong Kong has found that many of these entrepreneurs were immigrants from China with high educational attainment. But their credentials were not recognized in Hong Kong, thus forcing them to seek advancement through industrial endeavours instead (Sit and Wong, 1989:97–100). In the present wave of emigration from Hong Kong, the educated and professional elites are facing a similar barrier overseas where their qualifications and experience are not fully recognized. A substantial number of them are thus turning themselves into entrepreneurs by setting up small businesses in destination countries such as Australia (see Lever-Tracy et al. 1991).

However, the direction of conversion is by no means one way only. We have found that there is nearly a universal concern expressed by our respondents for their children's education. Hong Kong Chinese entrepreneurs, whether potential or actual, share with others the same preoccupation with the cultivation of cultural capital for themselves and among their offspring (see Ong, 1992). Thus there appears to exist a cyclical process of intergenerational conversion of network into cultural capital and vice versa. But how precisely is network capital reproduced in the family and passed through the generations? What role does gender play in particular in the accumulation and transmission of this type of capital? We know very little about these issues and clearly more research is needed.

## Conceptions of Home

While many Hong Kong people have left the territory in the past few years, a sizeable portion of them are coming back. However, the precise magnitude of this reverse flow is not known because the Hong Kong government does not collect systematic migration statistics.

We have an official estimate that about 12 percent of those who emigrated during the 1980s have returned. But an academic study suggests that the return rate for that period is much higher, probably close to 30 percent (Kee and Skeldon, 1994). Whatever their exact numbers, they are substantial enough to have confounded the official population projections. In 1996, the Census and Statistics Department in Hong Kong revealed that the local population has grown much faster than expected. It has reached the 6.31 million mark, exceeding the official projection by more than 7 percent. This big discrepancy was attributed mainly to a large-scale return migration, said to be amounting to more than 100,000 in the single year of 1995–96.[6]

Those who are coming back to Hong Kong are often called "returnees". But this is actually a misnomer because nobody knows whether they are coming back permanently to stay (Kwong, 1993:151–52). Furthermore, it is unlikely that they would be giving up the citizenship they have acquired abroad. It seems that, for most of them, the decision either to leave or to stay has been deferred indefinitely. They are thus neither "migrants" nor "returnees" in the strict sense. Rather, they are engaged in a form of "experimental migration" (Wang, 1993:133), made possible by the growing permeability of national borders and advancements in global transportation and communication.

## The "Astronauts"

The fluidity of their status is better captured by the new and figurative term of "astronauts" which carries a double meaning. At one level, it is a Cantonese pun, which means literally "persons with absentee wives", highlighting the fact that many of those who come back are leaving their spouses and children abroad. At another level, it refers to their frequent long distance flights of shuttling back and forth between Hong Kong and their new countries of adoption.

These "astronauts" constitute a novel phenomenon with several significant features. First of all, they tend to possess more versatile skills and valuable assets that set them apart from the traditional Chinese migrants who were predominantly coolies and traders. Mostly educated and bilingual, they have quite a number of professionals and entrepreneurs in their midst. Their talents are being actively courted by Hong Kong and the various destination countries which compete to attract them to their fold. They can, therefore, afford to pick and choose, and to move to and fro. Together, they form a horde of "roaming yuppies" in the contemporary world (S.L.Wong, 1994a).

Second, they are creating a pattern of migratory movement which is unprecedented in Chinese communities. Instead of individuals, families are now on the move at the same time. In the past, the usual pattern was for able-bodied men to venture overseas to seek a better livelihood. Parents, wives and children were generally left in the native communities, sustained and cared for by relatives and neighbours. The current practice is to have the entire family relocated abroad. In many instances, the able-bodied men would then come back to work, leaving the women, the young, and sometimes even the old to fend for themselves and adjust as much as they can to the new environment. The gruesome murder of an elderly couple from Hong Kong in their Canadian home in April 1997 provides a poignant example of this shift in migration pattern. The couple, both in their seventies, were due to return to Hong Kong to celebrate their newly acquired Canadian citizenship when they were apparently beaten to death by burglars. Their eldest son, who emigrated to Vancouver in 1989 and who sponsored them to join him in 1992, moved back to Hong Kong with his wife and children in 1995 after securing a job in one of the local universities. Therefore, at the time of the tragedy, the elderly couple, living by themselves in their house in Vancouver, were vulnerable to attack.[7]

## Homelessness?

When families rather than individuals are on the move, the notion of home base inevitably undergoes change. The contemporary Hong Kong migrants have to confront the question: where is home ? For their predecessors, the Chinese sojourners going overseas in the past, the answer was unambiguous. Home was the native village in China, where one's ancestors were buried. They would maintain a distinction between what G.W. Skinner (1971:275) calls residence and abode. The former was permanent while the latter was temporary. Should they be unfortunate enough to die overseas in their place of abode, it was imperative that their bodies, or at least their bones, be sent home for a proper burial (see Sinn, 1989:71).

For the present day "astronauts" from Hong Kong, however, the matter is far less clear cut. Their conceptions of home are more divergent. Some still uphold the traditional idea that the most desirable resting place remains the native village. Failing that, they should at least be returned to Hong Kong for burial, with their native place engraved on their tombstones as symbolic reminders of home.

Then there are those who have uprooted themselves and found their home in their adopted land. A recent obituary published in the *South China Morning Post* is illustrative. It reads: "CHAN, SHUN, born in China, lived in Hong Kong and settled in Vancouver since 1989, passed away peacefully on May 25, 1997. Survived by his loving wife, sons Tom and Caleb, daughters Helen, Esther, and Jacqueline, and 17 grandchildren." The memorial service was held at the Chan Shun concert hall, which was built with his endowment at the University of British Columbia, and he was buried in a cemetery in Vancouver.[8]

Yet, for the majority of the Hong Kong migrants, the idea of home is probably more slippery and less definite. They tend to maintain multiple abodes in various places, not being sure in their own minds where they would call home. In a study based on in-depth interviews with 18 returned migrants from Canada working in Hong Kong, Wendy Chan (1996:abstract) sums up their feelings of uncertainty and anguish in this way:

> The results of my study suggest that the returned migrants were "reluctant exiles" in the first place, and they are now living in a state of migrancy and "homelessness". However, while my subjects have failed to find home in the rationalist sense of the term, they still cannot accept homelessness as celebrated in the postmodernist view, and hence, the search for home continues. For they are "home but not home".

In their search for home as described by Wendy Chan, one place is conspicuous by its absence. They may be agonizing over the choice between Vancouver, Toronto or Hong Kong, but none of them mentions their native village in the Chinese Mainland as a possibility to be considered. It is apparent that China is no longer home to them. Such an orientation and sense of estrangement from China has been captured by Cheung Yuen-ting, the director of the movie, *The Soong Sisters*. In the programme publicizing the gala premiere of her film, Cheung (1997) writes:

> Born and raised in the British Colony of Hong Kong, I have never set foot on China until 1989, only to discover a country and a people I did not understand. With the coming of 1997 (the year that Hong Kong will stop being a colony and go back as part of China), I try to re-establish a link with the past, to study the history of China as we step towards the future, and to find out who I really am. During this search, I discovered three women who lived at the turn of the century, the Soong Sisters, whose situation bore striking resemblance to our predicament. Sent by their pioneering father to study abroad during their childhood, when most Chinese women still had their feet bound, they came back from the west as total strangers to a country they called their home — a home they

197

hardly recognised, and a home that hardly recognised them ...
As film-maker facing the imminent handover, and all the
unknowns of the future, I can understand and share the
sentiment of these women living a century before me. And by
writing about them and China of the time, it seems that I have
come to understand more about myself and China now.

## Cultural Affinity and Economic Rationality

It is this weakened emotional attachment that has enabled many
roaming yuppies from Hong Kong to venture into China as
investors in the past decade, and to approach the Mainland as an
economic frontier. Probably for the first time in the history of
Chinese migration overseas, these Hong Kong migrants are not
returning to China as their home. Unlike the sojourners before
them, they are not going back to their native village to have their
status confirmed and achievements celebrated. They do not feel
the urge to display their wealth and glorify their ancestors. They
are free from the heavy bondage of kinship and community
obligations. Thus they are able to combine cultural affinity with
economic rationality. They can mobilize social networks with
flexibility, as these networks are no longer firmly embedded in
strong and established relationships. Moving into China as
entrepreneurs, they can look for economic opportunities
dispassionately, unclouded by emotional bonds and insulated with
psychological distance. We may say that they are engaging in a
form of secular rather than sacred return. China is no longer the
normative centre of their cultural universe. As a result, they are
able to forge a cosmopolitan form of Chineseness and
entrepreneurship that is emerging as a potent, transnational force
in the global economy today.

## Conclusion

With the handover in 1997, the political status of Hong Kong
has changed. Yet the subjective identities of its people remain
as complex and diverse as ever. They show more signs of
continuity and persistence than sudden rupture and conversion.

This should not be surprising, as identities are multifaceted. They are composites of political, physical, economic and cultural elements, which are not simply haphazard products of situational or whimsical choices. As Wang Gungwu (1988) points out, identities are governed by norms. These norms, as I have demonstrated above, are embedded in family experiences, personal networks and cultural constructions of home and origin. Thus identities are rather enduring, and changes would only occur gradually.

For Hong Kong, the multiplicity of identities is nothing new. Since its early colonial days, Chinese traders had been flying flags of convenience on their ships. Merchants had been diversifying their assets by purchasing properties in various countries. The search for a cut-and-dried form of identity is nothing new either. In the heydays of student activism in the 1960s, the question of a Hong Kong versus Chinese identity had been debated endlessly. So it seems that the collective sense of ambivalence, unease, anguish and insecurity is very much part and parcel of the Hong Kong way of life, a way of life that represents what may be called coastal Chinese modernity. Such a form of modernity has its own dynamism and its charm. Yet it may not be always endearing to others, be they in other parts of China or other parts of the world. Those who yearn for purity and homogeneity in matters pertaining to identities may find the Hong Kong way of life too much of a hybrid that is distasteful, messy, and even morally corrupt. That is probably the real challenge that Hong Kong would face in the future, both in the new Chinese political framework of "one country, two systems", as well as in the new world order where identities are becoming sites of tension and conflict.

## NOTES

1. An earlier version of this paper was presented at the University of Washington on 6 May 1997 as "Deciding to leave, deciding to stay, deciding not to decide". The research was funded by the Hong Kong Research Grants Council through the project on "Emigration from Hong Kong: Families, Networks, and Returnees".

2. *Daily Information Bulletin*, 12 June 1998; *South China Morning Post*, 13 June 1998.

3. *The Standard*, 2 October 1998. For similar findings, see S.K. Lau, 1997; M.K. Lee, 1998; C.K. Lau, 1998.

4. *South China Morning Post*, 5 April 1997:1; *Ming Pao Daily News*, 5 April 1997:A1.

5. This section draws on my recent article, co-authored with Janet Salaff, entitled "Network Capital: Emigration from Hong Kong" in *The British Journal of Sociology*, vol. 49, no. 3, September 1998, pp. 358–74.

6. *Ming Pao Daily News*, 18 September 1996:A2.

7. *South China Morning Post*, 2 April 1997.

8. *South China Morning Post*, 29 May 1997:8; *The Hong Kong Economic Journal*, 29 May 1997:14.

## REFERENCES

Bourdieu, P. (1986). "The Forms of Capital." In J. Richardson (ed.), *Handbook of Theory and Research for the Sociology of Education* (New York: Greenwood Press).

Burt, Ronald (1992). *Structural Holes: The Social Structure of Competition* (Cambridge: Harvard University Press).

Chan, Wendy W.Y. (1996). "Home But Not Home: A Case Study of Some Canadian Returnees in Hong Kong". Unpublished M. Phil. thesis. Hong Kong University of Science and Technology.

Cheung, Yuen-ting (1997). "Director's Notes". Mimeographed leaflet on the Gala Premiere of *The Soong Sisters*. The University of Hong Kong Foundation for Educational Development and Research.

Chu, G.C. and Ju, Y. (1993). *The Great Wall in Ruins: Communication and Cultural Change in China* (Albany: State University of New York Press).

Coleman, J.S. (1988). "Social Capital in the Creation of Human Capital". *American Journal of Sociology*, 94 (Supplement):S95–S120.

Ghai, Yash (1996). "Nationality and Right of Abode". *The Hong Kong Law Journal*, 26(2):155–61.

Granovetter, Mark (1982). "The Strength of Weak Ties: A Network Theory Revisited." In Peter V. Marsden and Nan Lin (eds.), *Social Structure and Network Analysis* (Beverly Hills, CA: Sage).

Hamilton, Gary G. (1996). "Overseas Chinese Capitalism." In Tu Wei-ming (ed.), *Confucian Traditions in East Asian Modernity* (Cambridge: Harvard University Press).

Kee, P.K. and R. Skeldon (1994). "The Migration and Settlement of Hong Kong Chinese in Australia." In R. Skeldon (ed.), *Reluctant Exiles? Migration from Hong Kong and the New Overseas Chinese* (New York: M.E. Sharpe and Hong Kong: Hong Kong University Press).

Kwong, Paul C.K. (1993). "Internationalization of Population and Globalization of Families." In Choi Po-king and Ho Lok-sang (eds.), *The Other Hong Kong Report* (Hong Kong: Chinese University Press).

Lam, Kit-chun, Yiu-kwan Fan and Ronald Skeldon (1995). "The Tendency to Emigrate From Hong Kong." In Ronald Skeldon (ed.), *Emigration from Hong Kong* (Hong Kong: The Chinese University Press).

Lau, C.K. (1998). "Understanding the Fickle Nature of Our Patriotism." *South China Morning Post*, 5 July.

Lau, Siu-kai (1997). "Hongkongese or Chinese: The Problem of Identity on the Eve of Resumption of Chinese Sovereignty over Hong Kong." Occasional Paper No. 65. Hong Kong: Hong Kong Institute of Asia-Pacific Studies, The Chinese University of Hong Kong.

Lee, Ming-kwan (1998). "Hong Kong Identity — Past and Present." In Wong Siu-lun and T. Maruya (eds.), *Hong Kong Economy and Society : Challenges in the New Era* (Hong Kong: Centre of Asian Studies, The University of Hong Kong).

Leung, Tammy, Fung Mei-ling and Wong Siu-lun (1998). "Legal Issues of Migration in Hong Kong." Paper presented at the Second International Conference of the Asia-Pacific Migration Research Network, The University of Hong Kong, 23–25 February.

Lever-Tracy, C., David Ip, Jim Kitay, Irene Phillips and Noel Tracy (1991). *Asian Entrepreneurs in Australia: Ethnic Small Business in the Indian and Chinese Communities of Brisbane and Sydney* (Canberra: Australian Government Publishing Service).

Luhmann, Niklas (1979). *Trust and Power* (Chichester: John Wiley & Sons).

Ng, Chi-sum, Jane C.Y. Lee and Alison Ayang Qu (1997). *Nationality and Right of Abode of Hong Kong Residents: Continuity and Change Before and After 1997* (Hong Kong: Centre of Asian Studies, The University of Hong Kong).

Ong, Aihwa (1992). "Limits to Cultural Accumulation: Chinese Capitalists on the American Pacific Rim." *Annals of the New York Academy of Sciences*, 645:125–43.

Salaff, Janet W. and Wong Siu-lun (1997). "Migration and Identities in Hong Kong's Transition." Paper presented at the Conference on Hong Kong in Transition, Chatham House, London, England. 15 December.

Sinn, Elizabeth (1989). *Power and Charity: The Early History of the Tung Wah Hospital, Hong Kong* (Hong Kong: Oxford University Press).

Sit, Victor F.S. and Siu-lun Wong (1989). *Small and Medium Industries in an Export-Oriented Economy: The Case of Hong Kong* (Hong Kong: Centre of Asian Studies, University of Hong Kong).

Skinner, G. William (1971). "Chinese Peasants and the Closed Community: An Open and Shut Case." *Comparative Studies in Society and History*, 13(3):271–81.

Smart, Josephine (1994). "Business Immigration to Canada: Deception and Exploitation." In Ronald Skeldon (ed.), *Reluctant Exiles? Migration from Hong Kong and the New Overseas Chinese* (Hong Kong: Hong Kong University Press).

Smart, Josephine and Alan Smart (1991). "Personal Relations and Divergent Economies: A Case Study of Hong Kong Investment in South China". *International Journal of Urban and Regional Research*, 15:216–33.

Wang, Gungwu (1988). "The Study of Chinese Identities in Southeast Asia." In Jennifer Cushman and Wang Gungwu (eds.), *Changing Identities of the Southeast Asian Chinese Since World War II* (Hong Kong: Hong Kong University Press).

———— (1993). "Migration and Its Enemies." In Bruce Mazlish and Ralph Buultjens (eds.), *Conceptualizing Global History* (Boulder: Westview Press).

Wong, Siu-lun (1988). *Emigrant Entrepreneurs: Shanghai Industrialists in Hong Kong* (Hong Kong: Oxford University Press).

———— (1991). "Chinese Entrepreneurs and Business Trust". In Gary G. Hamilton (ed.), *Business Networks and Economic Development in East and Southeast Asia* (Hong Kong: Centre of Asian Studies, University of Hong Kong).

———— (1992). "Migration and Stability in Hong Kong". *Asian Survey*, 32(10):918–33.

———— (1994a). "Roaming Yuppies: Hong Kong Migration to Australia". *Asian and Pacific Migration Journal*, 3(2–3):373–92.

———— (1994b). "Business and Politics in Hong Kong during the Transition." In B.K.P. Leung and T.Y.C. Wong (eds.), *25 Years of Social and Economic Development in Hong Kong* (Hong Kong: Centre of Asian Studies, University of Hong Kong).

———— (1995a). "Political Attitudes and Identity." In Ronald Skeldon (ed.), *Emigration from Hong Kong* (Hong Kong: The Chinese University Press).

———— (1995b). "Business Networks, Cultural Values and the State in Hong Kong and Singapore." In R.A. Brown (ed.), *Chinese Business Enterprise in Asia* (London and New York: Routledge).

Wong, Thomas W.P. (1991). "Inequality, Stratification and Mobility." In Lau Siu-kai et.al. (eds.), *Indicators of Social Development: Hong Kong 1988* (Hong Kong: Institute of Asia-Pacific Studies, The Chinese University of Hong Kong).

Yang, Mayfair M.H. (1994). *Gifts, Favors and Banquets: The Art of Social Relationships in China* (Ithaca and London: Cornell University Press).

# CHAPTER 9

# THE SPLIT-FAMILY PHENOMENON: A NEW IMMIGRANT FAMILY STRUCTURE

Kuah Khun Eng

## Introduction

Hong Kong has since the 19th century been a safe sanctuary for the Chinese immigrants who wanted to leave the Mainland for both political and economic reasons. Since then, the flow of migrants into Hong Kong has not stopped. Even with political obstacles placed in their way, the migrants would continue to devise strategies that would get them into Hong Kong, both legally and illegally. In this paper, I would like to explore the split-family phenomenon — which came about as a result of Hong Kong men marrying mainland wives (including the sea-brides) and keeping mainland mistresses. Inevitably this impacted greatly on the changing lifestyle and family patterns of the migrants and continue to be seen as part of the emerging new family structure in Hong Kong, however dysfunctional it maybe.

# Touch-Base Mentality and Immigration Policies

## *The Touch-Base Mentality and Anxiety*

Hong Kong people have emigrated overseas because of anxiety in the run-up to the 1997 change of sovereignty from British rule to Chinese rule.[1] This anxiety has led many to rush to apply for emigration and to obtain a foreign passport. This move has great implications on the stability of the family structure. It resulted in the creation of the so-called "astronaut" family as well as changing the marriage patterns among the Hong Kong Chinese. Among Hong Kong Chinese women, some have forsaken the security offered by the registry of marriage and opted for a traditional Chinese marriage with social witnessing as the key to the legitimacy of the marriage though such a marriage is not legally-binding.

A contrasting picture can be painted, on the other hand, for the new immigrants from the Mainland to Hong Kong, who experience a different kind of anxiety. Many of them view Hong Kong as a land of opportunities and, therefore, a desirable place to emigrate. Many have risked their lives trying to enter Hong Kong illegally when the legal avenues were not opened to them. It has been reported regularly that the mainland illegal immigrants, also known commonly as IIs, have managed to skirt around the security officers of both the Mainland and Hong Kong authorities and made their way into Hong Kong.

In the months before the change of sovereignty, many mainland Chinese who have legal rights to settle in Hong Kong felt that they needed to be physically present in Hong Kong to ensure that their status as rightful immigrants is confirmed immediately after Hong Kong returned to Chinese rule. Among those eligible were the wives and children of Hong Kong men or the new immigrants who had applied for a one-way permit to join their families in Hong Kong. An official Chinese source estimated that there are over 80,000 mainland wives married to Hong Kong men and over 200,000 mainland Chinese waiting to be resettled in Hong Kong.[2] There was thus the anxiety to "touch base" or "reach base" in Hong Kong before 1 July 1997. As a result of this "touch base" anxiety, many mainland wives, including some who were advanced in their pregnancy and children risked their lives by entering Hong Kong through illegal means. They placed themselves in the hands of the snake-heads (triad leaders) who smuggled them in for a high price. Some made it to Hong Kong while others were caught and repatriated immediately across the border. One main reason for taking such high risks is their perceived understanding of the immigration policies under the Basic Law that would come into operation after 1 July. Under the Basic Law, children and wives of Hong Kong men and all new immigrants would be entitled to settlement in Hong Kong. Hence, the assumption that after the changeover, if the immigrants were physically in Hong Kong, then they would be entitled to obtain permanent residence immediately. To understand such a mentality, we will now turn to examine briefly the immigration policies towards mainland Chinese from the advent of British colonial rule to the present situation.

## *Immigration Policies and Control in Historical Perspective*

During the early years of British colonial rule, the mainland Chinese could move freely in and out of Hong Kong. Indeed, there were several waves of migration from the Mainland into Hong Kong in times of political and economic hardship. The Taiping Rebellion from 1850–64 and the 1911 Revolution were two examples where large-scale migration to Hong Kong took place. The result was a large increase in the population of Hong Kong that strained the existing infrastructure and drained the resources of the colonial administration in its efforts to cope with the influx. Population doubled from the existing 300,000 to over 600,000 during the period between 1901 to 1921. As a result of the periodic waves of large-scale migration from the Mainland, the British began introducing immigration control to impede the flow of mainland migrants into Hong Kong.

The Passports Ordinance in 1923 was the first act passed to control immigration. However, despite the introduction of this ordinance and subsequent ones, the colonial administration continued to adopt a fairly liberal attitude towards mainland immigrants where they were exempted from such restrictions (Chen, 1988:635). For example, the 1923 Passports Ordinance, stipulated that all persons entering Hong Kong required a passport except for persons of Chinese race (ibid.:635). Likewise, the new ordinances introduced in 1935 — namely the Immigration and Passports Ordinance and the Registration of Persons Ordinance — set out nine categories of undesirable immigrants who might be refused permission to land upon arrival, but they again exclude the Chinese (ibid.:636). There was thus little effort by the British to seriously restrict the entry of mainland Chinese. It was only during the 1930s when the Japanese Occupation brought about an even greater number of Chinese migrants (estimated at over 800,000) into the colony and the population of Hong Kong exceeded 1.5 million, that some form of restriction was imposed (ibid.:637).

In 1940, the Hong Kong government changed its policy and introduced the Immigration Control Ordinance which refused entry to the Chinese who did not possess the relevant visa, entry permits, frontier passes or certificates of residence issued under the ordinance (ibid.:638). This was seen as a watershed event in the Hong Kong government's policy towards the mainland migrants. The immigrant officers, however, continued to treat the Chinese migrants liberally and mainland migrants continued to make their way into Hong Kong. Nevertheless, the ordinance signaled for the first time that the colonial government was not giving any form of preferential immigration treatment to the mainland migrants. Under this new ordinance, illegal immigrants were given stricter treatment and could be deported.

After the Second World War and with communist victory on the Mainland, the influx of mainland Chinese into Hong Kong increased at an even greater rate. By 1950, the population of Hong Kong stood at 2.4 million (ibid.). The Hong Kong government was once again forced to reassess its immigration policy. This time, it introduced a new system of immigration control under the Immigrants Control Ordinance 1949. It stipulated that no person, including the Chinese, could enter the colony without a permit issued by the immigration officer. It required the registration of all aliens, including the Chinese. It also made it a criminal offence for those who entered Hong Kong illegally so that they were liable for expulsion when caught (ibid.:639)

In order to effectively control immigration from the Mainland, the Hong Kong government used this ordinance to establish a daily quota system for the entry of mainland Chinese at the Hong Kong–China border in 1950. Under this daily quota system, those who had been issued permits by the Hong Kong immigration authorities were considered bona fide migrants who could enter the colony legally, although residents of Guangdong continued to enter Hong Kong with little restrictions. While Hong Kong was trying to restrict entry of mainland migrants, the mainland government, too, was trying to stop the flow of mainland Chinese into Hong Kong by imposing strict exit controls. The result was that the 1950s and 1960s witnessed a sharp drop in the number of mainland migrants migrating to Hong Kong (ibid.:640).

In 1971, the Hong Kong government introduced the Immigration Ordinance 1971 which for the first time defined three categories of Hong Kong residents, namely Hong Kong belongers, Chinese residents and Resident United Kingdom belongers. Hong Kong belongers referred to those British subjects born in Hong Kong. They had "the right to land in Hong Kong and could not be refused entry by the immigration authorities and they could not be removed or deported from the colony (ibid.:643–44). Chinese residents were those born outside Hong Kong but had emigrated to Hong Kong and stayed for seven years or more (ibid.:644). They had earned the right to live in Hong Kong but could be deported when found guilty of various seditious or criminal activities (ibid.). The resident United Kingdom belongers referred to those who were born, adopted or naturalized in the United Kingdom and who had been residents in Hong Kong for seven years or more (ibid.:644–45). A fourth category, Others, did not have the right to enter Hong Kong unless they had been given permission by the immigration authorities.

One of the characteristics of the Immigration Ordinance 1971 was the issuing of "one-way permits" to mainland Chinese. Those entering from this period onwards with a one-way permit would be regarded as legal immigrants and were permitted to live and work in Hong Kong. Others entering without a one-way permit would thus be branded as illegal immigrants and subjected to deportation. The immigration authorities also issued "two way permits" for mainland Chinese to visit and stay in Hong Kong for a short period of time, after which they were expected to leave Hong Kong. If they failed to do so, they would also be branded as illegal immigrants and treated as thus (ibid.:648). However, this ordinance did not stop the flow of migrants from the Mainland but what it did was to create a large category of illegal immigrants. As such, there was a need to revise such a policy in order to eliminate the large number of illegal immigrants.

In 1974, another policy was introduced. This became known as the "touch-base" or "reach-base" policy. Under this policy, those migrants who did not have a one-way permit but who managed to enter the urban areas and resided with relatives or managed to find some sort of permanent accommodation would be considered to have "reached base" and thus were permitted to live in Hong Kong. However, those who were caught at the border or in the surrounding seas would be repatriated to the Mainland.

From the 1980s, the political climate in the Mainland became more relaxed as a result of the open-door policy. Many mainland Chinese attempted and successfully "touched base" in Hong Kong, leading to a surge in the number of mainland immigrants from 6,000 in 1977 to 108,000 in 1979 (ibid.:653). Thus, the Immigration (Amendment) (No. 2) Ordinance 1980 was introduced where it abolished the "touch base" policy and where all illegal immigrants would be repatriated (ibid.:654). It also stipulated that the maximum number of legal migrants to Hong Kong be restricted to 150 persons per day. This policy remained until shortly before 1 July 1997 when China resumed sovereignty of Hong Kong.

## The Basic Law and Its Immigration Policies

Under the Basic Law, drafted between the governments of the People's Republic of China (PRC) and the United Kingdom (UK), children who were born of Hong Kong parents are allowed to live in Hong Kong. This resulted in a sudden influx of illegal children migrants from across the borders in the two to three years leading to the changeover of sovereignty, prompting the immigration authorities to reassess its immigration policy towards these children. Under the Basic Law Article 24, a person of Chinese nationality born in Hong Kong will automatically get the right of abode in Hong Kong. However, the proposed revised immigration bill, Immigration (Amendment) (No. 3) Bill 1997, reaffirmed that mainland children of Hong Kong residents will be granted the right of abode.[3] However, it also stipulates that illegal immigrants would not be allowed to stay in Hong Kong even if the immigration authorities had allowed them to stay for seven years. It further stipulates that a person of Chinese nationality born in Hong Kong would only be eligible for the right of abode when one parent became a permanent resident.[4] This bill was passed into law on 21 June 1997.[5]

Of particular concern here is the issue of the mainland children born of Hong Kong parents and of the new immigrants who are not yet permanent residents of Hong Kong. In another proposal, citing Section 2a of the Immigration (Amendment) Bill, it was suggested that children of new immigrant parents would be given rights of abode while their parents would have to fulfil the seven-year residence before they were granted permanent residence status.[6] However, the status of these immigrant children remained somewhat confused as a result of various interpretations given to the clause within the Basic Law. This confusion was further worsened by the various groups of people, ranging from the legislators, welfare workers to the media personnel, who offered their public comments on the issue, as well as the various actions taken by the immigration authorities. In the run-up to the changeover and the immediate period after the changeover, some legislators have argued that under the Basic Law, the children of new immigrants, where either one of the parents is a permanent resident, would be entitled to right of abode. Any action by the immigration authorities to deny the right of abode to these children would be subjected to legal challenges. A second confusion arises over the fact that, as a result of public pressure, the immigration authorities have decided to grant more than 1,000 mainland Chinese temporary reprieve based on humanitarian grounds.[7] This has created false hope among the hopeful migrants and led to a substantial number of children crossing the border illegally through various means. These illegal immigrant children are commonly known as the "small snake people", *xiao-ren-she*.[8]

After the changeover, with the new immigration policies in place, the immigration authorities encouraged the illegal immigrant children to report to the immigration department. The parents of those children who had crossed the borders prior to the changeover brought their children to report to the immigration department. The large number of these illegal children shocked the immigrant officers who were given the task of deciding the fate of these children.

Within two weeks of the changeover, the Provisional Legislative Council passed the Immigration (Amendment) (No. 5) Bill on 9 July 1997. It empowered the SAR government to repatriate mainland-born children who were eligible for right of abode but had arrived without proper documents in Hong Kong from 1 July.[9] This bill has the support of the central government in Beijing. The Public Security Ministry stated that "this requirement will be conducive to the correct implementation of right of abode under the Basic Law".[10]

Under this bill, over 1,000 people, including 424 children, who were entitled the right of abode under the Basic Law and who have surrendered to the immigration department, would be returned to China and they have to apply formally to live in Hong Kong (ibid.). This bill was backdated to 1 July and those who entered Hong Kong from 1 July must carry a "certificate of entitlement" issued by the Department of Immigration. It was estimated that a total of about 2,000 children have entered Hong Kong illegally prior to the changeover.

It was estimated that there are about 66,000 mainland children waiting to be settled in Hong Kong. Among the legislators, some suggested that if the quota of one-way permits for the children is raised from 66 to 90 out of the 150 a day set in the quota, then, they could all be settled in Hong Kong within the next two years.[11] This quota was finally approved by the Beijing government.

The implementation of such a bill created anger and anxiety among various sectors of the population. Foremost is the Society for Community Organisation (SOCO) who mounted a legal challenge against this law claiming that it violated human rights and the rights of illegal minors who were given the right of abode in Hong Kong.[12] Furthermore, the director of Hong Kong Human Rights argued that "such an abrogation of these children's rights is particularly serious because it sets a precedent ... of denying by administrative measures the constitutional rights of Hong Kong people guaranteed in the Basic Law" (ibid.).

Apart from the challenges mounted by the various community groups in Hong Kong, individuals take the matter to court and challenge the legality of the deported persons under the Basic Law. In a test case of legal challenge, a nine-year-old mainland Chinese girl maintained her right as a permanent resident that is enshrined in the Basic Law and argued that new legislation cannot change that status.[13] The girl's father has right of abode in Hong Kong and she has arrived in Hong Kong half a year prior to the changeover under a two-way permit.

In the fight against deportation, the Hong Kong Legal Aid Department has approved providing legal aid to these children. After its announcement, 194 applications were filed.[14] Likewise, over 100 lawyers from the Bar Association and the Law Society have also joined in this legal battle against the SAR government if the children's legal aid applications failed.[15]

The plight of these illegal immigrant children has shed lights on wider issues pertaining to the immigration policies that have been questioned by some of the human rights groups. They see this as a violation of the basic rights of these children. It is often argued that these mainland Chinese children were treated unfairly compared to other groups, such as the spouses and children of Hong Kong residents who are mainland Chinese and those who are non-Chinese nationals. The present policy allows the spouses and children of Hong Kong residents who are non-Chinese nationals to apply for resident visas for entry to the SAR and it usually takes about four to six weeks for approval to take place. This short waiting time is possible because there is no quota system applied to them. The same arrangement is also accorded to the spouses and children of foreign nationals who entered Hong Kong on an employment visa.[16]

Both the mainland spouses and the children of Hong Kong residents need to apply to the Chinese government for permission to emigrate to Hong Kong. They are also subjected to a quota system that differs from province to province and county to county (ibid.). Furthermore, the quotas for spouses and children are separate, resulting in a situation where the children become separated from their mothers. It is also commonly known that corrupt officials would demand payments before issuing the exit permit. Thus those who have the resources and money and political connections could literally buy their way out while those without would be locked into an indefinite queue, with many waiting over seven or more years before getting the exit permit (ibid.).

# Implications on the Family Structure and Lifestyle of the New Immigrants

## *The Split-family Phenomenon*

As mentioned earlier, only those who have been given a one-way permit are considered as entering Hong Kong legally. Under such a situation, the new immigrants would, in theory, be given much assistance from the various agencies, including the immigration authorities and social welfare agencies, to assist them to adapt to a new environment. But in practice, a lack of information often leads to ignorance of the facilities available to the new immigrants.

However, there were several problems outlined by some politicians. Elsie Tu has commented openly on the social cost of allowing children to enter Hong Kong without their parents.[17] Others argue that there is a need to take into consideration the interests and wishes of these children. They argue that these children are not given a choice as to whether they wish to remain behind in the Mainland with their mothers or go to Hong Kong to a father whom many do not know and who is a stranger to them.

The immigration policies have great implications on the family structure and the lifestyle of the new immigrants who have arrived to settle down permanently in Hong Kong and to build a new life for themselves and their family. When they arrived in Hong Kong, they faced great difficulties in adjusting to a new environment, an unfamiliar language, a variant of the Chinese culture, employment and schooling for their children. In addition, they also have to deal with the immigrant policies that often resulted in splitting the family and locating the members in two regions — one in Hong Kong and the other on the Mainland. The outcome has been the split-family phenomenon.

In the split-family structure, there are three scenarios where the family members are scattered in both Hong Kong and the Mainland:

(1) In Hong Kong, there is usually a father-dominated household. A small number of the fathers are Hong Kong born but most fathers are Hong Kong residents born in China. He usually lives with one or two of his children who are either Hong Kong born or have obtained a one-way permit to join the father. They usually live in cramped housing — either in public housing, a rented apartment or room. In a majority of cases, the father holds a low-skill job and has a low wage. Many of these fathers work a full day and have little time to spend with their children. Many of these children are left alone to look after themselves. The girls often have to do additional household duties, including cooking and sometimes, looking after their younger siblings.

(2) In the Mainland, it is usually a female mother-dominated household. Here, the mother is mainland-born and either marries a Hong Kong-born husband or a Hong Kong resident born in the Mainland. She is able to obtain a two-way permit to visit and stay in Hong Kong on a temporary basis from one to three months. She may go over to Hong Kong to give birth in order that their child becomes a Hong Kong-born resident. It was not uncommon for women in advanced pregnancy to smuggle themselves into Hong Kong.[18] If this is the case, the children will remain behind with the father. Some of these women may choose to become illegal immigrants and continue to live in Hong Kong, especially if the couple has no other children in the Mainland. Many, however, return to the Mainland to look after their children who have been left behind in the care of the grandparents or relatives while the mother was away visiting Hong Kong.

The mother would also have applied for a one-way permit to join the husband. Likewise, the mainland-born children would also have applied for a one-way permit to join their father.

(3)  In Hong Kong, there are families where the mother has joined the husband after obtaining a one-way permit. However, the mainland-born children continue to wait for their one-way permit in the village. The result is that the children are left to the care of the grandparents or other relatives.

As a result of the immigration policies, a normal family has split into two sub-family structures, each living on either side of the border. This has become even more common today as a result of greater integration between Hong Kong and the Mainland, especially in the Guangdong region. It is estimated that 70 percent of the immigrants come from Guangdong alone.[19] There are several reasons that account for cross-border marriages. Romantic love is one reason that some cited for marrying a mainland Chinese. However, it is more common among the older men, and increasingly among the younger age group, who could not find a bride in Hong Kong, to try their luck in the Mainland. Having found a suitable wife, many married in the Mainland. It is, therefore, not uncommon for men to marry a young wife half their age. Why do mainland women want to marry Hong Kong men? The most common reason given is that they want to get out of China and marrying Hong Kong men would provide them with an opportunity to do so (see section on second wives or mistresses).

## Social Implications of the Split-family Phenomenon

As the married couple cannot live together in a single household, there is an emerging trend towards a new form of family structure — the split family, *fen-ju-jia-ting*. The result of living under separate households has great implications on the psychological and social well-being of not only the husband and wife, but also the children. There is often a lack of communication between husband and wife. Likewise, the parent-children relationship has often been strained. This is particularly so when the children live with one of the parent, usually the mother and where the other, often the father, is a total stranger to the children.

Another consequence of the split-family phenomenon is the difficulties faced by the family members when they finally obtain a one-way permit to live in Hong Kong permanently. Wives often suffer from problems of social and psychological dislocations arising from a combination of factors. First, the high expectation of better living standards in Hong Kong is often shattered by the poor living conditions that they are exposed to. Unlike the village dwelling which tends to be big and spacious, the apartments they occupy in Hong Kong are dwarf-sized in comparison. For those who live on their own in public housing, life can be bearable. However, for those who share rented apartments or rent only a single room, life is miserable. So, many wives, upon arrival, were disappointed by the living conditions and social experiences awaiting them.[20] Crammed housing with little or no social and personal space often results in tension and resentment. Quarrels are not uncommon among the couples. Often, the children are caught in between the parents who vent their frustrations on them.

Many of the wives are often housebound as they cannot find jobs. This has turned even more acute with the present economic downturn when part-time or hourly jobs are also not available.[21] Compounding this is the meagre financial resources of these households that make simple chores, such as food shopping, a less than pleasant task for these mainland wives. Furthermore, domestic chores, especially cooking, is especially difficult when the kitchen is a shared space with each family wanting to use the facilities at the same time. It often results in arguments among the wives.

Outside the home, these wives have found that Hong Kong is an unfamiliar territory and getting around the place is not easy. Some are also not fluent in the Cantonese dialect, especially those who come from Fujian and elsewhere and speak a different Chinese dialect. They are unable to make themselves understood and find the experience frustrating. They have problems learning a new dialect. As a result, they feel that they are outsiders living in the periphery of the Hong Kong society.

When they moved to Hong Kong, these wives left behind their kinship and social network which has been important to their overall emotional and spiritual well-being. By coming to Hong Kong, they can no longer draw on their kins-people and friends for emotional and other forms of support. This lack of support has resulted in many of the wives facing social and emotional problems. Often, by the time they seek help from the social workers or professional health workers, many are already in a state of depression. Many of them also suffer from physical health problems as a result of this emotional dislocation. The government welfare and some privately-run welfare agencies, such as Caritas Counselling Service, have social workers devoted to helping this group of women and helping them to adapt and adjust to life in Hong Kong. This is done through promoting mutual support and strengthening the support network structure for the immigrant women.

The immigrant children too suffer from a split-family structure. Many children have to wait for years for a one-way permit although the new immigrant policy after 1 July has stipulated that the waiting period to rejoin their parents in Hong Kong would be reduced to a maximum of two years. These children who are now in Hong Kong can be divided into two groups: the first group consists of those who have entered Hong Kong legally with the one-way permit; and the second group consists of those who entered Hong Kong illegally. Some continue to live illegally while others have surrendered themselves to the Immigration Department after 1 July in the hope of obtaining the right of abode as stipulated under the Basic Law. The influx of immigrant children is a second area that has become a great concern to the general Hong Kong population. This is especially so after the announcement that the quota for the number of immigrant children has been raised from 45 to 60 before the changeover and to 90 after the changeover.

Let us deal with the first group of children who entered Hong Kong legally. They face problems of adjustment and adaptation. Many of them come from a village environment and have to adjust to the completely urbanized setting. Like the mainland wives, these children too find that the lack of space has prevented them from becoming socially and physically active. This is further compounded by the fact that they are unfamiliar with their immediate outside environment, making venturing out a difficult task. Often, they are prevented from venturing out by their parents or relatives for fear that they may get lost.

A second problem these children face is schooling. There have been much concern by the Hong Kong general population that the immigrant children will take up extra space and educational resources, thereby depriving the Hong Kong children of their educational opportunities. There are also others who have expressed concern over the need to provide special and additional educational facilities for these children.[22] One of the primary concerns here is to find a suitable school for these immigrant children in the vicinity where they live. The Education Department operated a referral system but many immigrant parents have little knowledge of the system and so do not use it. It has been accused by the immigrants and some political leaders for failing to inform the immigrants of this service. Furthermore, the department officers have also been accused of being partial when they referred only those immigrant students whom they considered as having good potential to the better schools in favour of those whom they considered as lacking potential. The department credited itself with a 100 percent success rate in the referral system but it was accused of counting only those whom they have success with while those they failed were categorized as "parents seeking advice only".[23]

The success of the immigrant children remains a controversial issue. Some of these immigrant children do not do well in school and drop out at an early age.[24] School dropouts may then end up getting involved in triads. In some schools, additional tuition lessons have been arranged for these children to help them integrate into the system. A large sector of the immigrant children do complete secondary school to go on to tertiary education through their own diligence, although special attention given by the schools and additional facilities given by the Education Department may have also assisted them.[25]

Once they begin school, these immigrant children face many problems. When they first arrived in Hong Kong, they were not competent in the Cantonese dialect and many were also poor in the English language, making schooling an extremely unpleasant experience. Several welfare organizations are holding language classes to help the immigrants acquire language skills. Many of the immigrant children tend to pick up the Cantonese dialect quickly. As a result, it is not uncommon that these immigrant children soon act as translators and interpreters for their immigrant parents, many of whom continue to have poor Cantonese language skills. The government has been criticized for not providing the new immigrants with sufficient language training facilities.[26]

In mainland China, some of the wives and children of these immigrants had waited as long as 7 to 10 years before they were successful in getting a one-way permit to enter Hong Kong. One consolation among them is that their Hong Kong resident husband could easily make trips to visit them across the border. However, the problem is more of an emotional one for those wives who do not find it easy to have to endure a separation. Many also fear that their husband might look for other women in their absence. Furthermore, they have to manage a household on their own, creating a female-centred household. As many of the immigrant husbands living in Hong Kong are not wealthy and do not have much financial resources to send to their mainland wives and children, these wives have to work for an income.

Apart from this, they also have to look after their children. One wife said that the most difficult aspect is explaining the absence of the father to the children. She said, "You have to tell the child that the father is away working in Hong Kong and can only come to visit you once in a few weeks. However, it is often very difficult to expect the children to understand when all the fathers of the other children are around them everyday". She went on further to say, "the situation gets worse if I, the mother, go on a visit to Hong Kong after successfully obtaining a two-way permit. It is very difficult to explain that the mother has to go and join the father on a temporary basis and that they cannot come along. Not only this, they now have to go and live with their grandparents or aunt. The children feel that they are not wanted and do not have the family warmth that other children have."

In Hong Kong, the Hong Kong fathers have to manage a male-centred household. Many end up having to look after their young children, as their mothers remain in China, and at the same time hold on to a full-time job. Most of them cannot afford any kind of domestic help. The result is that the young children are left on their own at home during the day and sometimes at night too. Some of these children left alone are as young as 2 to 3 years old. There was a case when a young girl fell to her death from her flat when her father left her alone to go to work.

The effects of the split-family structure have great implications on the families involved. All members of the family are affected to some degree. It is misery for some and frustration for others. But, as long as the immigration law continues to bar the wives and children from joining their Hong Kong-based fathers, then such problems will continue. The wives will continue to live without the husband and the children without their father. Unlike the "astronaut" family of the Hong Kong immigrants in the Western countries in their quest for a foreign passport, the separation in the case of the split-family phenomenon is an involuntary one. Above all, it is a discriminatory one when compared to the immigration policy governing the issuing of visas to wives and children of foreign nationals who come to work in Hong Kong under an employment visa. While the immigration authorities argue that the quota system is the best solution for the large number of mainland Chinese who want to migrate to Hong Kong, it nevertheless overlooks the issue that it is inconsistent with the overall immigration framework of treating spouses and children. Moreover, it also neglects the very humane aspect of migration where apart from resettling people, it should also help to reunite families and make them a coherent whole within the new environment that they have chosen to call home. The present immigration policy serves to reinforce the broken family phenomenon.

The second group of immigrant children are those who entered Hong Kong illegally without the one-way permit. The exact number in this group remains unknown. Immediately after the changeover, over 2,000 illegal immigrant children surrendered themselves to the Immigration Department in the hope that they would be allowed the right of abode under the Basic Law. Following 1 July 1998, however, the immigration authorities deported these children. The department confronted strong public reaction arguing against their inhumane actions and their violation of the Basic Law. Under a string of criticisms, the Immigration Department issued "walking papers" to some of these illegal immigrant children which permitted them to move around Hong Kong as "legitimate" residents. This has resulted in more children being smuggled into Hong Kong by the "snake-heads".[27] The Immigration Bill was subsequently amended and adopted and these children now stand to be deported back to the Mainland.

As they are residing illegally in Hong Kong, these children lead a fearful life. Many of them are kept at home and dare not venture outside for fear of being caught and deported. The result is that many of these immigrant children feel bored at home. Life in Hong Kong is confinement in restricted space instead of the anticipated lively city life that they had envisaged. They have very few friends and many do not have an opportunity to build up a network of friends. Many of them are unhappy and some suffer from psychological problems related to isolation.

There is also a problem with schooling for the immigrant children. Under the existing policy, these illegal immigrant children are not accepted into government schools. The result is that these immigrant children are forced to stay at home when they should be attending school. There is very little the children or the immigrant parents can do unless the policies pertaining to accepting immigrant children are changed. At present, the policy is unlikely to change given the outcry by the general public over the amount of resources allocated to helping the legal immigrant children in schools.[28]

There were many cases of the wives and children of immigrants who entered Hong Kong illegally. Once caught, they are routinely deported to the Mainland. This has created much tension and anxiety among those who are caught. While some appealed to the Immigration Department and others sought legal aid to help them obtain right of abode, almost all of them were unsuccessful. The great trauma that they experience cannot be underestimated.

In one case, a girl who was smuggled into Hong Kong when she was three months old and lived for eight years in Hong Kong.

After 1 July, her father surrendered her to the Immigration Department in the belief that she would be able to obtain the right of abode under the Basic Law. However, the new immigration policy required her to be deported even though the father and two brothers are Hong Kong residents. In a media report, after she was served with a deportation order, several immigration officers went to her apartment and literally dragged her out of her house and put her on a van and whisked her off to the border. Understandably she was in great distress as she was sent to Guangzhou, a place of which she has little knowledge as she was brought up in Hong Kong.[29]

Such stories were abundant immediately after the changeover when the young children were deported as a matter of routine. These emotional episodes touched the hearts of the public. However, such sympathy did not translate into much action by the Hong Kong people. Thus, the lack of pressure from external agencies has meant that the immigration authorities could carry out its harsh immigration policies without much hindrance. Besides, there is also a lack of moral reasoning behind such an act. This lack of moral accountability and the respect for the family as a social unit tend to be subsumed under the bureaucratic functioning of the Immigration Department.

## Mainland Mistresses

It is now accepted knowledge that with the opening up of South China and the easy access to Shenzhen and other parts of Guangdong, an increasing number of Chinese men are setting up a domestic or second domestic hearth across the border. Most of them have found it easier to find a wife or to keep a "mistress", *bao-er-nai*, in South China. Several villages in Southern China have now become known as "lovers' nests" where most of the women are mistresses to Hong Kong men. This has resulted in the original households moving out of the village to avoid embarrassment to themselves and their families. At the same time, single women who envied the luxurious lifestyle of the mistresses would move into these villages in the hope of getting a Hong Kong boyfriend or husband. These Hong Kong men are not only businessmen and professionals but they are also from the lower socio-economic stratum, including truck drivers and workers.

There are different reasons as to why the men have opted to get a wife in South China. One main reason given is that Hong Kong women are very demanding and choosy and many do not want to marry blue collar workers. Demographically, as well, there is a slight sex imbalance in the female to male ratio as 1:1.5 indicating that there are more men than women in Hong Kong. Thus some Hong Kong men begin looking for a wife in Shenzhen, or other parts of Guangdong, which is an attractive alternative. Likewise, the frequent visits to South China by businessmen, truck drivers, workers and others have also encouraged married men to acquire a "mistress". For those men with wealth, acquiring a mistress across the border is relatively inexpensive. However, for those at the lower socio-economic ladder, this has created substantial problems for the families in Hong Kong.

It is interesting to note that in traditional Chinese society, having a mistress was confined to the upper social stratum, often among the elite. In present day Hong Kong, however, having a mistress is becoming increasingly common among the lower socio-economic groups. There are two considerations here. First, the Hong Kong men, even those from the lower socio-economic groups, are wealthier than their counterparts in Guangdong. Socially, the women from Guangdong are seen to be marrying up the social and economic ladder. They could, therefore, lead a life of leisure and are materially better off. Second, by marrying Hong Kong men, these women hope that it will provide them with an opportunity to become eligible to apply for a one-way permit to migrate and live in Hong Kong, a much preferred place than mainland China. Here, the ability to migrate to Hong Kong serves as an important consideration for those willing to become wife or mistress of Hong Kong Chinese men. Even though most of the mistresses are probably aware that their Hong Kong men are already legally married to someone else, they are waiting in line in the hope that one day they, too, might become the lawful wives of their Hong Kong men. For the time being, they are content with a life of material well-being.

The effects of having a mistress across the border have led to several problems in the Hong Kong family, foremost of which is the effect that this has on the wives of these men. Emotional distress and quarrels become the norm rather than the exception in the household. The social welfare department and other welfare groups have set up special services to offer support and counsel this group of distressed wives. A second effect is that when the men have to maintain two households, it becomes inevitable that the financial resources are divided between the two households. Often quarrels centre around insufficient money for household expenses and the children. A third effect is that these men spend very little time with the Hong Kong households, especially during the weekends when they would travel up north to visit their mistress and their mainland children.

Some of the marriages in Hong Kong end in divorce because of men having mainland families. Others experience marital discord within the Hong Kong families and many wives suffer from depression. The social welfare department and Caritas Family Service provide counselling for these wives. Apart from these, the Hong Kong government is powerless to do anything to stop men from going across the border and having mistresses or concubines. As long as they do not legally marry the mainland wives, they cannot be accused of bigamy. This second wives' phenomenon has been a concern of many welfare groups in Hong Kong who regard it as a primary problem for family breakdown and divorce.[30] In a recent move, the Guangdong Provincial Women's Federation provided a radical formula to stop Hong Kong men and others from other parts of China from having mistresses and second homes in Guangdong. They proposed that the men guilty of bigamous relationships be rehabilitated in a re-education camp, a move supported by some Hong Kong wives but condemned by some welfare groups in Hong Kong who see such moves as being counterproductive.[31]

## Sea-brides (shui-shan xin-niang)

There are also cases where the boat people, commonly known as the Tanka, married mainland wives. These mainland wives have been given a permit by the Guangdong provincial government

223

and the Hong Kong immigration authorities to live on board their boats in Hong Kong waters. However, they are not permitted to live on land.

Over time, however, many of the Tanka boatpeople have forgone the fishermen lifestyle and have "landed" where they live permanently on land. These sea-brides, too, come onshore and live on land. However, living on land is considered illegal and they thus become illegal immigrants. Some of these sea-brides are caught and deported to the Mainland, again creating the split-family phenomenon. Their children again become separated from the mother as they are considered Hong Kong born and are thus permitted to live in Hong Kong. These sea-brides, like the other mainland wives, have to apply for a one-way permit to join their family in Hong Kong.[32]

## Comments and Analyses

The split-family phenomenon has become a new immigrant family structure that straddles across the Hong Kong-Chinese (especially Guangdong) border. And it is an emerging new structure that warrants more attention from both sides of the government, especially the Hong Kong government where the new immigrants will finally reside permanently in Hong Kong. As the situation stands today, many of them will have to wait for a long period of time before being allowed to settle in Hong Kong. Given the large number of wives and children waiting to be resettled in Hong Kong, the Immigration Department has a moral obligation to assist them in the rapid resettling process. At the very least, they should be able to process their one-way permit at an acceptable rate instead of expecting these wives and children to wait indefinitely.

The time frame for resettling in Hong Kong is an important issue to consider here. Otherwise, they would enter Hong Kong as illegal immigrants and lead a life in constant fear of being caught by the authorities. What is needed is the establishment of an overall immigration framework to deal with these would-be new immigrants so that they know exactly how long the waiting period is. This is important as it would allow both the men in Hong Kong and their wives and children on the Mainland to plan their resettlement and adjustment process. Furthermore, it would also stop them from taking risks by illegally entering Hong Kong or entrusting their children to the triads who operate smuggling rings to smuggle their children into Hong Kong.

In a modern society like Hong Kong, which prides itself on efficiency and which champions various rights such as human rights and freedom, the government therefore has a moral obligation to ensure that these mainland wives and children are given the type of protection necessary before and after their arrival in Hong Kong. One of these is to make sure that they do not take unnecessary risks to come into Hong Kong. The policies for issuing one-way permits, the waiting period, information on Hong Kong, employment, education and welfare facilities should be given to these would-be new immigrants long beforehand in order that they can better prepare themselves for a new life in Hong Kong.

Another issue of concern here is the involvement of the Chinese government in the issuing of exit permits for these hopeful immigrants. It is common knowledge that those who can afford to pay bribes of HK$20,000 to HK$30,000 and at times, over HK$200,000 to the relevant officials can shorten their wait considerably and join their husband and family in Hong Kong sooner than those who cannot afford to bribe the officials. While the waiting time is usually three years on average, there were cases where the wives have to wait for over 25 years before they were given a one-way permit.[33] In order to ensure that such queue jumping is stamped out, a reasonable framework would help to reassure these hopeful immigrants of their waiting status. Better coordination between the Hong Kong and the Chinese immigration authorities is essential.

It is also important for the government to provide the new immigrants with initial assistance when they first settle in Hong Kong, especially in the areas of housing, language learning, social networking and education for their children. Many of the new immigrants live in cramped housing and when the other mainland members join them, the living quarters become inadequate. Often tension and domestic violence are the result of living in cramped housing. Chief Executive Tung Chee-hwa's plan for more housing should help ease the shortage of housing which would also lower the price for housing. This will make it possible for the new immigrants to afford reasonable accommodation in Hong Kong. It is pointless to accept these new immigrants if they cannot have decent living conditions and a fair standard of living in Hong Kong.

There is also a need to provide a coordinated language programme so that these new immigrants can learn the Cantonese language within a reasonable period of time after arrival. After all, language is essential in facilitating integration into a community. At present, there are some forms of language courses planned for the new immigrants. However, they are not readily accessible to them and the courses are often held in places distant from the homes of these new immigrants. One way to ensure that the new migrants benefit most from the language programme is to conduct Cantonese language classes in the neighbourhood associations (*kaifong* associations) which are located close to where the immigrants live. Another possible avenue is to conduct Cantonese language courses in the clan and dialect associations *(tongxianghui)* which many of the new immigrants visit on a regular basis.

One main problem faced by the mainland wives and children is their inability to integrate into the wider Hong Kong society. As such, many of the new immigrants, especially the wives, feel socially dislocated when they move to Hong Kong. Such anomie has resulted in the wives suffering from ill heath and depression. There is a need to assist them in establishing a new social network. One possible way is to tap into the existing social networks, especially the *tongxianghui*, which have been a meeting place for many of these new immigrants. However, there is a need to encourage these *tongxianghui* to structure some of their activities to cater to the needs of the wives and children as these associations continue to cater largely to the male immigrants. Neighbourhood associations could organize social activities and encourage the new immigrants to participate and help them integrate into the wider community.

Education for the mainland children has been one of the hottest debated topics in Hong Kong, especially in the immediately after 1 July. While the public has expressed apprehension over the amount of resources spent on these mainland children, it is nevertheless important to recognize that these children are now part of Hong Kong society and should be given all the assistance and adequate resources to help them become full-fledged Hong Kong residents. They, like the Hong Kong-born children, will grow up in Hong Kong and will eventually contribute to the Hong Kong society. With adequate educational training, they will eventually become fully integrated into the wider Hong Kong society and be able to contribute fully to the social, economic and political life of their adopted home.

## Conclusion

With the return of sovereignty to China, Hong Kong is now an important part of China, yet its status as a "Special Administrative Region" has enabled it to continue to remain distinct from the rest of the Mainland. The wealth and lifestyle in Hong Kong continue to be viewed as desirable and sought after by the mainlander. Given the opportunity, many mainland Chinese would want to emigrate and live in Hong Kong. Many have already tried, some successfully but many failed to enter Hong Kong illegally. Yet, others are considered as more fortunate by their mainland village counterparts when they marry Hong Kong men or become their mistresses and are given the opportunity to apply for a one-way permit to live in Hong Kong.

Irrespective of whether they marry Hong Kong men or become their mistresses, these women have to pay a high price for the opportunity to move to Hong Kong — that they have to become a variant of single motherhood and run a female-dominated household during the waiting period. In short, they have to endure the split-family phenomenon. Furthermore, they have to shoulder all the social and emotional burdens on their own without the support of their husband. They also have to look after the children and often contribute financially to their mainland household. However, in a very pragmatic way, many view this as a tradeoff for the ultimate prize of a higher standard of living for themselves and their children in Hong Kong. This imagined sense of a better life in Hong Kong is a sufficient force that pushes them to endure the long wait to Hong Kong.

For some, Hong Kong presents hope and opportunity and for many others, nightmare and despair. Yet, many continue to persevere and cling on to the dreams of a better tomorrow and they work hard to attain such a goal.

## NOTES

1. Kuah, K.E., "Negotiating Emigration and the Family: Individual Solutions to the 1997 Anxiety", *The Annals*, vol. 547 (September 1996), Thousand Oaks: Sage Periodicals Press, pp. 54–67.

2. *Hong Kong Economic Journal*, 3 April 1997:58; *Hu-bao*, 15 April 1997:52 and *Wen Wei Pao*, 16 April 1997:54.

3. *Hu-bao*, 6 June 1997:10.

4. Ibid., 7 June 1997:15.

5. *South China Morning Post*, 22 June 1997:52.

6. Ibid., 9 June 1997:11.

7. *Hu-Bao*, 6 July 97:42.

8. *Ming Pao*, 5 April 1997:56; 10 April 97:61; *Xin Bao*, 8 April 1997:61; *Shin Bao*, 9 April 1997:58.

9. *South China Morning Post*, 10 July 1997:34.

10. Ibid., 15 July 1997:37.

11. Ibid., 10 July 1997:37.

12. *Hua-bao*, 10 July 1997:35.

13. *South China Morning Post*, 10 July 1997:36.

14. Ibid., 13 July 1997:27.

15. *Hu-bao*, 14 July 1997:36.

16. *South China Morning Post*, 17 July 1997:38.

17. *Hu-bao*, 16 February 1998:57.

18. *Ming Pao*, 17 March 1997:57 & 58; *Kuai-bao*, 11 February 1997:52.

19. Ibid., 24 April 1997:56.

20. Ibid., 2 April 1997:58.

21. *Sing Tao Daily*, 12 April 1997:55.

22. *Hong Kong Economic Journal*, 3 April 1997:58.

23. *Hu-bao*, 11 July 1997:1.

24. *Kuai-bao*, 4 June 1997:7.

25. *Hong Kong Economic Journal*, 13 March 1997:11; 10 April 1997:12; *Ming Pao*, 10 March 1997:5.

26. *Hu-bao*, 5 March 1997:4.

27. *Sing Tao Daily*, 6 July 1997:44; *Economic Journal*, 3 July 1997:61; *Xin Bao*, 5 August 1997:64.

28. *South China Morning Post*, 15 August 1997:11.

29. *Ming Pao*, 20 April 1997:41; 23 April 1997:50 & 52; *Catholic News*, 25 April 1997:62; *South China Morning Post*, 23 April 1997:47; 26 April 1997:50.

30. *Sing Tao*, 18 April 1997:65.

31. *South China Morning Post*, 4 October 1998:4.

32. *Kuai-bao*, 13 July 1997:47.

33. *Hu-bao*, 1 April 1997:59.

## REFERENCES

Chen, A.H.Y. (1988). "The Development of Immigration Law and Policy: The Hong Kong Experience". *McGill Law Journal*, vol. 33 (4):631–75.

Chung, Yau-Ling (1982). "Media and the Illegal Immigrants from China". Unpublished M.Phil. (Comm.) dissertation.

Ho, H.K. (1994). "The Earnings and Employment Pattern of New Immigrants from China". Unpublished M.Phil. (Econ.) dissertation.

Hong Kong Council of Social Service (The Working Party on Women) (1990). *Report on the Needs and Problems of Women in Temporary Housing Area*. Hong Kong.

————— (The Working Party on Arrival, Community Development Division) and Social Sciences Department of Lingnan College (1985). *Report on the Social and Economic Adaptation of the Chinese New Arrivals in Hong Kong*. Hong Kong.

Kuah, K.E. (1996). "Negotiating Emigration and the Family: Individual Solutions to the 1997 Anxiety". *The Annals*, vol. 547 (September). (Thousand Oaks: Sage Periodical Press). pp. 54–67.

Lai, P.C.Y. (1995). "The Stress of Migration, Social Support, and Depression: An Exploratory Study on Chinese Immigrant Women in Hong Kong". Unpublished M.Social Work dissertation. Chinese University of Hong Kong.

Lee, M.T. (1993). "Programme Design for Adult Chinese Immigrants Learning English as a Second Language". Unpublished MA dissertation. Department of English, Chinese University of Hong Kong.

Li, L.Y. (1990). "An Exploratory Study of the Marital Adjustment of Chinese Female New Arrivals in Hong Kong". Unpublished M.Social Work dissertation. Department of Social Work, University of Hong Kong.

Lo Yongjian (1981). *"Zhongguo he fai yi ming zai xianggang zi shi ying wen ti"* (Chinese legal immigrants in Hong Kong and their problems of adaptation). Unpublished M.Phil. (Soc.) dissertation. Chinese University of Hong Kong.

Pang, T.S.F. (1984). "An Exploratory Study of the Relationship between the Adjustment Problems of New Immigrants from China and Crime in Hong Kong". Unpublished M.Social Work dissertation. (In Chinese) Chinese University of Hong Kong.

Wong, P.H. (1996). "An Exploratory Study on the Social Impact and Health Status of the Chinese Female Immigrants in Hong Kong: A Case Study of Those Living in Temporary Housing Areas". Unpublished M.Social Work dissertation. Division of Social Work, Chinese University of Hong Kong.

Yung, D.Y.Y. (1991). "Mainlanders in Hong Kong Films of the Eighties: A Study of their Changing Depictions". Unpublished M.Phil. (Comm.) dissertation.

# CHAPTER 10

# WHITHER HONG KONG'S MIDDLE CLASS?

Lee Ming-kwan

The Hong Kong new middle class on the eve of 1997 are cynical and retreatist in orientation. They are distrustful of political leaders and political authority ... They either stay aloof from politics or submit to an institutional environment from which they feel increasingly estranged. They maintain their distance from political matters ... Whether they are returnees, applicants for foreign passports, or people who have never thought of leaving, they do not constitute a bourgeois social force which has the commitment and vision to defend a liberal social and political order ... The story of Hong Kong's new middle class in the period of political transition is one of quiescence and inaction. If there is a lesson to be drawn from this story, it is an early warning to the future SAR government and the Chief Executive — can "one country, two systems" be viable without an active, dynamic, and hopeful middle class?

Lui Tai-lok (1997:224–25)

Lui was looking at the new middle class — salaried professionals, managers and administrators, and, in general, white collar employees[1] — on the eve of 1997. His analysis led him to conclude that this was not a class which would stand up to defend the capitalist system and its way of life in post-1997 Hong Kong.[2] This paper takes up where Lui leaves off.

# The Politics of Identity

Lui was, of course, writing in the final hours of British rule, when the drama of the politics of identity was into its last scene and the audience was held in suspense about what would happen when the inevitable moment came.

This inevitable moment was 1997. After 140 years of British rule, the reality had finally dawned on the Hong Kong Chinese that, like it or not, Hong Kong would cease to be a British colony and become part of China, and they would cease to be colonial subjects, becoming citizens of the People's Republic of China. "The new reality upsets taken-for-granted identities. Perforce the Hong Kong people will have to redefine who they are and how they are to relate to one another, to the outgoing colonial authority, to the incoming Chinese government, to the Chinese across the border, and to the neighbouring countries. The experience reinvigorates ... old questions like: Who am I? Am I Chinese or Hongkongese? What kind of Chinese am I?" (Lee, 1995:120–21). Questions also arose as to "whether the Hong Kong people are prepared to pledge their loyalty and commitment, as Chinese citizens, to the government of the People's Republic, whether they take pride in this new identity, (and) whether they are ready to accord to national political leaders, institutions, and symbols the respect expected from them" (ibid.:121). The reality was hard to accept because the Hong Kong Chinese, in fact, identified themselves less as "Chinese" than as "Hongkongese" (Lau and Kuan, 1988:178–87; Lee and Leung, 1995; Lau, 1997a) and had less trust in the Chinese than in the Hong Kong government (Lee and Leung, 1995; Lau, 1997b). It was a Hong Kong identity that they cherished.

The full story of the rise of the Hong Kong identity[3] (see, for example, Wong 1997 and Lee, 1998) cannot be re-told here. Suffice it to say that it was largely the outcome of three sets of post-war experiences: first, the eclipse of national identity and the increasing alienation of the Hong Kong Chinese from

Chinese national politics; second, "decolonization", changes redefining their rights and statuses, making them less colonial subjects than citizens of their own government; and third, the transformation of the colonial government into a modern polity characterized by relative openness and democracy and by its commitment to its responsibility to its citizens. The result was that towards the last years of British rule, a new relationship had come between the government and its people. "The Hong Kong people no longer saw themselves as the 'subjects' of the British colonial government, when they began to see this government less as a government superimposed from the outside by an alien power than as a government of their own, and when they began to see themselves as its people" (Lee 1998:155). This new relationship signified the beginning of the Hong Kong identity.

The irony of history was that the Hong Kong identity should take shape just when British rule was about to end and when China was about to resume sovereignty over the territory. It was, therefore, not without a sense of agony and bewilderment that the Hong Kong Chinese pondered the prospect of the city's reunion with China. Would Hong Kong become not what it was? Would there no longer be the Hong Kong way of life? Would Hong Kong become just another coastal Chinese city? Expressing these concerns, a 1988 survey found that, indeed, across the board, Hong Kong people foresaw deterioration in every front after 1997. They anticipated curtailment of civil rights, reduction of personal liberties, deterioration of the legal system, and stagnation or lowering of living standards. There was a pervasive sense of foreboding.

The stage was set, therefore, for the *politics of identity* — Hong Kong people pondering their alternatives and choices, debating what should be done, taking sides, and seeking to shape political outcomes affecting their future. The issue dominating these debates was democracy — whether there could be autonomy without democracy; whether democracy-as-buffers would work; how democratic should the government be both before and after 1997; and how political reforms should be brought about.[4] These debates pitched the "liberals" against the "conservatives". In the final months of British rule, as the relationship between the two sovereign powers deteriorated, debates over the reform proposals championed by the colony's last governor, Chris Patten, further forced the conservatives and the liberals to take sides as either "pro-China" or "pro-Britain".

In these debates, the middle class "was not mobilized and remained unpoliticized" (Lui, 1997:219). This was despite the fact that compared with the other classes, professionals and managers were actually more liberal in their political attitudes and more ready to identify with the Hong Kong than with the national identity (Lee and Leung, 1995). Such inaction can be explained by a combination of factors. Political inaction was, first of all, not just a middle-class malaise. It followed from the more widely shared culture of "utilitarianistic familism" (Lau, 1981): devotion of the Hong Kong Chinese to the pursuits of familial economic interests in the post-war years. Such devotion siphoned off their interests in politics. Political inaction followed also from the "ideology of success" (Lui, 1997:214), the belief among Hong Kong people in competition, personal effort and individual achievement. They did not see the need to act collectively to advance their interest.

When "voice" (Hirschman, 1970), or taking political action, was largely disliked, the options left to most Hong Kong Chinese as they pondered what to do in the face of an uncertain political future were either "exit", i.e. emigrate or securing foreign passports, or "loyalty", i.e. staying behind and braving whatever might happen. Exit was, however, not a viable option for many either did not have the wealth, or the skills, or the connections to enable them to emigrate. Perforce they had to stay. Successful emigrants were, consequently, mainly the "best educated, well trained, and highly skilled" (Skeldon, 1997:31–32). Exit was very much a middle-class option.

But, most importantly, the middle class was not mobilized for political action because class was not the issue in the politics of identity. The issue was rather democracy. Mobilization for political action on this issue was not on a class basis, but rather on the basis of whether one was "pro-China" or "pro-democracy" or, in the last months of British rule, "pro-Patten". Political opinions were split and, among political actors, battle-lines were drawn between the "pro-China" camp — an across-class alliance of pro-Beijing organizations, political parties, trade unions and activists — and the "pro-democracy" camp of liberal intellectuals, trade unions and political parties with the Democratic Party as its flagship. It was the political community rather than the classes which was in conflict and it was political rather than class identity which was the basis of solidarity and mobilization.

The politics of identity had been complicated by the fact that the two sovereign powers were actively involved. It was not just the Hong Kong Chinese arguing among themselves about democracy and Hong Kong's future. In contention were also the two governments, each seeking to shape public opinions and rally political support as they fought each other, both publicly and behind the scene, over every conceivable issue — from building the new airport to the protocol of the handover ceremony — in events leading up to 1997. Their involvement served both to harden the battle-lines between the two contending camps and enhance the solidarity of each.

As we shall see, such solidarity would not last long. Time was ticking away and the British factor would soon be irrelevant. As Hong Kong became the Special Administrative Region (HKSAR), and as experience proved that China was honouring its words, i.e. not interfering in Hong Kong affairs, much of what had so far been at the back of Hong Kong people's anxiety and a sense of foreboding would dissipate. This would erode the support enjoyed by the pro-democracy camp. As support for the pro-democracy camp declined, and with the British quickly becoming irrelevant, the pro-China camp would lose the factor which had hitherto helped to hold its disparate elements together: some common antagonists. Before long the alliance of pro-China business organizations, political parties and trade unions would break up. It did not take long for these to happen. What had hastened the process, however, was economic decline and the entry of class politics.

# Economic Decline and
# The Entry of Class Politics

Hong Kong had had nearly three decades of uninterrupted economic growth when it was hit by the worst economic crisis since the Second World War. Such had been the rate of growth that in a relatively short span of time, Hong Kong had catapulted into one of the wealthiest places, its residents enjoying a standard of living envied by most countries in the world.[5] It was this growth and prosperity that had made possible the "Hong Kong experience" (Lui and Wong, 1995), the opportunity to "make it" in Hong Kong through personal effort. As one sociologist astutely puts it, "Hong Kong's spectacular economic development in the 1960s and 1970s seemed to bring about social advancement for many without a serious opposite and downward effect on others. Prosperity and growth generated a benign external environment, inducing optimism that one's turn to move ahead was to come soon" (Wong,1996:389).

This growth and prosperity was conducive to interclass relations. When everyone had a growing share of the economic pie, no one felt strong deprivation. The capitalists, the middle class and the working class were all able to pursue their economic interests without provoking and encountering hostile reactions from the other classes. Each did not see the need for collective action and each did not present itself as an organized force which might threaten the interests of the other classes. Growth and prosperity had, in other words, discouraged class-based collective action and "put a lid " on class conflicts. This was remarkable given the fact that, in all these years, the gap between the rich and the poor had actually widened and Hong Kong is now among the most unequal countries in the world.[6]

The "benign external environment" is, however, becoming a thing of the past. The worst economic crisis in many years has induced radical changes in the political economy. These changes are impacting on pre-existing class relations, upsetting what had hitherto been taken for granted and questioning established values and practices.

Economic recession has, first of all, wiped out a big part of Hong Kong's wealth, the total loss amounting to some HK$300 billion, roughly equivalent to all the deposits in the local banks.[7] Property owners and investors have been hard hit. Many shares have halved in value since August 1997 and many mortgaged homes have become negative assets. The middle class are among the heavy losers.[8] This sudden and huge loss of wealth is just the most ostensible part of the problem. Many workers now face pay cuts and loss of their jobs. Unemployment rate has reached the fifteen-year high of 5.3 percent.[9] As many as 188,000 workers are unemployed,[10] the number increasing as more and more workers are laid off, as firms cut cost, and as a growing number of loss-making companies wind up.[11] More workers have been asked to work longer hours.[12] Many others face cuts in fringe benefits and welfare.[13]

Middle-class jobs, especially professional jobs, were well paid and secure. They no longer are. Even "established professions" — like architects, lawyers, accountants — face pay cuts and job loss just the same.[14] White-collar layoffs have increased and white-collar salaries have plunged as the economic crisis takes a tighter hold. Compared with the April–June figures, the median wage of administrators and managers in August was down by 6.6 per cent.[15] Finance, insurance, property and business services employees have suffered the biggest set-back.[16]

These are unprecedented. The assumption that there is a share of the economic pie for every one, and a bigger one, too, over time, no longer holds. Perforce there is the need to get organized and to act collectively to defend one's interests which would provoke and encounter hostile reactions from the other classes. The ground rules for interclass relations are no longer the same.

The stage has been set, therefore, for class politics. On 17 September 1998, Hong Kong Telecom, the city's biggest private-sector employer, announced that its 13,800 employees would take a 10 percent pay cut in November. The decision evoked angry responses. In its editorial, the *South China Morning Post* summed up the prevailing sentiments: "Pay cuts have become increasingly common as Hong Kong struggles to adjust to the dismal economic climate ... But the spread of this trend to profitable companies, which can scarcely argue pay cuts are an alternative to bankruptcy, is unjustified and alarming. Worse still, is the way they are imposed: without consultation or warning".[17] The telecommunications giant had just reported a HK$17-billion net profit. On 20 September, 2,000 Hong Kong Telecom employees staged a protest outside Telecom House against their "rich but not benevolent" employer. Under mounting public and political pressure,[18] the company admitted defeat and rescinded its unpopular plan.

The first major stand-off between employers and employees since 1967 ended with the defeat of the former. It was, however, signalling the beginning of more of the same to come. No sooner had Hong Kong Telecom admitted its defeat then the Hong Kong Chamber of Commerce and the Hong Kong Retail Management Association, whose members together employed over 1,600,000 workers, called for a wage freeze the following year. This invited an angry response from union leaders. "If the employers don't stop what they are doing," warned Chan Yuen-han of the Hong Kong Federation of Trade Unions, "employees may be forced to take extreme action." Lee Kai-ming, union leader-cum-legislator, also warned that if this situation continued, there could be the kind of riots which rocked Hong Kong in 1967.[19] On the national day, seven hundred demonstrators marched to the government offices in Central District in protest against "pay cuts and unemployment".

In the wake of the economic downturn and worsening industrial relations, trade unions registered record growth of membership. In just the first six months of the year, a total of 44,000 new members joined the Hong Kong Federation of Trade Unions, The Confederation of Trade Unions and the Federation of Hong Kong and Kowloon Labour Unions, increasing their membership by 10 per cent.[20] "Workers are more united in difficult times like these," said union leader Lee Kai-ming. "They join unions so that they can better defend their rights and rice bowls in their struggles against employers. This is high time for membership drive".[21]

Unionists have also warned of social instability in the face of worsening economic situations. "The seeds of unrest have been sown," said the Confederation of Trade Unions. It urged the government to introduce laws on collective bargaining, increase welfare spending, create more jobs and set up an employment insurance system. The Federation of Hong Kong and Kowloon Labour Unions said it was extremely concerned over the unprecedented livelihood of all employees. It called on the government to stop importing foreign workers and review immigration policies, such as the return of migrants and the daily quota allowing 150 migrants from the Mainland.[22]

Class politics does not just "take to the street". It has also been taken into the Legislative Council. The democrats and unionists are prepared to give a thumbs-down to Chief Executive Tung Chee-hwa's earlier policy address (1998) for having said very little on what his government plans to do to solve the unemployment problem. Business legislators, on the hand, rally behind Tung. The Legislative Council is becoming divided along class lines.

For about 15 years, the politics of identity had so dominated Hong Kong's political agenda that class issues had been very much sidelined and overshadowed. But as the "China factor" (Leung 1993; 1996; Lee, 1993), or, more specifically, "the local mistrust of the Chinese central government" (Wong, 1998) subsides, and as economic conditions rapidly deteriorate, the issue of class has surged to the fore. Class has, as one study confirms, emerged as the most salient issue in the 1998 Legislative Council election (ibid.).

The middle class is caught unprepared in these developments. For many of them, "exit" no longer seems the feasible option because "recession bites"[23] and many have been left less rich and less confident to move.[24] "Voice" does not seem to be the feasible option either because they are, as Lui (1997) describes them, individualistic, cynical and retreatist. In the main spectators and "rear-guarders" (Mills, 1951:353), the middle class are little organized and unprepared to act collectively to defend their interests. In the looming battles between organized business and labour, and caught in crossfires, they seem certain to lose. The middle class have never been as vulnerable. Not surprisingly there was a "sense of plight"[25] in the middle class. Their economic situation has already been undermined by the fact that the "utilitarian value of education has depreciated" (Lau, 1997c:429) as a result of the rapid expansion of higher education in the last two decades. It has been further hit by economic recession.

# Conclusion

What have happened a year after 1997 can perhaps be couched in the terms of "paradigm shift": Hong Kong politics has made a radical shift from the politics of identity to class politics. This radical change has many implications for Hong Kong politics and the Hong Kong political economy. It means the redefinition of political realities, the social construction of a new set of political agenda, the reconfiguration of political interests, and the formation of new patterns of political alignments and solidarity. It could mean the "politicization of welfare"[26] and political debates and conflicts around welfare issues.[27] The full implications of the change have yet to be explored, described and analysed.

For the researchers, perforce this also means that they must rethink old views, question taken-for-granted assumptions, and ask new research questions. In this perspective, one must reconsider what has been said about the middle class amid the politics of identity. Lui's contention, that "[t]he story of Hong Kong's new middle class in the period of political transition is one of quiescence and inaction" (1997:225), perhaps true in the earlier period, may no longer be true in a period during which the politics of class has taken centre stage.

In this sense, one may also reconsider the "lesson" which Lui learns from his study of the middle class, the lesson that "it is an early warning to the future SAR government and the chief executive — can 'one country, two systems' be viable without an active, dynamic, and hopeful middle class?" (ibid.). The question, meaningful in the context of the politics of identity, no longer seems so now, when it is not so much democracy as class issues which dominate Hong Kong's political agenda. Also, it is clearer than ever that "one country, two systems" cannot be viable without a viable capitalist economy. Hong Kong may fall not because there is no democracy, but because its economy lets it down. Whether there is an "active, dynamic, and hopeful" middle class is neither a necessary nor a sufficient condition for an economy that has made Hong Kong the prosperous and dynamic place that it is.

Whither the middle class? I hesitate to give an answer, let alone a lesson. My educated guess is that, with looming "social disharmony and friction among socio-economic groups, [with] perhaps even a visible sense of class antagonism" (Lau, 1997c:429), as class politics unfolds, and under mounting economic and political pressures, the middle class will increasingly be forced to act collectively to defend their interests, reluctant though they may be. The way has been paved for middle-class "class formation".

# NOTES

1. The new middle class is also referred to as "the service class" (Goldthorpe, 1982; Goldthorpe et al., 1987). In this chapter, the terms *middle class, the new middle class,* and *the service class* are used interchangeably.

2. Such doubt — of the political clout and stamina of the middle class — is neither new nor exceptional. As early as 1951, C. Wright Mills lamented that "there is no probability of the new middle class forming or inaugurating or leading any political movement" (Mills, 1951). Echoing Mills, Goldthorpe argues, some 30 years later, that in terms of structural but "empirically determinable" interests in relation to other classes, the service class is fundamentally conservative (1982:179–85).

3. The view is taken here that identity is the relationship between nation and state that obtains when the people of that nation identify with the state (Dittmer and Kim, 1993:13). In this perspective, the Hong Kong identity is what obtains when the people of this society regard the Hong Kong government as their government and the Hong Kong people as the people of this government (Lee, 1998:154).

4. These debates began from as early as the mid-1980s on the so-called *representative government* and how it should be brought about. This was followed by debates on whether direct elections should be introduced in elections to the Legislative Council in 1998, on the Basic Law, Hong Kong's mini-constitution, and, since 1992, around governor Chris Patten's political reform proposals.

5. Hong Kong's per capita income in 1998 is US$24,540. This ranks Hong Kong among the top four countries with the highest per capita income (*Ming Pao,* 17 October 1998).

6. The Gini Index, one way of expressing income distribution, was 0.49 in 1960. It falls to 0.43 in 1971. Between 1971 and 1976, it stayed at 0.43, gradually rising to 0.45 in 1981. In 1991, it rose to 0.48. From this it rose to 0.518 in 1996. This placed Hong Kong in the 79th position, just ahead of Honduras and Columbia (*Ming Pao,* 17 October 1998). However, the Gini Index "must have substantially underestimated the actual magnitude of economic inequality in Hong Kong, for it relies solely upon the income figures collected in censuses and by-censuses, whereas the grossly unequal distribution of wealth is not taken into account" (Lau, 1997c).

7. *The Economist,* 27 June 1998:28.

8. *Yazhou Zhoukan,* 31 August–6 September 1998).

9. The unemployment rate stayed more or less around 2 percent throughout the greater part of the 1980s (Ng, 1989:120).

10. *Ming Pao,* 17 November 1998.

11. Among firms which have folded up or which are about to fold up are such big names in the department stores business, such as Daimaru, Yaohan and Matsuzakaiya. Wing On, the other big name, has been laying off

workers. Hundreds of workers have lost their jobs as a result. There could be many firms which have closed down without being noticed.

12. The clothing chain, Bossini, for example, had asked sales staff and other employees to work 40 hours extra each month without more pay. The company reported a HK$45.5 million net loss for the year ended in March against a HK$64.5 million net profit the previous year (*South China Morning Post*, 17 October 1998).

13. For example, the two leading banks, Hong Kong Bank and Chartered Bank, have been reviewing staff welfare and benefits (*Hong Kong Economic Journal*, 19 September 1998).

14. Between April and August 1998, around 400 architects had lost their jobs. Those who kept their jobs faced a 20 percent pay cut (*Hong Kong Economic Journal*, 19 September 1998). In March, a big law firm also required its employees to take a 20 percent pay-cut (*Yazhou Zhoukan*, 31 August–6 September 1998:17).

15. *Ming Pao,* 20 October 1998.

16. The average earnings of finance, insurance, property and business services workers have fallen 5.1 percent in a year (*South China Morning Post*, 17 October 1998).

17. *South China Morning Post,* 19 September 1998).

18. The chief executive, Tung Chee-hwa, was concerned and was said to have intervened. The Financial Secretary openly criticized the move of the Hong Kong Telecom. Union leaders who met Linus Cheung, the company's chief executive officer, told him they disapproved the pay-cut.

19. *Yazhou Zhoukan,* 12–18 October 1998).

20. *Ming Pao,* 4. October 1998.

21. *Ming Pao,* 4 October 1998.

22. *South China Morning Post,* 17 November 1998.

23. *South China Morning Post,* 9 September 1998.

24. Migration to Canada has dropped by 69 percent in the first nine months of the year. Only 3,397 professionals emigrated, compared to 10,003 last year. A Canadian immigration official attributed the fall to "the current fiscal uncertainty and roller-coaster stock markets" (*South China Morning Post,* 9 October 1998).

25. Lau, 1997c:429.

26. Nelson Chow first referred to the "politicization of welfare" in an article which appeared in the *Hong Kong Economic Journal,* 26 May 1993.

27. A looming issue is around the government's plan to cut the unemployment benefits provided through the "Comprehensive Social Security and Assistance" Scheme for the unemployed.

# REFERENCES

Dittmer, Lowell and Samuel S. Kim (1993). "In Search of a Theory of National Identity." In Lowell Dittmer and Samuel S. Kim (eds.), *China's Quest for National Identity*. Ithaca and London: Cornell University Press. pp. 1–31.

*Economist*. 27 June 1998. London.

Goldthorpe, John (1982). "On the Service Class, Its Formation and Future." In A. Giddens and G. MacKenzie (eds.), *Classes and the Division of Labour: Essays in Honour of Ilya Neustadt*. Cambridge: Cambridge University Press. pp. 162–85.

Goldthorpe, John, C. Llewellyn and C. Payne (1987). *Social Mobility and Class Structure in Modern Britain* (2nd edn). Oxford: Clarendon Press.

Hirschman, Albert O. (1970). *Exit, Voice and Loyalty*. Cambridge: Harvard University Press.

Lau, Siu-kai (1981). "Utilitarianistic Familism: The Basis of Political Stability." In Ambrose Y.C. King and Rance P.L. Lee (eds.), *Social Life and Development in Hong Kong*. Hong Kong: The Chinese University Press. pp. 195–216.

———— (1997a). "Hongkongese or Chinese: The Problem of Identity on the Eve of Resumption of Chinese Sovereignty over Hong Kong." Occasional Paper No. 65. Hong Kong: Hong Kong Institute of Asia–Pacific Studies, The Chinese University of Hong Kong.

———— (1997b). "Democratization and Decline of Trust in Public Institutions in Hong Kong." In Lau Siu-kai, Wan Po-san, F.H. Siu, Wong Siu-lun, Ng Chun-hung, Lui Tai-lok, Thomas Wong and Lee Ming-kwan, *Decline of Authority, Social Conflict, and Social Reintegration in Hong Kong: Patterns of Social Change in the Last Years of British Rule*. Research report submitted to the Research Grant Council of the Universities Grants Committee.

———— (1997c). "The Fraying of the Socio-economic Fabric of Hong Kong." *Pacific Review*, vol. 10, no. 3:426–41.

Lau Siu-kai and Kuan Hsin-chi (1988). *The Ethos of the Hong Kong Chinese*. Hong Kong: The Chinese University Press.

Lee, M.K. (1998). "Hong Kong Identity — Past and Present." In Wong Siu-lun & Toypjiro Maruya (eds.), *Hong Kong Economy and Society: Challenges in the New Era*. Hong Kong: Center of Asian Studies, The University of Hong Kong. pp. 152–75.

Lee, Ming-kwan (1993). "Issue-Positions in the 1991 Legislative Council Election." In Lau Siu-kai and Louie Kin-shuen (eds.), *Hong Kong Tried Democracy: The 1991 Elections in Hong Kong*. Hong Kong: The Hong Kong Institute of Asia–Pacific Studies, The Chinese University of Hong Kong. pp. 237–48.

———— (1995). "Community and Identity in Transition in Hong Kong." In Reginald Kwok and Alvin So (eds.), *The Hong Kong–Guangdong Link: Partnership in Flux*. Armonk and London: M.E. Sharpe. pp. 119–34.

Lee, Ming-kwan and Leung Sai-wing (1995). "Democracy, Capitalism and National Identity in Public Attitudes." Occasional Papers Series No. 4. Hong Kong: Department of Applied Social Studies, The Hong Kong Polytechnic University.

Leung, Sai-wing (1993). "The 'China Factor' in the 1991 Legislative Council Election: The June 4th Incident and Anti-Communist China Syndrome." In Lau Siu-kai and Louie Kin-shuen (eds.), *Hong Kong Tried Democracy: The 1991 Elections in Hong Kong*. Hong Kong: Hong Kong Institute of Asia-Pacific Studies, The Chinese University of Hong Kong. pp.187–236.

———— (1996). "The 'China Factors' and the Voters' Choice in the 1995 Legislative Council Election." In Kuan Hsin-chi (ed.), *The 1995 Legislative Council Elections in Hong Kong*. Hong Kong: Hong Kong Institute of Asia-Pacific Studies, The Chinese University of Hong Kong. pp. 201–44.

Lui, Tai-lok (1997). "The Hong Kong New Middle Class on the Eve of 1997." In Joseph Y.S. Cheng (ed.), *The Other Hong Kong Report 1997*. Hong Kong: The Chinese University Press. pp. 207–25.

Lui, Tai-lok and Thomas W.P. Wong (1995). "The 'Hong Kong Experience': Class, Inequality and Morality in Political Transition." *Asiatische Studien Etudes Asiatiques*. vol. 49, no. 1.

Mills, C. Wright (1951). *White Collar*. New York: Oxford University Press.

Ng, Sek-hong (1989). "Labour and Employment." In T.L. Tsim and Bernard H.K. Luk (eds.), *The Other Hong Kong Report*. Hong Kong: The Chinese University Press. pp. 119–44.

Skeldon, Ronald (1994). "Hong Kong in an International Migration System." In Ronald Skeldon (ed.), *Reluctant Exiles?* Hong Kong: Hong Kong University Press. pp. 31–32.

Wong, Ka-ying, Timothy (1998). "Issue Voting in the 1998 Legislative Council Election." Paper presented to the Conference on the 1998 Legislative Council Elections. Hong Kong Institute of Asia-Pacific Studies, The Chinese University of Hong Kong. 24 September 1998.

Wong, Thomas W.P. (1996). "Economic Culture and Distributive Justice." In Lau Siu-kai, Lee Ming-kwan, Wan Po-san and Wong Siu-lun (eds.), *Indicators of Social Development: Hong Kong 1993*. Hong Kong: The Hong Kong Institute of Asia–Pacific Studies, The Chinese University of Hong Kong. pp. 367–98.

———— (1997). "Colonial Governance and the Hong Kong Story." Paper presented at the 2nd Asia–Pacific Regional Conference of Sociology (APRCS). University of Malaya, Kuala Lumpur, Malaysia. 18–20 September. (Mimeograph).

# CHAPTER 11

# A SEARCH FOR IDENTITY: LEGAL DEVELOPMENT SINCE 1 JULY 1997

Johannes Man-mun Chan

In September 1984, after two years of confidential negotiations between the British and the Chinese governments over the future of Hong Kong, the eagerly-awaited Sino-British Joint Declaration was published. It formally announced the termination of British rule over Hong Kong on 30 June 1997, and the beginning of an unprecedented experiment of "one country, two systems". The key to this experiment is that "Hong Kong will enjoy a high degree of autonomy. It will be vested with executive, legislative and independent judicial power, including that of final adjudication. The laws currently in force in Hong Kong will remain basically unchanged." The blueprint set out in the Joint Declaration was elaborated (or to some extent, re-interpreted) and constitutionalized in the Basic Law, which was promulgated in April 1990. The Basic Law contains various provisions to define the respective responsibilities of the central government and the Hong Kong Special Administrative Region (HKSAR), to preserve the legislative and the judicial system prior to the changeover, and to entrench certain fundamental rights of Hong Kong permanent residents.

The passage of transition was rough and turbulent. The suppression of the students' movement in Beijing in the summer of 1989 not only crushed the confidence of the people in the future of Hong Kong, but it had also bred serious suspicion and distrust between the central government and the Democratic Party in Hong Kong. This contributed to the removal of their members from the Legislative Council on the eve of the changeover despite their landslide victory in the general election of 1995. Beijing continued to refuse to have dialogue with them even after their return to the legislature in 1998. The arrival of Chris Patten, the last governor, and the change of British policy towards China in the early 1990s only added fuel to the already tensed Sino-British relationship. Political reform proposed by Patten was said to be in contravention of the Basic Law, the Joint Declaration and the understanding contained in seven letters exchanged between the Chinese and the British governments in 1991 — the famous "three-contraventions". Implementation of the political reform in 1995, despite strong opposition from the Chinese government, led to the derailing of the "through train" model: the terms of office of the last Legislative Council would terminate on 30 June 1997, and the Chinese government would, and did, set up its own political machinery to carry through Hong Kong's transition from a colony to a special administrative region.

Against this background, it comes as no surprise that the first HKSAR government regards a smooth transition as its primary and most important task. A smooth transition is understood in terms of social stability and continuity. There should be no major social or political unrest or disorder. At the same time, the political reform introduced by Patten and the practical constraints faced by the outgoing government have considerably weakened the power and credibility of the executive government, which had been branded a "lame-duck government". Thus, another major task of the first HKSAR government is to rebuild the credibility of the executive government and to reassert leadership. These two main themes of governance, namely maintenance of social stability and restoration of an executive-led government, dominate the legal development in the first year of the HKSAR.

# The Provisional Legislative Council

The breakdown of the Sino-British negotiations on the composition of Legislative Council in 1995 led to the abandonment of the "through train model" as anticipated in the Basic Law, that is, members of the last legislature of Hong Kong could not automatically become members of the first legislature of the HKSAR.[1] On the other hand, it is necessary to have a legislature on 1 July 1997 to carry out a number of specific tasks, such as endorsement of the chief justice and judges of the Court of Final Appeal. Without the cooperation of the British government, the Chinese government considered that it would not be possible to form the first legislature in accordance with the Basic Law. Accordingly, it decided to form a Provisional Legislative Council (PLC) whose members were "elected" by an election committee of 400 members who were themselves "elected" by a selection committee of 800 members appointed by the Chinese government. The selection committee was asked to elect from a nomination list which contained 20 percent extra candidates for election to the election committee. It is, therefore, not surprising that this elaborate mode of "election" is generally regarded by the Hong Kong community as an appointment in disguise, and from the very beginning the PLC suffered from the problems of lack of legitimacy and credibility.

The PLC began to operate in Shenzhen in January 1997. Shenzhen was chosen to avoid creating an impression of having two legislatures simultaneously operating in Hong Kong. This decision turned out to be crucial in due course. Instead of just preparing the necessary legislation for the transition, the PLC functioned as a formal legislature by adopting similar legislative procedures practised in Hong Kong and by embarking on a vigorous legislative programme, completing the three readings of a total of 13 bills before 1 July 1997. In June 1997, the Democratic Party applied for a declaration that Rita Fan, president of the Provisional Legislative Council, had unlawfully usurped the functions of the legislature in Hong Kong. The application was refused on the grounds that the geographical jurisdiction of the Hong Kong courts did not extend to Shenzhen.[2]

This defeat was by no means the end of the litigation. In less than 10 days after the establishment of the HKSAR, the legality of the PLC was again challenged in court.[3] It arose in the most unexpected manner. Three defendants were charged with the offence of conspiracy to defraud, a common law offence. The trial began in June 1997 and ran through July. Counsel for the defendants argued that the common law offence of conspiracy to defraud no longer existed because there was no act of adoption of the common law when the HKSAR was established. Alternatively, if the common law was adopted by the Hong Kong Reunification Ordinance enacted by the PLC on 1 July 1997, the ordinance was null and void and the adoption ineffective because the ordinance was passed by the PLC which, not being provided for in the Basic Law, was illegal. The alternative argument raised squarely the issue of the legality of the PLC. In view of the constitutional importance of the issues raised, the case was referred directly to the Court of Appeal.

On 29 July 1997, the Court of Appeal decided that no act of adoption of the common law was required. Under articles 8 and 18 of the Basic Law, the common law previously in force in Hong Kong automatically became part of the laws of the HKSAR, except those which were inconsistent with the Basic Law. This part of the decision was uncontroversial, and was in general accord with the prevailing wisdom in the legal profession. This ruling was sufficient to dispose of the case. However, the Court of Appeal decided to go further to deal with the alternative argument.

The Court of Appeal accepted that the PLC was not provided for in the Basic Law. Nor could it be regarded as the first Legislative Council, as the method of constitution and its composition were radically different from that of the first Legislative Council. Therefore, it could not derive its legality from the Basic Law. However, as the political reality was that it was not possible to form the first Legislative Council in accordance with the Basic Law, the Standing Committee of the National People's Congress (NPCSC) might, in the exercise of its sovereign power, mandate the establishment of the PLC. The Court of Appeal found that the mandate could be found in a decision of the NPCSC in 1994, and in any event, the PLC was ratified by the adoption of the report of the Preparatory Committee in 1996 which contained detailed coverage on the establishment of the PLC. Once it was decided that the PLC was set up pursuant to the sovereign power of the NPCSC, it was not open to the Hong Kong court to query whether this power was exercised consistently with the Basic Law. That is, even if what the NPCSC had done was outside the scope of the Basic Law, the Hong Kong court had no jurisdiction to challenge its validity.

This part of the decision attracted strong criticism from the legal community.[4] If the PLC did not derive its legality from the Basic Law, where could it derive its legality from? Article 18 of the Basic Law provides that the laws of the HKSAR are the laws previously in force in Hong Kong, the laws enacted by the legislature of the HKSAR, and the national law as set out in Annex III of the Basic Law. It is generally believed that article 18 defines exhaustively the sources of law of the HKSAR. What the Court of Appeal has decided is that there is a fourth source of law, namely, an undefined notion of sovereign power, which is to be exercised by the NPC or the NPCSC when the NPC is not in session. This sovereign power is apparently over and above the Basic Law. To aggravate the situation, the exercise of this power, even when it goes beyond the Basic Law, cannot be challenged in Hong Kong courts. The Court of Appeal has accepted uncritically the applicability of the common law doctrine of supremacy of Parliament, and applied it to the NPC, which was regarded as the equivalent of Parliament in the common law. This reasoning is most dubious because while Parliament in England is supreme, the NPC in the People's Republic of China (PRC) is subject to the PRC Constitution and bound by the Basic Law (at least until the Basic Law is amended). The doctrine of supremacy of Parliament cannot be applied without modification to a system where there is a written constitution. The existence of this sovereign power alongside the Basic Law makes the elaborate provisions on the relationship between the central government and the HKSAR in the Basic Law almost a mockery. As Yash Ghai forcefully argued, the decision of the Court of Appeal was a surrender of the high degree of autonomy promised to the HKSAR.[5]

Ten months later, the Court of Appeal had a chance to revisit its decision.[6] Unfortunately, instead of re-examining its earlier reasoning, the Court of Appeal decided the issue on a technical point, namely, that it was bound by its previous decision and that the issue could only be reopened at the Court of Final Appeal. However, the chief judge did accept that some of his analogy based on the doctrine of supremacy of Parliament was problematic. The issue is now pending before the Court of Final Appeal.

# Legislation

Despite the fact that the PLC is only short term, it has enacted a number of controversial legislation. Even if one is prepared to assume that the PLC is legally constituted, it is still not a full legislature in that its jurisdiction is confined to "enact laws which are essential for ensuring the proper operation of the HKSAR" and to "handle all matters which must be handled by the Provisional Legislative Council for the HKSAR before the formation of the first Legislative Council".[7] Some of the legislation it enacted hardly fell within this description, and no doubt, in appropriate cases, such legislation might be challenged for being *ultra vires* the PLC.

## *Freedom of Assembly and Demonstration*

Among the legislation passed by the Provisional Legislative Council before 30 June 1997 was the Societies (Amendment) Ordinance 1997 and the Public Order (Amendment) Ordinance 1997. The Societies Ordinance and the Public Order Ordinance were respectively amended in 1992 and 1995 in order to bring them in line with the Bill of Rights. While the effect of the amendments was to liberalize the repressive regime operating under the previous law in respect of control of societies and regulations of public assemblies and demonstrations, the amendments were perceived by the Chinese government as an attempt to undermine the ability of the HKSAR government in maintaining public order and social stability. As a result, the 1992 and 1995 amendments were declared by the NPCSC, pursuant to article 160 of the Basic Law, to be inconsistent with the Basic Law and, therefore, not adopted as the law of the HKSAR. Non-adoption of these amendments did not automatically revive the previous law repealed by these amendments, and some members of the PLC, therefore, proposed the restoration of the former law. This had attracted strong opposition from the community. The Societies (Amendment) Ordinance 1997 and the Public Order (Amendment) Ordinance 1997 represented a compromised position.[8]

The Public Order (Amendment) Ordinance 1997 re-introduces a licensing system for holding any public demonstration, with "national security" as a ground to justify the banning of public demonstrations. It is well established in international human rights law that "national security" as a ground for justifying restrictions to fundamental rights has to be construed narrowly and is confined to those situations where "the existence of a nation or its territorial integrity or political independence is endangered by force or threat of force".[9] It refers to forces or threats of forces endangering the security of the entire nation, and not certain regions of the nation. Seen in this light, it is difficult to see how any public demonstration in Hong Kong could threaten the national security of the PRC. Unfortunately, the vague and undefined notion of national security means that its interpretation is largely left to the police in their day-to-day enforcement of the Public Order Ordinance (at least until the decision of the police is challenged in court). In an internal guideline, the Commissioner of Police stated that he "will take into consideration, among other things, whether or not the declared purpose of the notified public meeting or procession is to advocate separation from the People's Republic of China including advocacy of the independence of Taiwan or Tibet."[10] Mere expression which is lawful before the changeover (and which is still lawful after the changeover in the sense that there is as yet no law restricting such expression) is now grounds for banning public assemblies and demonstrations.

Indeed, the police has tightened up its control over public assemblies and demonstrations after the changeover.[11] On a number of occasions when senior leaders from Beijing were in Hong Kong and when non-governmental organizations wished to stage a demonstration, not only did the police designate a place for public demonstrations which was far away from the leaders, but the demonstrators were surrounded by walls of policemen so that the demonstrators could hardly be seen. On one occasion, the police even put on Beethoven's *Fifth Symphony* to drown the slogans chanted by the demonstrators. They explained that classical music was played to put policemen on duty at ease — the explanation was rightly rejected by the Independent Police Complaints Council as ludicrous![12]

## Freedom of Association

The Societies (Amendment) Ordinance 1997 is even more controversial. It reintroduces the registration of all lawful societies; failing to do so is a criminal offence on the part of the office bearers. "Societies" is widely defined to cover "any club, company, partnership or association of persons, whatever the nature or objects".[13] The Societies Officer may refuse to register a society on the grounds of "national security". It is generally believed that this power is to outlaw those organizations which support the democratic movement in China. Indeed, the Hong Kong Bar Association forcefully argued that if a society is engaged in illegal activities, its responsible members could be prosecuted; but if a society engages in perfectly lawful activities, why should its office bearers be guilty of a criminal offence for failing to register their organization, an offence which may have been committed out of inadvertence or ignorance of the law?[14] It is difficult to see what public interest a registration system of lawful and non-trading societies would serve.[15]

Another controversial aspect of the amendment is that it prohibits a society from having any connections with a foreign political organization or a political organization in Taiwan. "Connection" is widely defined to cover any financial support or affiliation or control of the decision-making process. "Foreign political organization" covers an agent of a foreign government or a political party in a foreign country. The Consultation Document states explicitly that the concern was not so much foreign political influences in Hong Kong domestic affairs, but their influence in China.[16]

Hong Kong is an international cosmopolitan city. Coupled with freedom of movement both in and out, Hong Kong is open to influences and opinions from different directions. Indeed, we attach importance to developing an international outlook among the people of Hong Kong, and in building social, economic and cultural ties with other countries. This is essential to our economic growth. On the other hand, we must also take steps to prevent Hong Kong from being used for political activities against China. This has been a long-standing policy of the Hong Kong Government. This policy should be maintained after the establishment of the HKSAR.

Interestingly, there is no prohibition of any connection with a political organization, including the Communist Party, in the Mainland. It is perhaps ironical that when the Societies Ordinance was first enacted in 1949, the repressive regime contained in the Ordinance was targeted at communist activities in Hong Kong. Almost half a century later, a similarly repressive regime was reintroduced for exactly the opposite reason — to curb any attempt to affect party leadership in the Mainland.

Despite strong opposition from the community, the Public Order (Amendment) Ordinance 1997 and the Societies (Amendment) Ordinance 1997 were passed and came into effect on 1 July 1997. The amendments were destined, as they were motivated by the worries of the HKSAR government that Hong Kong could be used as a base for anti-communist activities, either from pro-democratic activists or from Taiwanese political factions. Such activities would only shake the stability of the HKSAR, something which the first HKSAR government could not afford.

## Bill of Rights

The Bill of Rights Ordinance was enacted as a confidence-saving measure in the aftermath of the suppression of democratic movements in China in 1989. Therefore, it was perceived by the Chinese officials as a slap in the face for China. As soon as the Ordinance was passed by the Legislative Council, the Foreign Ministry of the PRC issued a statement suggesting that the Bill of Rights would not be adopted as law in the HKSAR.[17]

In February 1997, the NPC, pursuant to article 160 of the Basic Law, declared that sections 2(3), 3 and 4 of the Bill of Rights

Ordinance were inconsistent with the Basic Law and, therefore, would not be adopted as law in the HKSAR. This was said to be a compromise already — a repeal of three provisions rather than declaring the entire Ordinance to be inconsistent with the Basic Law. Section 2(3) provides that the purpose of the Ordinance is to incorporate into Hong Kong law the provisions of the International Covenant on Civil and Political Rights (ICCPR). This is merely an interpretation clause and in any event, the purpose of the Ordinance is obvious, given that the substantive rights provisions in Part II of the Ordinance are almost a verbatim replica of the corresponding provisions in the ICCPR. There is, indeed, a direct reference at the end of each of the substantive rights clause to the corresponding provisions in the ICCPR. Section 3 provides that all legislation which existed at the time of the commencement of the Bill of Rights Ordinance shall be construed consistently with the Bill of Rights. Otherwise they shall be repealed to the extent of inconsistency. This is a codification of the long standing common law principle that if two statutory provisions are in conflict and the conflict cannot be resolved by the ordinary principles of interpretation, it will be assumed that the provision which is later in time reflects the intention of the legislature to repeal the earlier provision. Conflict in legislative provisions is inevitable, and it is difficult to see why a codification of this common law principle of interpretation is inconsistent with the Basic Law. Finally, section 4 provides that all future legislation shall be construed consistently with the ICCPR as applied to Hong Kong. It is another well-established principle of interpretation that the legislature does not intend to legislate contrary to the State's international obligations and, therefore, a domestic legislative provision is to be construed consistently with an international treaty — the ICCPR as applied to Hong Kong in this case. Hence, it is difficult to see how these three provisions contravene the Basic Law. The repeal is also ineffective. Since these provisions are nothing but codifications of common law principles of long standing, the court could easily achieve the same result via the common law route even if they are repealed.

The PRC government's argument that these three provisions effectively entrenched the Bill of Rights is misconceived. The entrenchment is achieved by the Letters Patent, which provides that any subsequent legislation (enacted after the commencement of the Bill of Rights Ordinance) which is inconsistent with the ICCPR as applied to Hong Kong is *ultra vires* the legislature and hence, null and void. The Letters Patent, of course, lapsed on 30 June 1997. If the Bill of Rights continues to enjoy any special status after 1 July 1997, that special status is conferred by article 39 of the Basic Law, and not because of the three sections which have not been adopted by the NPC. Indeed, what is entrenched is not the Bill of Rights, but the ICCPR as applied to Hong Kong, and this is the result of article 39 of the Basic Law.

The Attorney General Chambers of the Hong Kong government and the Hong Kong Bar Association each issued a strong public statement refuting any legal basis for holding that sections 2(3), 3 and 4 of the Bill of Rights Ordinance were inconsistent with the Basic Law.[18] Despite the heavy weight of these legal opinions, these three sections disappeared from the statute books of the HKSAR on 1 July 1997. As expected, the non-adoption of these three sections makes virtually no impact on the operation of the Bill of Rights in the post-1997 regime.[19]

Section 7 of the Bill of Rights Ordinance provides that the Ordinance shall apply to government and public authority. In *Tam Hing-yee v. Wu Tai Wai*,[20] a judgment creditor applied, pursuant to section 52E of the District Court Ordinance, for a stop order restraining the judgment debtor from leaving the territory until the judgment debt had been satisfied. Notwithstanding that the power to prevent the judgment debtor from leaving the territory stemmed from a legislative provision, the Court of Appeal held that the Bill of Rights Ordinance had no application to that case which involved a dispute between two private individuals. In so holding, the court accepted that the Bill of Rights would fall short of implementing the ICCPR as applied to Hong Kong. This decision was heavily criticized, and even the drafter of the Bill of Rights accepted that the court had misinterpreted the intention of the legislature.[21] In June 1997, the private member's bill was successfully moved. It reversed the effect of *Tam Hing-yee* by providing expressly that a court would have jurisdiction to consider the consistency of any legislation with the Bill of Rights, irrespective of the capacity of the parties concerned. The amendment came into effect on 27 June 1997, and lasted less than three weeks. It was first suspended by the PLC on 18 July 1997, and then repealed on 28 February 1998.

The repeal might be *ultra vires* the PLC. Once the amendment had been suspended and could not have any effect on the operation of the HKSAR, it could hardly be seen why its repeal would be "essential for ensuring the proper operation of the HKSAR", or that it would be a matter "which must be handled by the Provisional Legislative Council before the formation of the first Legislative Council."[22] Moreover, since *Tam Hing-yee* had already been reversed by the Bill of Rights (Amendment) Ordinance 1997, the repeal of the amendment ordinance in 1998 would not revive *Tam Hing-yee*. Hence, the application of the Bill of Rights to inter-citizen dispute is, by 1998, open to arguments.

## Other Human Rights Legislation

Apart from the Bill of Rights Ordinance, the PLC also suspended (and subsequently repealed) a number of other human rights legislation.[23] They were mainly concerned with labour rights, notably the right to collective bargaining which is enshrined in the International Labour Organization Convention No. 98. Ironically, Convention No. 98 has been extended to Hong Kong by the PRC.

Another two pieces of controversial legislation enacted by the PLC are the Immigration (Amendment)(No 3) Ordinance 1997 and the Adaptation of Laws (Interpretative Provision) Ordinance 1998, which will developed further in this chapter.

## An Executive-led Government

Since the electoral reform in 1995, the government has lost virtually all control over the legislature. There is no longer any appointed or official members on the Legislative Council. Party politics become more prominent, and there is no guarantee that any bill introduced by the government would be passed in its original form, or even in an amended form. Legislative councillors are more ready and willing to resort to the weapon of introducing private members' bills, and on a number of occasions, the government had to withdraw a bill altogether when it failed to stop or defeat an amendment introduced by private members. Members of the Legislative Council are also getting more critical of the government and are more ready to initiate or engage in debate on motions on government policies. Although these motion debates are not legally binding on the government, they did create an enormous pressure on the civil servants and the government. As 1 July 1997 approached, the out-going government, which was already working under great political constraints when making long-term policies, appeared defenceless in the light of growing criticisms from the legislature, and was generally labelled as a "lame-duck government"

In order to reassert the authority of the executive government and to ensure that the Legislative Council plays only a monitoring and not a leadership role, the SAR government decided to attack the two most important instruments of the Legislative Council, namely, the power to introduce motion debates and private members' bills. Indeed, restrictions already exist in the Basic Law, and the executive government has only to elaborate on these restrictions. It was unnecessary to do this to the PLC, which was first, a temporary body, and second, an appointed body which was unlikely to pose any threat to the executive government. However, as soon as the first Legislative Council was elected in May 1998, the executive government lost no time in proposing restrictions to curtail the powers of the Legislative Council, resulting in a rather tensed executive-legislative relationship.

One of the first tasks of the first Legislative Council was to agree on its own Rules of Procedures. On 30 June 1998, the Solicitor-General, in an unusual move, wrote to the Legal Advisor of the Legislative Council tendering the view of the Department of Justice on the incompatibility of certain aspects of the Rules of Procedures with the Basic Law. His concern was in four respects.

First, article 74 of the Basic Law provides that members of the Legislative Council may only introduce bills which do not relate to public expenditure or political structure or the operation of the government. The written consent of the chief executive shall be required before bills relating to government policies are

257

introduced. The Solicitor-General took the view that the restrictions in article 74 apply not only to the introduction of a bill, but also to the introduction of any amendment to a bill at the committee stage.

While article 74 may on its own appear ambiguous, it seems clear that it applies only to bills and not amendments to bills when the Basic Law is considered as a whole, including Annex II which clearly draws a distinction between bills and amendments to bills. The Solicitor-General argued that this would create an anomaly as members of the Legislative Council could achieve by way of a committee stage amendment which they could not introduce by way of a private member's bill. This argument is hardly convincing. A member cannot introduce any amendment he wishes; there are restrictions on the nature of an amendment that can be introduced. For example, an amendment must be relevant to the subject matter of the bill and to the subject matter of the clause to which it relates; it must be consistent with other clauses of the bill already agreed to, and must not be frivolous or meaningless.[24] Besides, unlike a private member's bill which the government cannot stop once it has been introduced, the government can withdraw any bill if it is not satisfied with the amendment introduced by a member. This has, indeed, been done on a number of occasions. Therefore, confining the scope of article 74 to bills and not committee stage amendments will not create any anomaly, especially when there are further self-imposed restrictions on the nature of amendments that can be introduced.

Second, rules 31 and 57(6) of the Rules of Procedures introduce a self-imposed restriction that no motion or amendment to motion or amendment to a bill may be introduced by a member, which has the object or effect of disposing of or charging any part of the revenue or other public moneys of Hong Kong, unless it has the written consent of the chief executive. This is generally known as the "charging effect test". The Solicitor-General held the view that these provisions were inconsistent with article 48(1) of the Basic Law, which regulates motions which have any effect on revenue or expenditure (that is, increases or decreases in revenue as well as increases or decreases in expenditure) as well as motions which are related to any other aspects of revenue or expenditure. In contrast, the charging effect test was narrower and more specific than the formulation of "regarding revenues or expenditure" specified in article 48(10) of the Basic Law.

This argument seems to be based on an erroneous reading of article 48(10) of the Basic Law. This article sets out the powers of the chief executive as follows: "to approve the introduction of motions regarding revenues or expenditure to the Legislative Council". Article 48(10) is about introduction of motions *to* the Legislative Council. It has nothing to do with introduction of motions by the Legislative Council. Thus, the effect of this article is that no public official can introduce a motion regarding revenues or expenditure *to* the Legislative Council without the approval of the chief executive, who is the head of the executive government of the HKSAR.

It is a well established constitutional practice in many common law jurisdictions that the Crown demands money, the Commons grant it, but the Commons do not authorize expenditure or seek to impose taxes unless required by the Crown.[25] This principle applied to the former Legislative Council. Clause XXIV of the Royal Instructions stipulated that "every ordinance, vote, resolution, or question, the object or effect of which may be to dispose of or charge any part of Our revenue arising ... shall be proposed by the Governor, unless the proposal of the same shall have been expressly allowed or directed by him." The same formulation is adopted in the Rules of Procedures of the Legislative Council of the HKSAR regarding the introduction of motions or amendments to motions (rule 31), and amendments to bills (rule 57(6)). Known as the charging effect test, it restricts members from introducing motions or amendments which would have the effect of reducing revenue or increasing expenditure. However, it does not cover motions or amendments which have the effect of increasing revenue or reducing expenditure.

As the Court of Appeal in *HKSAR v. David Ma* observed, the key element in the Basic Law is continuity.[26] Rules 31 and 57(6) faithfully reproduce the system prevailing before 1 July 1997. It is, therefore, difficult to see how these rules are in conflict with the Basic Law in general, or article 48(10) in particular, if it applies at all. In the absence of any evidence to the contrary, the phrase "regarding revenues or expenditure" must be construed in the light of the previous system in Hong Kong. Moreover, the proposal of the Solicitor-General is exceedingly wide and would deprive the Legislative Council of its right to debate on many motions dealing with matters of public interest in the absence of written consent from the chief executive.[27]

Third, the Solicitor-General argued that the chief executive, rather than the president or chairman of the Legislative Council, shall decide whether a bill is related to public expenditure or political structure or the operation of the government or government policies under article 74, or whether a motion falls within the ambit of article 48(10) of the Basic Law. This argument is so absurd that it needs only be stated to be rejected. The Legislative Council must be the master of its own house. Therefore, the question whether any bill or motion falls within the ambit of its own rules must be decided by the Legislative Council itself through its president. No doubt the president of the Legislative Council would consider the views of the government before it rules on such a question. If the government disagrees with the decision of the president of the Legislative Council, it may bring the matter to court, as ultimately it is a question of statutory interpretation. The argument that the chief executive is the best person to decide whether any bill relates to government policies is clearly misconceived. Taking this argument to its logical end, if the legislature disagrees with the government on the nature of a bill and takes the matter to court, it must follow, on the argument of the Solicitor-General, that the chief executive will be in the best position to construe the meaning of articles 48(1) and 74 of the Basic Law and, therefore, the interpretation and application of these provisions should be left to the government and not the judiciary. Such an absurd argument has been rejected time and again by the court.

The powers of the Legislative Council are set out in article 73, which includes raising questions on the work of the government, and receiving and debating the policy addresses of the chief executive. In order to achieve its role of monitoring the government, the Legislative Council should be an autonomous body independent of the executive government. It is, therefore, obvious that the chief executive should not have any power to dictate how the legislature is going to transact its business, subject only to whatever restraint there is regarding the introduction of bills.

260

Finally, relying on the difference between the Chinese language text and the English language text in Annex II of the Basic Law, the Solicitor-General argued that as far as the passage of government bills was concerned, which required a majority vote of members present, abstentions could not be counted in determining the voting outcome. However, for private members' bills which required a majority of those present, abstentions should be counted and, therefore, the majority had to be a majority of those present, including those who were present and abstained. Private members' bills are already subject to the requirement of a majority support of two separate groups of legislators. The effect of this argument is that it would be more difficult for private members' bills to be carried.

This argument is probably the best example of the "austerity of tabulated legalism".[28] It turns on the appearance of an extra Chinese character in the Chinese text of the Basic Law and draws a distinction between "a simple majority vote" and "a simple majority". It was argued that "a simple majority" referred to a simple majority of members present at a meeting, and this included those who were present but abstained. In contrast, "a simple majority vote" referred to the votes, and an abstention was not a vote and, therefore, should not be counted. The English language version does not draw such a distinction, but it was argued that the Chinese language version prevails.

It is well established that a constitution, such as the Basic Law, must be given a generous and purposive interpretation as opposed to a narrow, literal and technical meaning.[29] It is obvious that the broad purpose of the voting procedure as set out in Annex II of the Basic Law is that government proposals require only a simple majority, whereas a "two-house system" was introduced insofar as the passage of private members' proposals is concerned. This is, indeed, confirmed by Ji Peng Fei, Chairman of the Drafting Committee for the Basic Law of the HKSAR, when he introduced the draft Basic Law to the National People's Congress on 28 March 1990. He said:

> Annex II also stipulates that different voting procedures shall be adopted by the Legislative Council in handling bills introduced by the government and motions and bills

introduced by individual members of the Legislative Council. The passage of bills introduced by the government requires a simple majority vote of the members of the Legislative Council present. The passage of motions, bills or amendments to government bills introduced by individual members of the Legislative Council requires at least a simple majority vote by each of the two groups of members present, i.e., members returned by functional constituencies and those returned by geographical constituencies through direct elections and by the Election Committee. Such provisions take into consideration the interests of all social strata and will prevent endless debates over government bills, thus helping the government work with efficiency.

No such distinction has been drawn in the voting procedures of the Legislative Council prior to the changeover, and it was believed that the introduction of the "two-house system" was sufficient to curb the a number of amendments to government bills by private members. It did not appear that the drafters contemplated a further restriction on the power of private members to introduce bills or amendments by laying down different methods of vote counting for government bills and private members' bills. In neither the official English translation nor the original Chinese speech of Ji Peng Fei did he draw a distinction in the method of vote counting between the two types of bills.

All four proposals were rejected by the Legislative Council. However, the most interesting and, perhaps, the more important issue is the fact that these proposals were made in the first place. It is obvious that they represented not merely a technical view of the Department of Justice but a considered policy of the executive government.[30] They attempted to redefine the relationship between the executive government and the legislature by severely curtailing the ability of the Legislative Council to interfere with government bills or policies, thereby upsetting the existing checks and balances system. The attempt of the executive government to assert authority over the Legislative Council to the extent that the legislature is relegated to an opposition group is a retrograde step in the democratic movement of Hong Kong. It also resulted in a tense relationship between the legislature and the executive.

# Central-Local Relationship

While there were a lot of speculation, prior to the changeover, as to the degree of interference Beijing would exercise after it had resumed sovereignty over Hong Kong, the restraint displayed by the Beijing leaders in the last 20 months surprised even the most sceptical observers. Apart from the decision of the NPC declaring, in February 1997, that certain ordinances in Hong Kong were inconsistent with the Basic Law and the promulgation of the Garrison Law and its extension to Hong Kong in late 1996, Beijing has, on the whole, stayed away from the domestic affairs of the HKSAR. The most dramatic incident concerned the role of the Radio and Television Hong Kong (RTHK). RTHK is a government-owned and financed radio and television, yet it enjoys virtually complete editorial independence and produces high-quality programmes which are well received in Hong Kong. Among its current affairs programmes are various programmes which are very critical of the government of the HKSAR, and this has led to numerous criticisms on the proper role of the RTHK. It was argued that public funds should not be spent on a station which keeps producing satirical programmes and making sarcastic remarks about the government. When Xu Si-min, a long-time veteran supporter of the Beijing government and an influential public figure in Hong Kong, voiced his dissatisfaction at the RTHK at a meeting of the National Committee of the Chinese People's Political Consultative Conference (CPPCC), he was told that this was not a matter for the CPPCC. Both the chairman of the CPPCC and the president of the PRC reminded the people of Hong Kong that the domestic affairs of Hong Kong should be resolved in Hong Kong, and not in Beijing.

The restrained attitude of the Beijing leaders is partly due to their determination to uphold the principle of "one country, two systems", and partly due to their confidence in the chief executive in keeping Hong Kong within the confines of its autonomy. Indeed, on a number of occasions, the HKSAR government may have gone farther than necessary to protect perceived Beijing interest. A particularly pertinent example is the exemption of state organs from the HKSAR laws.

About eight months after the transfer of sovereignty over Hong Kong, the HKSAR government introduced an amendment to section 66 of the Interpretation and General Clauses Ordinance.[31] The original section 66 read:

> No Ordinance shall in any manner whatsoever affect the right of or be binding on the Crown unless it is therein expressly provided or unless it appears by necessary implication that the Crown is bound thereby.

The amendment sought to substitute the word "State" for "Crown". "State" is defined to include any central authorities of the PRC or any of their *subordinate organs* that exercise executive functions for which the central people's government has responsibility under the Basic Law and which do not exercise any commercial function. According to the HKSAR government, the amendment was purely technical: "Its effect is to reflect the reunification, but otherwise to maintain the legal position as it was immediately before, and after, the reunification ... this is not an exercise of law reform. The Bill does no more than to retain and adapt to the common law principle in section 66."[32] Therefore, in one stroke, PRC organs exercising executive functions are now equated with the "Crown" and inherit the colonial principle that they are not subject to the ordinary law of the land unless otherwise stated.

The principle that the Crown is not bound by statutes, save by express words or necessary implication, has its origin as a prerogative immunity.[33] Without going into the historical and legal details,[34] it suffices to point out that it is at least highly doubtful whether this presumption of Crown immunity from legislation could survive the change of sovereignty. The constitutional rationale for the exemption, namely that the Crown made law for its subject, has no application to the State in the post-1997 constitutional regime of the HKSAR. Under the Basic Law, the State has no power to make law for the HKSAR, save perhaps, the power to remit local legislation for being inconsistent with the Basic Law and the power to amend the Basic Law.[35] Yet even in these situations the power is vested only in the Standing Committee of the NPC, and not in any of its subordinate organs.

The HKSAR government admitted that there could be different views on the wisdom or desirability of retaining section 66, but it insisted that this would be law reform and not adaptation of the law and is hence outside the scope of the amendment exercise. This kind of formal distinction hardly addresses the issue. At heart, the issue is whether state organs, as defined in the Bill, should be presumed not to be subject to Hong Kong laws unless otherwise stated. To draw a hair-splitting distinction between law reform and the adaptation of law on such a crucial and fundamental matter of principle is to push formality to its extremity.[36]

There are more fundamental grounds of objection. Article 22 of the Basic Law expressly provides that "All offices set up in the Hong Kong Special Administrative Region by departments of the Central Government, or by provinces, autonomous regions, or municipalities directly under the Central Government, and the personnel of these offices shall abide by the laws of the Region." This article was introduced to allay the fears of the people of Hong Kong that central organs stationed in Hong Kong after the change of sovereignty would be above the law. The new section 66 reverses the presumption in article 22 of the Basic Law. The HKSAR government argued that PRC organs which fell within the definition of "State" would continue to be bound by Hong Kong laws, as the general criminal law, the Bill of Rights, civil law and ordinances which bind the Crown would apply to the State.[37] Yet it was a particularly disturbing coincidence that the amendment came shortly after the Secretary for Justice decided not to prosecute Xinhua News Agency, the *de facto* PRC embassy in Hong Kong before 1997, for a breach of the Personal Data (Privacy) Ordinance.[38] There is a huge body of law which has not been expressly stated to be applicable to the Crown, such as those relating to fire services, third-party motor insurance, personal data protection, town planning, building construction, and environmental protection. Do they apply to the State? It would be highly undesirable to leave such an important question to "necessary implication".[39] Even if the State is prepared to comply with these laws which do not apply to it explicitly or by necessary implication, the effect of section 66 is that the State obeys the law not as a matter of necessity, but as a matter of grace, a proposition which "would reverse the result of the Civil War".[40]

Indeed, the new section 66 expands the scope of the common law. The "State" is a new concept and not a mere adaptation. It covers the central people's authorities in the exercise of their "executive functions", which is undefined. Under the Basic Law, the central people's government is already responsible for national defence and foreign affairs, which are outside the scope of autonomy of the HKSAR.[41] The HKSAR legislature and the judiciary have no jurisdiction in these areas.[42] What other "executive functions" should the central people's authorities and their subordinate organs have and exercise in the HKSAR which should not be regulated by the laws of the HKSAR? So far the HKSAR government is unable to give a satisfactory answer.

Despite strong criticisms from the legal profession and from many quarters of the community, the amendment was passed by the Provisional Legislative Council by an overwhelming majority on the second last day of its short and controversial life.[43] The resumed second debates were over in less than 30 minutes.[44]

# The Judiciary

## Court of Final Appeal

Despite the many destructive consequences of British imperialism, a positive contribution it has made is the transplantation of the common law to its colonies and occupied territories. A rational legal system imbued with the common law characterized by its concern for procedural justice and fairness was invariably set up, with the judicial committee of the Privy Council situated in London as the court of final appeal. Although it is not the court of final appeal in England, the Privy Council comprises the finest legal brains in the House of Lords and the courts of final appeal of many Commonwealth countries. Thus, it is of no coincidence that a number of former colonies still retain the Privy Council as their court of final appeal even after they have become independent. Apart from the fine quality of the judgments rendered by the Privy Council, which is no doubt enhanced by the stature and eminence of the judges thereon, the Privy Council sometimes also serves a political function of stabilizing the domestic legal system, especially one in its infancy, because of its renowned independence and impartiality as it is unlikely to be vulnerable to domestic politics or executive influences.

Until 30 June 1997, the Privy Council was the court of final appeal for Hong Kong. It was regarded as unacceptable, as a matter of sovereignty, to retain the Privy Council as the court of final appeal for Hong Kong after the changeover. Hence, the Sino-British Joint Declaration 1984 provides that the HKSAR would set up its own court of final appeal, which may, if required, invite judges from other common law jurisdictions to sit on it. This promise was written into the Basic Law in due course as article 84.[45]

The Court of Final Appeal Ordinance, which was a result of a prolonged negotiation between China and the United Kingdom, was enacted in 1995 but only came into force on 1 July 1997. As required by the Basic Law, the chief justice has to be a Chinese citizen who is a Hong Kong permanent resident with no right of abode in any foreign country. The Court of Final Appeal comprises a panel of local judges, which includes four permanent judges and a panel of non-permanent local judges, mostly former judges of Hong Kong, and a panel of overseas judges. Each hearing will be presided by five judges, amongst whom there can only be one overseas judge.

Shortly before the changeover, there was anxiety as to whether the Court of Final Appeal would be able to maintain its independence, especially when the PRC government had shown a keen interest and determination to have its voice heard on its composition and jurisdiction when the Court of Final Appeal Ordinance was drafted.[46] Indeed, in the last two years preceding the changeover, there was a dramatic rise in the number of appeals to the Privy Council and a frantic attempt to meet the deadline for the last hearing before the Privy Council, which rendered its last judgment as the final court of appeal of Hong Kong on 26 June 1997.[47] Thus, the Court of Final Appeal has to establish its own reputation against the tide of speculation.

Similar to the previous system of appealing to the Privy Council, leave is required for an appeal to the Court of Final Appeal. Leave will only be granted when the appeal involves a point of law of great and general importance, or when the amount of claims in civil cases exceed HK$1 million.[48] Like the court of final appeal in other jurisdictions, decisions are made by a majority vote, and dissenting opinions are permitted. The Court of Final Appeal is also determined to have the best legal arguments and has shown a keen interest in having *amicus curiae* in appropriate cases to address the court.[49] By 1 October 1998, the Court of Final Appeal has rendered only eight substantive judgments.

The nature of cases before the Court of Final Appeal is not much different from that presented before the Privy Council before the changeover. Indeed, most of them involved rather mundane technical issues. The quality of judgments varies somewhat though they are better than many judgments of the former Court of Appeal. The approach of the court is largely legalistic and technical. With perhaps one or two exceptions, the court has seldom considered the values underlying our system nor the issues in a wider context. Nor has the court shown itself to be a liberal institution.[50] The range of authorities considered by the court is also relatively narrow. Cases cited by the court are predominantly English authorities, with some references to Australian and New Zealand and Canadian authorities.

In *Tang Siu Man v. HKSAR*,[51] the issue was whether the trial judge, in directing the jury on the relevance of the good character of the appellant, was obliged to direct the jury not only on the relevance of credibility but also on his propensity to commit a crime, a standard direction known as the *Vye* directions. The court decided, by a majority, that it was not necessary to impose the *Vye* directions on trial judges. The majority held that the fundamental rule was that a summing up must be fair and balanced, so that the jury could properly weigh up the true issues. The appellate courts should be slow to impose artificial rules in criminal practices. After all, the jury must be presumed to be imbued with intelligence and common sense. Having considered the policy behind the *Vye* directions, the manner *Vye* directions was applied in practice, and the practice in Hong Kong and in other common law jurisdictions, the majority decided to depart from the more rigid approach in England and in New Zealand. Bokhary PJ, however, delivered a strong dissenting judgment. Building up a case on how an accused's character was handled in a jury trial in the present state of the law in Hong Kong, he concluded that notwithstanding the level of intelligence or common sense of the jury, the concern for protecting the innocent from being wrongfully convicted had always been answered by a reference to the features built into the system of criminal justice, and therefore there was a minimum content which must be included in all directions to the jury. He accepted that the form of the direction could be flexible, but the message was generally mandatory. In the facts of that case, Bokhary PJ found that the failure to give a *Vye* direction constituted a non-direction. In this regard he was influenced by the fact that the jury returned a verdict of a majority of five to two only.

This is by far the best judgment rendered by the Court of Final Appeal. In both the majority and the dissenting judgments, there is a general survey of law and practice, an analytical approach to precedents and an appreciation of common sense, without losing sight of the underlying policies, backed up by a comparative approach in the practice of common law jurisdictions. It is this kind of judgment that will enhance the reputation of the Court of Final Appeal.

On the whole, it is fair to say that the Court of Final Appeal has established its reputation as an independent and impartial tribunal and is eager to demonstrate its independence and its legal leadership. Indeed, the chief justice himself insisted on his presence in a number of important ceremonial occasions to demonstrate the presence of the judiciary and its role as one of the three branches of government. However, the court has not shown itself to be a liberal institution. Nor has it so far faced any real challenges in the sense that most of the cases before it involved largely technical/legal and not political issues. Time will come when the assertion of its independence comes into conflict with fundamental interests of the executive government or the central people's government. This will be the litmus test of its strength, and the first occasion is likely to arise in the coming appeal in *Cheung Lai Kwan v. Director of Immigration* (see below).

## A Few Controversial Decisions

It has been argued elsewhere that, on the whole, judicial attitude towards human rights even before the changeover is largely conservative, inward-looking and parochial.[52] There is nothing to suggest a change of this attitude in the first 12 months after the changeover. Indeed, the predominant concern of the judiciary during this period seems to be continuity and stability.

It has already been pointed out earlier that the HKSAR government appeared to be more willing to prosecute demonstrators who transgressed the law. A number of such prosecutions had taken place and most of them were successful. In *HKSAR v. Tam Chun-yin*,[53] the defendants wished to demonstrate against the World Bank and the International Monetary Fund which were holding their meetings in Hong Kong. The police refused to give permission to the defendants to demonstrate in areas outside the designated area. After an unsuccessful negotiation, the defendants attempted to get to an area nearer the meeting place by taking an alternative route. When they found that the alternative route had been cordoned off, they came into direct confrontation with the police. They were convicted of various offences, including obstructing police officers in the due execution of their duties and assaulting police officers. While the decision was largely factual, it is interesting to note what the magistrate expected the demonstrators to do when they were ordered by the police to leave the scene:

> D5 was in a similar position. Her position was significantly different as she was not an organiser [sic]. The video tape depicts her at the forefront of the protesters, shouting and chanting. She is blocked by a police cordon, she refused to retreat. A police woman, PW5, is seen approaching her and talking to her, still D5 remains at the police cordon. I did not accept all the testimony of PW5. Although she may have been telling the court the whole truth, the video tape did not support her complete testimony. PW5 stated that there was body contact between her and D5, the video tape does not show this. On this point I gave D5 the benefit of the doubt. I find that D5 should have retreated, that she should have gone back to the bulk of the protesters who were behind the two police cordons, as requested by the police to do so. The video

clearly illustrates that the police wanted her to retreat, she chooses not to do so.

It was the police duty to clear the walkway so that normal pedestrian traffic could be maintained. D5 chooses to stand her ground, her remonstrations are clearly seen on the video. I accept that she was agitated, this however is not a legally justifiable excuse. I found that D5 deliberately chooses to remain at the police cordon line, yelling and chanting, making it more difficult for the police to carry out their duties and that it was her intention to make it more difficult for the police to carry out their duties. It was for this reason that I convicted D5 of obstructing a police constable in the due execution of his duty.

In *HKSAR v. Ng Kung-siu*,[54] the defendants were convicted of two charges of desecrating the national flag and the regional flag, contrary to section 7 of the National Flag and National Emblem Ordinance and section 7 of the Regional Flag and Regional Emblem Ordinance. Both ordinances were passed by the Provisional Legislative Council and took effect on 1 July 1997. The defendants argued that the offences constituted an unjustifiable restriction on the freedom of expression under the ICCPR as applied to Hong Kong, which was entrenched by article 39 of the Basic Law. They relied on two flag burning cases by the United States Supreme Court, which held by majority that the respective state and federal legislation prohibiting desecration of the US flag were unconstitutional for being inconsistent with the First Amendment on free speech. In a disappointing and highly nationalistic judgment, the magistrate referred to a popular song composed during the suppression of the students' movement in Tiananmen Square in June 1989 to show that the national flag has been and should remain a sacred symbol respected by all Chinese regardless of their social, political or philosophical beliefs. Referring to some riots in the 1950s resulting from desecrating the Taiwanese Kuomintang (KMT) flag, and despite the fact that most events commemorating the 1989 democratic movement in Beijing were held in Hong Kong in a peaceful and orderly manner, the magistrate found that "the government should not overlook such real possibility of social disorder caused by desecration of the national flag in public." He further held that if the national flag represented the idea of one country, the HKSAR flag represented the idea of two systems within this concept and, therefore, the regional flag should enjoy no less protection than that of the national flag. He found no violation of the ICCPR or the Basic Law.

While the magistrate might be correct in his conclusion, what is worrying is the nationalistic tone of his judgment, his failure to discuss arguments contrary to his nationalistic view, and his cavalier approach to evidence. The judgment appears more like a political manifesto than a carefully reasoned and argued legal decision. There was no reference or analysis of the authorities relied upon by the defendants; instead, the magistrate was content to cite one sentence from the dissenting judgment of Rehnquist CJ in *Texas v. Johnson* that "the flag is not simply another 'idea' or 'point of view' competing for recognition in the marketplace of ideas." There was no evidence that desecrating the national or regional flag would attract a hostile audience, and regulation of hated speech is one of the most difficult issues in freedom of expression. Unfortunately, the judgment is devoid of any intellectual discussion on these issues. The defendants have since lodged an appeal.

The decision of the Court of Appeal in *HKSAR v. David Ma* has already been referred to in the section on the Provisional Legislative Council. In considering whether the Provisional Legislative Council was legally constituted, the Court of Appeal has repeatedly stressed that the main theme of the Basic Law was stability and continuity. The court rejected the relevance of the doctrine of necessity (which is a narrower doctrine in the common law), but the essence of its holding was that the establishment of the Provisional Legislative Council was necessary. The predominant concern of the Court of Appeal was that the transfer of sovereignty should not result in a chaotic situation in Hong Kong, and this concern prompted the court to rely on a vague notion of sovereignty to justify the establishment of the Provisional Legislative Council which the court admitted was outside the Basic Law.

A final decision which should be mentioned is *Cheung Lai Wah v. Director of Immigration*,[55] which raised the difficult question of the right of abode of children born to Hong Kong permanent residents in Mainland China and the one-way permit system. Over the years, many Hong Kong permanent residents[56] got married in Mainland China and have children born there. Prior to 1 July 1997, the PRC authorities operated a one-way exit permit system under which a certain quota of persons living in Mainland China were permitted to settle in Hong Kong. The one-way exit permit system was handled entirely by the public security bureau in Mainland China, and the Immigration Department in Hong Kong had no part to play on the issue or in the allocation of permits, though it was generally consulted on the size of the quota. Children born in Mainland China to Hong Kong permanent residents did not acquire any right of abode in Hong Kong before the changeover.

Under article 24 of the Basic Law, children born outside Hong Kong to a parent who is a Hong Kong permanent resident are qualified to be Hong Kong permanent residents. In anticipation of the coming into effect of the Basic Law on 1 July 1997, many of these children entered Hong Kong clandestinely or overstayed in Hong Kong under a visitor permit system (the two-way permit system). After 1 July 1997, they approached the Immigration Department seeking recognition of their status as permanent residents of the HKSAR and the issuance of identity cards.

On 10 July 1997, the Provisional Legislative Council enacted the Immigration (Amendment) (No. 3) Ordinance 1997.[57] The amendment introduced a certificate of entitlement scheme under which the status of a claimant of HKSAR permanent resident can only be established by holding a valid travel document and a valid certificate of entitlement affixed to such travel document, unless he can produce a valid HKSAR passport or a valid permanent identity card issued to him. One can only apply for the certificate of entitlement in the Mainland. An application for a one-way exit permit would be regarded as an application for a certificate of entitlement, and the certificate will be affixed to the one-way exit permit at the immigration control point when the applicant arrives in Hong Kong. The result is that even if a child can prove that he satisfies the requirements under article 24 of the Basic Law to be a Hong Kong permanent resident, he is not eligible to make such a claim unless he is in possession of the necessary certificate of entitlement. Possession of the certificate becomes the sole and exclusive means of proof of the status of Hong Kong permanent residents. This requirement does not, of course, exist in article 24 of the Basic Law. The amendment went through all three readings in one day, and operated retrospectively on 1 July 1997.

As a result, all children already in Hong Kong on or before 10 July 1997, who were born in Mainland China to a Hong Kong permanent resident, are liable to immediate removal. For this group of children, the requirement of having been in possession of a certificate of entitlement before they can enjoy the right of abode in Hong Kong is an impossible requirement which they could in no way comply with before 10 July 1997. It is a fiction created to nullify their right of abode. Moreover, both the children and their parents could be guilty of various immigration offences. The Bar was outraged by such retrospective legislation and called for an emergency meeting. After the meeting, over a hundred barristers signed up to act for these children on a *pro bona* basis to prevent them from being summarily removed. Eventually, legal aid was granted and the Immigration Department undertook not to remove any of these children until the final determination of the judicial review. *Cheung Lai Wah v. Director of Immigration* was lodged as a test case.[58] The applicants argued, *inter alia*, that the amendment was inconsistent with article 24 of the Basic Law. One of the issues before the court was the retrospective operation of the amendment. It was argued that an unqualified constitutional right of abode in Hong Kong of those who were already in Hong Kong on or before 10 July 1997 was retrospectively taken away.

At first instance, Keith J held that the amendment could be justified by article 22(4) of the Basic Law, which provided:

> For entry into the Hong Kong Special Administrative Region, people from other parts of China must apply for approval. Among them, the number of persons who enter the Region for the purpose of settlement shall be determined by the competent authorities of the Central People's Government after consulting the government of the Region.

It was held that persons coming to Hong Kong "for the purpose of settlement" included those persons who enjoyed the right of abode under article 24 but who were living in Mainland China. Counsel for the applicants argued that article 22, being in the section on the relationship between the central government and the HKSAR, applied only to those who did not have a right of abode in Hong Kong and who wanted to come to the HKSAR for settlement. It did not apply to those who were already Hong Kong permanent residents under article 24. It was also powerfully argued that the reliance on article 22(4) was a "monumental afterthought", as neither the drafting documents of the Basic Law Drafting Committee nor the debates in the Provisional Legislative Council referred to this article at all. These arguments, however, did not persuade the judge.

On the question of retrospectivity, the reasoning of the trial judge is most curious. In the first place, he held that since the right of abode of these children were already curtailed by article 22 of the Basic Law, which came into effect on 1 July 1997, there was no retrospective denial of their right of abode. As to the other argument based on article 12(1) of the Hong Kong Bill of Rights, Keith J said:[59]

> This argument proceeds on the assumption that art 12(1) of the Hong Kong Bill of Rights prohibits legislation which exposes persons to the possibility of prosecution for conduct which was not criminal at the time of the conduct. I do not construe art 12(1) in that way. I construe art 12(1) as prohibiting the prosecution of persons for conduct which was not criminal at the time of the conduct. After all, if a person cannot be prosecuted for such conduct, no question of him being exposed to the possibility of prosecution arises. Indeed, that is far more consistent with the language of art 12(1): "No one shall be held guilty of any criminal offence ..." I know that two commentators on the equivalent provision (art 7(1)) in the European Convention on Human Rights take a different view, but the *travaux préparatoires* of art 15(1) of the ICCPR are inconclusive. Accordingly, the challenge to the No. 3 Ordinance on the basis of retrospectivity fails. What could be challenged successfully is any prosecution on the basis of a contravention between 1 and 10 July of s 38(1)(a) of the Immigration Ordinance.

In short, the legislature is free to enact retrospective provisions, but no one could be prosecuted for violating these retrospective provisions! With respect, this would be the most curious kind of reasoning. As counsel for the applicants forcefully argued on appeal, "if the judge were right, it would mean that the lawmakers could with impunity stigmatize as offences acts which were perfectly lawful at the time they occurred and deny these people the right to have the law declared invalid and their innocence vindicated in a court of law."[60]

The Court of Appeal confirmed the decision of Keith J that the new certificate system was justified by article 22 of the Basic Law, but differed on the issue of retrospectivity. Chan CJHC held that there was no justification whatsoever for the retrospective provision and found it unconstitutional. Accordingly, those who arrived in Hong Kong before 10 July 1997 could not have their constitutional right of abode taken away. He reaffirmed that the courts have always viewed retrospective provisions with caution and disfavour, and would be slow to uphold retrospective provisions unless there is clear and express provision to that effect, especially when they affect accrued rights.[61]

This strong conviction against retrospective application of legislation provision was not shared by the other two judges. Mortimer VP upheld the retrospective provision.[62] He found that "a retrospective provision in legislation is not *per se* unconstitutional or unlawful, or in breach of the Bill of Rights or the ICCPR, as applied in the Basic Law. [Accordingly], it cannot be said that the Ordinance has by its retrospective provision arbitrarily deprived the applicants of an accrued right of abode when the exercise of the right of abode is constitutionally limited and the provisions of Ordinance No. 3 are themselves consistent with the Basic Law." Nazareth VP adopted a halfway house solution. Having held that the amendment was constitutional because of article 22(4) of the Basic Law, he took the view that the amendment should not affect any person who had arrived in Hong Kong before 1 July 1997, but those who were here between 1 and 10 July 1997 would be caught by the amendment. Since article 22(4) came into effect on 1 July 1997, the retrospective provision was sanctioned by article 22(4) and accordingly it was not unconstitutional.[63]

The concern of the HKSAR government, which is shared by the judiciary, is a sudden influx of children into Hong Kong, which may exert tremendous pressure on the resources in housing, education, medical and other social services. The applicants argued that should their challenge be successful, it would only force the government to consider other means to accommodate the settlement of these children in the Mainland. Unfortunately, instead of working out these alternative measures, the government chose an easy way out by legislation. The new certificate system effectively means that only those who are approved by the PRC authorities to come to settle in Hong Kong under the one-way permit system will enjoy a right of abode in Hong Kong. Despite recent improvements, the one-way permit system, which is administered solely by the PRC authorities, has long been criticized for being administered in a corrupt and unfair manner. Yet under the new certificate system, the right of abode of a person in Hong Kong is now made dependent on the administrative decision of an authority outside the control of the HKSAR.

Even if the concern of the government and the judiciary, is justifiable, it is difficult to see what damages would have been done to Hong Kong to permit those children who have already arrived in Hong Kong before 10 July 1997, the date of the amendment introducing the new certificate system, to stay in Hong Kong. The number is finite, and the law is at best ambiguous. Yet the judiciary failed to uphold the time-honoured aspiration of the common law that retrospective legislation is to be sanctioned in the most critical manner. It is perhaps worth quoting fully the powerful view of the chief judge on this issue:

> The retrospective provision in the present case does not fit in comfortably with reality. How can the Ordinance say that the appellants do not have the status of permanent residents and the right of abode when in actual fact they can clearly show that they have? How can it be said that between 1st and 9th July 1997, a person (whether he be in Mainland China or in Hong Kong) could apply for a certificate of entitlement when the necessary forms were not even in existence until the 10th July when the law was passed or even 11th July 1997 when the Director's Notice was issued? The Director could not possibly have issued any certificates during that

period. If these appellants had applied for and had been issued permanent identity cards between 1st and 9th July 1997 before the amendment to the provisions of the Registration of Persons Regulations by the No. 3 Ordinance, would they have been able to fall within section 2AA of the No. 3 Ordinance? Presumably they would not. This is because the Ordinance was deemed to have taken effect on 1st July and these people did not have permanent identity cards on that date but only obtained them after that date. What then would their status be? What would happen to their accrued rights? As the authors of Bennion, *Statutory Interpretation*, 2nd ed., say at p. 215: "Retrospectivity is artificial, deeming a thing to be what it was not. Artificiality and make-believe are generally repugnant to law as the servant of human welfare".

The case is now on its way to the Court of Final Appeal. However, a difficult constitutional issue will arise there. Under article 158 of the Basic Law, before the HKSAR court renders its final judgment which is not subject to further appeal, and if the judgment raises an interpretation of a provision of the Basic Law concerning the responsibility of the central people's government or the relationship between the central authorities and the region, the court should seek an interpretation from the Standing Committee of the National People's Congress, whose interpretation will be binding on the Hong Kong court. The crux of the *Cheung Lai Wah* case turns on the meaning of article 22 of the Basic Law, which falls within the chapter on the relationship between the central authorities and the region. If article 158 applies, then the Court of Final Appeal will have to refer the interpretation of article 22 of the Basic Law to the NPCSC. However, once the NPCSC gives an interpretation of article 22 of the Basic Law, in this case whether this article permits the HKSAR authorities to introduce a new certificate system, there is not much left for the Court of Final Appeal to decide. This will raise all kinds of difficult issues, such as whether the parties to the appeal have a right to make submission to the NPCSC, whether the Court of Final Appeal should render an opinion to "help" the NPCSC in reaching its decision, as after all, it involves also the interpretation of the Hong Kong law. Apart from article 158 of the Basic Law, there is no procedure governing the referral to the NPCSC. Under article 158, the NPCSC has to consult the Basic Law committee, which comprises both Hong Kong and mainland members. What should the role of the Basic Law committee be? The Basic Law committee comprises non-lawyers and the NPCSC is basically a political organ, yet their interpretation of law is binding on the Court of Final Appeal and prevails over the collective wisdom of five eminent judges of the highest calibre. The credibility, or perceived credibility of the Court of Final Appeal, and that of "one country, two systems", will be subject to strenuous test when this issue arises in a few months' time.

# Conclusion

First July 1997 is a paradoxical date. It marks the end of the 150-year long British administration in Hong Kong and the beginning of a new era — a transition from a colony to a special administrative region with a high degree of autonomy, but very much under the umbrella of one sovereignty. To the ruling regime in Beijing, the date marks the accomplishment of one of the two most important tasks they set for themselves — the reunification of Hong Kong and the reunification of Taiwan. The experiment of "one country, two systems" has to be successful in order to show to the whole world in general and Taiwan in particular that Hong Kong continues to prosper after reuniting with the motherland. In this regard, success is measured largely by reference to economic prosperity and social stability. To the ruling regime in Hong Kong, 1 July 1997 is a date when Hong Kong people become masters of their own house. It is not only the beginning of a new era, but also the beginning of a new identity. With an affluent and thriving economy, it is time for the government to reassert its much damaged and challenged leadership immediately before the changeover and to lead Hong Kong to a new era when people in Hong Kong can enjoy the fruit of economic success.

The form of governance has to be executive-led, and the introduction and implementation of government policies should be subject to minimal interference, particularly from the legislature. Social stability is of equal importance, as it reinforces the credibility and competence of the ruling government and creates a vital environment for economic prosperity. It will also minimize the need for any direct interference from Beijing. A restrained central government and a harmonious central–local relationship can only be conducive to the establishment or re-establishment of the authority of the ruling government in Hong Kong. The acquisition of a new identity means something quite different to the legislature and the judiciary. The legislature, with a partial mandate from the people, demands an accountable government, and is not prepared to be downgraded as an opposition party. With the establishment of the Court of Final Appeal, the judiciary is equally eager to assert its role as one of the three branches of government, independent of the legislature and the executive. Replacing the Privy Council, the Court of Final Appeal may well regard itself as the final protector of the rule of law and human rights. To the business and other elite classes in Hong Kong, it is important to maintain continuity of the economic and legal systems, through which they have so far enjoyed much success. Assertion of a new identity is of little importance, and may even be dangerous. Whilst there are other players in the constitutional scenes, these different political forces largely shape the constitutional development in the first year of life of the HKSAR.

On the whole, the transition from a colony to a special administrative region has been smooth. The chief executive has won the confidence and the support of the Beijing government, a task which he regarded as excessively important. The price for this is that legislative and executive measures were taken to eliminate anything which might worry Beijing, particularly human rights legislation and control over public assemblies and demonstrations. Partly for this reason, the Beijing leadership has lived up to its promise not to interfere with the domestic affairs of Hong Kong. Indeed, to the credit of the Beijing leadership, it has exercised a high degree of self-restraint and positively avoided getting itself involved in Hong Kong's domestic affairs.

Domestically, the previous social, economic and legal systems are maintained without major changes. There is no major political crisis or suppression of human rights, notwithstanding the repeal of a number of human rights legislation and the stepping up in the control of public assemblies and demonstrations. It is perhaps ironic that apart from the illegal immigrant cases, there is a dearth of legal challenges relying on either the Basic Law or the Bill of Rights, which is in stark contrast with the situation when the Bill of Rights was first introduced in 1991. Indeed, it was unexpected that the major crisis faced by the HKSAR government concerned economic and financial issues. Yet these economic and financial crises have subjected the ability and leadership of the executive government to the most strenuous test.

The Provisional Legislative Council has suffered from a lack of legitimacy from the date of its inception, and it has never been able to recover from this handicap. With the establishment of the first Legislative Council in May 1998, the transition has largely been completed. As the chief executive designate, Tung Chee-hwa remarked that Hong Kong spends too much time on politics, it is therefore ironic that one of the programmes undertaken by the executive government is to build up a strong executive-led government, which necessarily reduces the power of the legislature. A weak and uncritical Provisional Legislative Council did help to create a strong executive-led government though an unintended consequence is that the political pressure, which used to be borne by politicians, now falls directly on the principal policy officials of the government, and the civil service is apparently not ready to take up such political pressure.

The lack of a dominating political party in the first Legislative Council reinforces the determination of the executive government to assert its leadership, an issue which has led to a rather tense relationship between the legislature and the executive government in recent months. On a number of occasions, the executive government has even threatened to take out judicial review against the decisions of the Legislative Council. The Legislative Council is not prepared to give way. It would be unfortunate if the judiciary is brought into the power struggle between the executive and the legislative bodies. It may perhaps be time for the executive government to reconsider what an executive-led government means, otherwise a political/constitutional crisis may easily develop. The judiciary has by and large remained rather conservative, and the Court of Final Appeal is largely untested on sensitive political or human rights affairs. At the same time, the recognition of a new identity on the part of the Court of Final Appeal and the determination of the chief justice to build up a strong Court of Final Appeal can easily result in an assertive and eager judiciary that may not find favour with the equally assertive executive. The balance of power has never been so delicate in the history of Hong Kong.

## NOTES

1. For a more detailed account, see J. Chan, "Representation in Dispute: Will Hong Kong People really Rule Hong Kong?", *China Rights Forum: The Journal of Human Rights in China* (1996), pp. 4–7, 38–39.

2. *Ng King Luen v. Rita Fan* (1997) 7 HKPLR 281.

3. *HKSAR v. David Ma* [1997] 2 HKC 315.

4. See, for example, J. Chan, "The Jurisdiction and Legality of the Provisional Legislative Council" (1997) 27 *Hong Kong Law Journal* 374; Y. Ghai, "Dark Day for our Rights", *South China Morning Post*, 30 July 1997.

5. See note 4 above.

6. *Cheung Lai Wah v. Director of Immigration (No. 2)* [1998] 2 HKC 382.

7. Decision of the Preparatory Committee, dated 24 March 1996, on the Establishment of a Provisional Legislative Council of the HKSAR, para 5, reproduced in (1997) 27 *Hong Kong Law Journal* 11.

8. For a detailed comment on these amendments, see J. Chan, "Human Rights: From One Era to Another", in Joseph Cheng (ed.), *The Other Hong Kong Report 1997* (Chinese University Press, 1997), pp. 137–67.

9. See "Siracusa Principles on the Limitation and Derogation Provisions in the ICCPR", (1985) 7 *Human Rights Quarterly* 3–14, and Erica-Irene Daes, *Freedom of the Individual under Law*, Special Rapporteur's Report to the United Nations Sub-Commission on Prevention of Discrimination and Protection of Minorities, UN Sales No E99.XIV.5 (United Nations, 1990).

10. Reported in Hong Kong Journalist Association, *Annual Report 1998*, p. 11.

11. See, for example, *HKSAR v. Tam Chun-yin* (1998) Mag, ESC 5206 of 1997 (3 June 1998).

12. See *South China Morning Post*, 26 May 1998.

13. Section 2, Societies Ordinance (Cap. 115). A society which is established solely for religious, charitable, social or recreational purposes or as a rural committee can be exempted, but even in such cases exemption has to be sought: section 5A.

14. Hong Kong Bar Association, *Submission on the Consultation Document on Civil Liberties and Social Order*, 23 April 1997.

15. To make things worse, any appeal against the decision of the Societies Officer shall be made to the chief executive in council, and not to an independent tribunal, which is the case when there is an appeal against the decision of the Police Commissioner under the Public Order Ordinance.

16. Chief Executive's Office, *Civil Liberties and Social Order: Consultation Document* (April 1997), para 4.4.

17. The Chinese press statement and an English translation can be found in J. Chan (ed.), "United Kingdom: British Dependent Territories — Hong Kong", Booklet 5, in A. Blaustein's *Constitutions of Dependencies and Special Sovereignties* (New York: Oceana Publications, 1995), pp. 87–88.

18. The papers of the Attorney-General's Chambers and the Hong Kong Bar Association are produced in J. Chan and G. Edwards (eds.), *Hong Kong's Bill of Rights: Two Years before 1997* (Faculty of Law, University of Hong Kong, 1995), Appendixes C and E respectively.

19. See, for example, *Secretary for Justice v. Oriental Press Group Ltd* [1998] 2 HKC 627, p. 672; *Cheung Lai Wah v. Director of Immigration* [1997] 3 HKC 64, pp. 88–89.

20. (1991) 1 *HKPLR* 276.

21. See Letter of the Hong Kong Bar Association to the Secretary for Justice dated 3 September 1997. For a criticism on *Tam Hing Yee v. Wu Tai-wai*, see for example, *Bill of Rights Bulletin*, v. 1, n. 2, pp. 1–4; J. Chan and Y. Ghai, "A Comparative Perspective on the Bill of Rights", in J. Chan & Y. Ghai (eds.), *The Hong Kong Bill of Rights: A Comparative Approach* (Singapore: Butterworths, 1993), pp. 23–26; A. Byrnes, "The Hong Kong Bill of Rights and Relations between Private Individuals", in Chan and Ghai, ibid., pp. 80–91; N. Jayawickrama, "Interpreting the Hong Kong Bill of Rights", in W. Angus and J. Chan (eds.), *Canada–Hong Kong: Human Rights and Privacy Law Issues* (Toronto: Joint Centre for Asia Pacific Studies, 1994), pp. 76–79.

22. Decision of the Preparatory Committee, dated 24 March 1996, on the Establishment of a Provisional Legislative Council of the HKSAR, para 5, reproduced in (1997) 27 *Hong Kong Law Journal* 11.

23. They were the Trade Unions (Amendment)(No. 2) Ordinance 1997 (Ord. No. 102 of 1997), Employee's Rights to Representation, Consultation and Collective Bargaining Ordinance 1997 (Ord. No. 101 of 1997), and Employment (Amendment)(No. 4) Ordinance 1997 (Ord. No. 98 of 1997). See Legislative Provisions (Suspension of Operation) Ordinance 1997 (Ord. No. 126 of 1997).

24. Rule 57(4), Rules of Procedures of the Legislative Council.

25. This forms the basic principles governing the financial relationship between the Crown and Parliament in the United Kingdom, Australia and Canada.

26. [1997] 2 HKC 315.

27. Under article 73(6) of the Basic Law, the Legislative Council can "debate any issue concerning public interests".

28. *Minister of Home Affairs v. Fisher* [1980] AC 319 at 328–29, per Lord Wilberforce.

29. *HKSAR v. David Ma* [1997] HKLRD 761 at 772; *Minister of Home Affairs v. Fisher* [1980] AC 319 at 328.

30. "A Soft Executive Council and a Tough Department of Justice", *Ming Pao*, 4 August 1998, p. B11.

31. Adaptation of Laws (Interpretative Provisions) Bill 1998, Legal Supplement No. 3, C512 (22 February 1998).

32. Speech by the Acting Secretary for Justice, Ian Wingfield, in the Provisional Legislative Council on 7 April 1998 on the resumption of the Second Reading Debate on the Adaptation of Laws (Interpretative Provisions) Bill.

33. See de Smith, *Constitutional and Administrative Law* (Harmondsworth: Penguins, 1985, 5th ed.), p. 134; F.A.P. Bennion, *Statutory Interpretation* (London: Butterworths, 1997, 3rd ed.), section 34.

34. For a more detailed discussion, see J. Chan, "Due Process in Hong Kong: The Prospect under Chinese Sovereignty", a paper for the Conference on Judicial Independence: St Anthony's College, Oxford, 12–13 June 1998.

35. Articles 17 and 158, Basic Law.

36. The consultative draft of the Bill which was published in October 1997 proposed to substitute "HKSAR Government" for "the Crown". It was unclear what led to the replacement of "HKSAR Government" by "the State" in the Bill. The change was obviously a political decision and the claim of the HKSAR government that the amendment was purely technical sounded hollow.

37. Speech of Ian Wingfield, supra, p. 3. It is unclear whether these laws apply by expressed provisions or by necessary implications. For example, there is nothing in the Bill of Rights Ordinance which says that it binds the Crown, nor is the Crown subject to any tortuous liabilities but for the Crown Proceedings Ordinance.

38. On 18 November 1998, the government decided that Xinhua News Agency fell within the meaning of a "State" and was, therefore, not subject to Hong Kong law unless otherwise expressly stated. *Ming Pao*, 19 November 1998.

39. Not surprisingly, the Independent Commission Against Corruption found it necessary to issue a press statement that the Corrupt and Illegal Practices Ordinance (Cap. 288) and the Prevention of Bribery Ordinance (Cap. 201) will apply to everyone in Hong Kong.

40. *In re M* [1994] AC 377 at 395.

41. Articles 13 and 14.

42. Articles 18 and 19. Foreign affairs and defence should be governed by national law which will be extended to the HKSAR through Annex III of the Basic Law.

43. 7 April 1998. For the controversy on the legality of the Provisional Legislative Council, see J. Chan, "The Jurisdiction and Legality of the Provisional Legislative Council" (1997) 27 *HKLJ* 374–87.

44. As a compromise, the HKSAR government promised to review about 90 ordinances which applied to the Crown before the changeover and consider whether they should apply to the State. This, however, does not address the concern that laws which did not apply to the Crown do not automatically mean that they should not apply to the State, which is now an enlarged concept. The exercise has not been completed yet, but on 20 October 1998, the government announced that, after consultation with the appropriate authorities of the Mainland, 15 ordinances would be made applicable to the State. *Ming Pao*, 21 October 1998, p. A10.

45. For a discussion on the controversies arising from article 84 and the composition of the Court of Final Appeal, see A. Cheung, "The Legal System: Falling Apart or Forging Ahead?" in S.Y.L. Cheung and S.M.H. Sze (eds.), *The Other Hong Kong Report 1995* (Chinese University Press, 1995), pp. 13–31.

46. See ibid.

47. Until 1995, the number of appeals to the Privy Council is about five appeals per year. The number at the very least doubled in 1996 and 1997.

48. Court of Final Appeal Ordinance (Cap. 484), s. 32(2). See also *Miu Po Chu v. HKSAR* [1997] 3 HKC 12.

49. The Official Receiver appeared as an *amicus* in *Max Share Ltd v. Ng Yat Chi* [1998] 2 HKC 251 which is the usual practice in liquidation cases.

50. See, for example, *Thang Thieu Quyen v. Director of Immigration* (1998) CFA, FACV No. 2 of 1998.

51. [1998] 1 HKC 371.

52. J. Chan, "Hong Kong's Bill of Rights: Its Reception of and Contribution to International and Comparative Jurisprudence" (1998) 47 *International and Comparative Law Quarterly* 306–36.

53. (1998) Mag, ESC No. 5206 of 1997 (3 June 1998).

54. (1998) Mag, WSS Nos. 5151 and 3152 of 1998 (17 May 1998).

55. [1997] 3 HKC 64 (CFI); CACV No. 203 of 1997 (CA).

56. By "Hong Kong permanent residents" I refer only to those persons of Chinese origin who have acquired the permanent resident status as a result of seven years' residence in Hong Kong. Those who acquired this status by way of British Dependent Territories citizenship are in a different category.

57. Ord No. 124 of 1997, *Gazette of the HKSAR*, Legal Supplement No. 1, p. A301 (10 July 1997).

58. There were in fact four different cases chosen to represent four typical categories of applicants.

59. [1997] 3 HKC 64 at 89. Article 12(1) of the Bill of Rights provides that "no one shall be held guilty of any criminal offence on account of any act or omission which did not constitute a criminal offence, under Hong Kong or international law, at the time when it was committed."

60. At p. 28.

61. At pp. 55–56.

62. At p. 69.

63. At p. 54. On article 12 of the Bill of Rights, he agreed with Keith J that "the necessity from time to time to make retrospective legislation should not be absolutely barred simply because some persons might be exposed to criminal prosecution; rather they should have immunity from prosecution, as in fact they here appear to do."

CHAPTER 12

# HONG KONG'S LEGAL SYSTEM IN TRANSITION: 1997–99

Albert H.Y. Chen

During the colonial era, Hong Kong was "borrowed time, borrowed place".[1] From the point of view of the people of Hong Kong, the colonial legal system was also a borrowed legal system. It was an alien imposition from the metropolitan power, and was completely separate and distinct from both the imperial Chinese legal tradition and the Marxist-Leninist legal system that was established on the Chinese mainland after 1949. Ironically, as the colonial era drew to an end, the people of Hong Kong had come to accept the transplanted legal system as their own. They cherished the values of the rule of law, the rights of the individual, equality under the law and the independence of the judiciary that were enshrined in the transplanted common law. They recognized that the existing legal system in Hong Kong was far superior to that in the Chinese mainland for the purpose of providing an infrastructure for economic prosperity and the protection of human rights. And so, in the course of the evolution of Hong Kong's public culture after the Sino-British Joint Declaration of 1984, particularly in the course of the drafting of the Basic Law of the Hong Kong Special Administrative Region (HKSAR) which was ultimately passed into law by China's National People's Congress in 1990 (although it would only come into effect in 1997), it soon became axiomatic that the future of the rule of law, of human rights and of economic prosperity in the post-1997 era would depend crucially on the maintenance of the pre-existing law and legal institutions of Hong Kong.

The Joint Declaration itself promised that Hong Kong's existing laws would "remain basically unchanged"[2] after the handover. There existed also other provisions that were designed to preserve the continuity of the legal and judicial systems. All these provisions have been incorporated into the Basic Law with some further elaboration. Looking back at Hong Kong's legal history in the two years of 1997 and 1998, one may ask whether the great promise of the continuity of Hong Kong's legal system has, indeed, been translated into reality, and whether such cherished values as the rule of law and human rights have continued to thrive in the HKSAR of the People's Republic of China (PRC). It is the purpose of this chapter to address these questions.

# A New Constitutional Foundation

The termination of Hong Kong's constitutional status as a British colony and the establishment of the HKSAR of the PRC at midnight between 30 June and 1 July 1997 was accompanied by a "revolution" in a technical legal sense. By this I refer to a shift in the "basic norm" (*Grundnorm* in German, as expounded in the writings of the German legal philosopher, Hans Kelsen) of Hong Kong's legal system.

According to Kelsen's analysis of the structure of legal systems, each legal system can be understood as a hierarchy of legal norms. The legal validity of norms at lower levels (e.g. legislation and subordinate legislation) is derived from norms situated at higher levels of the hierarchy (e.g. the constitution and legislation), which authorize relevant government institutions to make the norms at the lower levels. The validity of all norms within a legal system can be ultimately traced back to, and derived from, a "basic norm".

The basic norm unifies all these norms into one legal system, and serves as the ultimate source of validity for all these norms. Kelsen points out that in a country with a written constitution, the basic norm is a norm that presupposes the validity of the first constitution made by the founders of the state (from which the validity of the current constitution, if different from the first, is derived).

Before Hong Kong's reunification with China, the basic norm of Hong Kong's legal system was basically identical to that of the legal system of the United Kingdom. Thus this basic norm recognized the validity in Hong Kong of all Acts of Parliament that applied to Hong Kong by their express terms or by necessary implication. It also recognized the validity of "prerogative legislation" made by the "Crown", such as the Letters Patent and Royal Instructions which supplied the constitutional foundation of Hong Kong's colonial government institutions. On 1 July 1997, this basic norm was replaced by a new basic norm which refers to the Constitution of the PRC as the ultimate source of validity of all laws in Hong Kong. The validity in the HKSAR of laws such as the common law and legislation made by the Hong Kong legislature is now derived from the Basic Law. The validity of the Basic Law is, in turn, derived from the PRC Constitution, since the Basic Law was enacted by the National People's Congress (NPC) of the PRC in 1990 in pursuance of article 31 of the PRC Constitution.

# The Survival of Existing Laws

The shift in the basic norm of Hong Kong's legal system and the substitution of the Basic Law for the previous Letters Patent and Royal Instructions as the constitutional foundation of the government system in Hong Kong do not, however, have any significant impact on the laws that govern the daily life of the people of Hong Kong, their rights and liberties, or their commercial transactions. At the same time as prescribing the new political system in the HKSAR and delineating the scope of the HKSAR's autonomy with respect to the central government in Beijing, the Basic Law also provides for a high degree of *continuity* for Hong Kong's pre-existing laws and judicial institutions.

More particularly, article 8 of the Basic Law provides for the continued validity of the "laws previously in force in Hong Kong, that is, the common law, rules of equity, ordinances, subordinate legislation and customary law", except for any law that contravenes the Basic Law and subject to any amendment by the HKSAR legislature. Under article 160 of the Basic Law, the Standing Committee of the NPC may declare which of Hong Kong's pre-existing laws contravene the Basic Law and cannot, therefore, survive the 1997 transition. Such a declaration was made by the Standing Committee on 23 February 1997 in its Decision on the Treatment of the Laws Previously in Force in Hong Kong.[3]

The Decision identified a number of ordinances or portions thereof as laws that should not form part of the law of the HKSAR. It also provided rules for the purpose of adapting the wording, interpretation and application of existing laws for use in the HKSAR. These rules were subsequently re-enacted by the Provisional Legislative Council (PLC) of the HKSAR as part of the Hong Kong Reunification Ordinance, and are generally regarded as technical in nature and uncontroversial.[4] As regards the non-adoption of certain ordinances, the termination of the operation of some of the ordinances concerned is uncontroversial as it is generally accepted that they related to the very nature of the colonial regime and were not needed in the postcolonial era.[5] However, the non-adoption of certain electoral laws and human rights-related laws was, indeed, controversial and was the focus of much debate and criticism in early 1997.

The electoral laws that failed to survive the transition were laws enacted to implement former Governor Christopher Patten's political reform package, which was considered by the Chinese government as fundamental changes to Hong Kong's government system introduced unilaterally by the United Kingdom in a manner inconsistent with the spirit of the Joint Declaration, the Basic Law and the understanding reached by exchange of correspondence between the Chinese and British governments in early 1990. The vacuum resulting from the non-survival of some of these electoral laws was subsequently filled by new laws enacted by the Provisional Legislative Council, in accordance with which the first Legislative Council of the HKSAR was elected on 24 May 1998.

As regards the human rights-related laws, the NPC Standing Committee decided not to adopt the major amendments made to the Societies Ordinance and the Public Order Ordinance in July 1992 and July 1995 respectively. The amendments were part of a law reform exercise to bring Hong Kong's law in line with the standards enshrined in the International Covenant on Civil and Political Rights (ICCPR) as imported into Hong Kong's domestic law by the Hong Kong Bill of Rights Ordinance enacted by the Hong Kong legislature in 1991. In the view of the Chinese government, the amendments were maliciously motivated and aimed at reducing the legitimate public order regulatory powers of the HKSAR government, because the British government had represented to the Chinese side during the negotiations leading to the conclusion of the Joint Declaration that Hong Kong's laws at that time were already fully consistent with the ICCPR. At the same time as rejecting the amendments to the societies and public order legislation, the NPC Standing Committee also declared the non-adoption of three interpretative provisions in the Hong Kong Bill of Rights Ordinance on the ground that they purported to give the ordinance a superior status overriding other Hong Kong laws, which is inconsistent with the principle that only the Basic Law is superior to other Hong Kong laws.[6]

Although the NPC Standing Committee nullified the amendments introduced in the 1990s to the Societies Ordinance and Public Order Ordinance, it did not actually mandate the restoration of these laws to their pre-amendment version. The HKSAR government was given the freedom to make a new version of societies and public order legislation for the region. Rising to the challenge, the Office of the HKSAR chief executive-designate published a consultative document on 9 April 1997 proposing such a new version of the law on freedom of association and freedom of assembly and procession in Hong Kong. On the basis of the opinions collected in the consultative exercise, bills were drafted and finally enacted by the Provisional Legislative Council (PLC) on 14 June 1997 in the form of the Societies (Amendment) Ordinance 1997 and the Public Order (Amendment) Ordinance 1997. The new version largely preserved the improvements and liberalizations made in the 1992 and 1995 amendments. The significant changes introduced by the PLC to the existing law related to two areas. First, under the latest version of the law, the government has the power to prohibit a public meeting or procession or the operation of a society on the grounds of "national safety" (in addition to the pre-existing grounds of "public safety" and "public order"). Second, it is now provided that political bodies in Hong Kong may not have any connection with foreign or Taiwan political bodies (otherwise the former's existence may be prohibited). This provision reflects the requirements in article 23 of the Basic Law.[7]

To conclude this section of the chapter, it may be said that the body of Hong Kong's pre-existing law has remained basically intact after the 1997 transition. With the exception of the specific laws set out in the NPC Standing Committee's Decision of 23 February 1997, all other laws have survived the handover. The non-adoption of most of the laws specified in the Decision for use in the HKSAR is uncontroversial and generally accepted. On the other hand, electoral laws and human rights-related laws have, indeed, been areas of controversy. The legal vacuum resulting from the Decision in these areas has subsequently been filled by new electoral laws enacted by the PLC within the framework for the HKSAR political system established by the Basic Law and the Preparatory Committee for the HKSAR, and a new version of societies and public order legislation enacted by the PLC as discussed earlier.

# The Application of Mainland Chinese Law

According to article 18 of the Basic Law, the laws that are in force in the HKSAR are those pre-existing laws which survive the transition as discussed above, laws enacted by the HKSAR legislature, and the national laws listed in Annex III to the Basic Law. Article 18 also provides that the mainland Chinese laws listed in Annex III must be "confined to those relating to defence and foreign affairs as well as other matters outside the limits of the autonomy of" the HKSAR. It may be pointed out that the smaller the scope of application of these Annex III laws, the higher the degree of autonomy of the region's legislative system.

When the Basic Law was enacted in 1990, Annex III consisted of six items, including the nationality law and various enactments on the capital, national day, national flag and emblem, territorial sea and diplomatic privileges. With the introduction of some new mainland Chinese laws on defence and foreign affairs and certain national affairs after 1990, Annex III became out-of-date. On 1 July 1997, the NPC Standing Committee, after consulting the HKSAR government and the Committee for the Basic Law in accordance with article 18 of the Basic Law, amended Annex III by adding to it five new items: law on the garrisoning of the HKSAR, law on the national flag, law on the national emblem, and two other laws on the territorial sea and consular privileges.[8] Article 18 of the Basic Law provides that the Annex III laws should be applied in Hong Kong "by way of promulgation or legislation by the Region". In fact, the laws on the national flag and emblem have been applied in the HKSAR by ordinances enacted by the PLC for the purpose of adapting the national laws to local circumstances,[9] whereas all the other Annex III laws have been directly applied to Hong Kong by promulgation.[10]

It may, therefore, be seen that mainland Chinese laws only have a minor application to the HKSAR. Among those mainland laws that do apply in Hong Kong, the most significant ones are probably the nationality law and the law on the garrisoning of the HKSAR. The nationality law was enacted by the NPC in 1980, but the manner in which it applies to the HKSAR was governed by the NPC Standing Committee's Interpretations on the nationality law dated 15 May 1996. As regards the law on the garrisoning of the HKSAR, this was enacted by the NPC Standing Committee on 30 December 1996 after fairly extensive consultation with the Hong Kong people and research into the legal position of the British forces in Hong Kong. This law regulates the activities and behaviour of members of the Chinese military forces stationed in Hong Kong, and affirms the jurisdiction of the courts in the region in handling cases involving acts done by these members otherwise than in the execution of their official duties.

Unlike the nationality law and the garrison law which both apply to Hong Kong directly by promulgation, the PRC law on the national flag and law on the national emblem mentioned earlier have been applied by the enactment of a local ordinance, the National Flag and National Emblem Ordinance.[11] In the case of *HKSAR v. Ng Kung-siu and Lee Kin-yun*,[12] the defendants had participated in a demonstration for democracy in China during which they displayed a defaced national flag (of the PRC) and a defaced regional flag (of the HKSAR). They were subsequently charged with violations of section 7 of the National Flag and National Emblem Ordinance and section 7 of the Regional Flag and Regional Emblem Ordinance.[13] The sections provide for the offences of desecration of the national flag or emblem and of the regional flag or emblem. The former section was basically reproduced from article 19 of the PRC law on the national flag and article 13 of the PRC law on the national emblem.[14]

The defendants were convicted by the magistrate; they were not fined nor imprisoned, but bound over to keep the peace on a recognizance of HK$2000 for each of the two charges for 12 months. They successfully appealed against their conviction before the Court of Appeal. The court held that the sections under which they were charged are contrary to the guarantee of freedom of expression in article 19 of the International Covenant on Civil and Political Rights as applied by article 39 of the Basic Law. In the court's opinion, the prohibition of desecration of the national or regional flag, being a restriction on freedom of expression, cannot be justified by any necessity to protect public order.

At the time of writing, this case is in the process of being appealed to the Court of Final Appeal. The final decision in this case will be of far-reaching constitutional significance, for the question raised is the extent to which national laws listed in Annex III to the Basic Law are enforceable in Hong Kong, where specific provisions therein are determined by the Hong Kong court to be inconsistent with other provisions in the Basic Law.

# Reversal of certain Laws Passed by the previous LegCo

The principle in article 8 of the Basic Law to preserve those existing laws which do not contravene the Basic Law is subject to the proviso that the HKSAR legislature can change any existing law. Immediately after the establishment of the HKSAR, the HKSAR government introduced a bill in the PLC proposing to freeze the operation of seven ordinances passed by the former Legislative Council (LegCo) as private members' bills (i.e. bills originally drafted and introduced into the legislature by an individual LegCo member rather than by the government), on the grounds that these laws were hastily passed by LegCo during its last week of operation in June 1997 without adequate discussion in bills committees, public consultation, and, in the case of the five labour law-related ordinances among them, prior consideration by the Labour Advisory Board. The PLC did not support the government's proposal in its entirety, and only agreed to freeze four of the ordinances concerned when it passed on 16 July 1997 the Legislative Provisions (Suspension of Operation) Ordinance 1997.[15]

This ordinance only provided for a temporary suspension of the four ordinances pending their further review by the government and the PLC. The review of the three labour law-related ordinances among them was completed by the end of October 1997, when the PLC passed the Employment and Labour Relations (Miscellaneous Amendments) Ordinance.[16] This ordinance, in effect, repealed the Employee's Rights to Representation, Consultation and Collective Bargaining Ordinance 1997 (which introduced, for the first time in Hong Kong's history, a legal right on the part of trade unions to collective bargaining with employers) and the Employment (Amendment)(No. 4) Ordinance 1997 (which strengthened the anti-discrimination remedies for members of trade unions). With regard to the change in rules regarding the registration and operation of trade unions introduced by the Trade Unions (Amendment)(No. 2) Ordinance 1997, the Employment and Labour Relations (Miscellaneous Amendments) Ordinance did not abolish it entirely but introduced a modified, compromise version of the trade union law.

The remainder of the four frozen ordinances was the Hong Kong Bill of Rights (Amendment) Ordinance 1997,[17] and this was dealt with by the PLC when it enacted the Hong Kong Bill of Rights (Amendment) Ordinance 1998[18] on 25 February 1998. The previous amendment ordinance had extended the scope of application of the Bill of Rights to legislation affecting only relations between private persons (as distinguished from legislation governing the relations between the government or public authorities, on the one hand, and citizens, on the other hand). This extension has now been removed by the 1998 amendment ordinance.

The suspension and subsequent partial repeal by the PLC of these labour law-related and human rights-related laws enacted by the former LegCo was one of the most controversial acts of the PLC in its one-year lifespan, particularly in view of the fact that the PLC had less democratic legitimacy in the eyes of the Hong Kong people than the former LegCo. It should, however, be noted in this regard that the initiative and the driving force behind this move came from HKSAR government officials who were the same officials in the pre-July 1997 government. These officials' position was consistent before and after the handover. They had opposed the private members' bills before the bills were passed by the pre-July LegCo, and it just so happened that the PLC was more sympathetic to their views and concerns than the pre-July LegCo. However, even the PLC did not accept all of their proposed suspensions, and the final version of the law that ultimately emerged represents, to some extent (albeit a relatively minor extent), a compromise from the government's point of view.

## "Crown", "State" and Adaptation of Laws

Another highly controversial law passed by the PLC was the Adaptation of Laws (Interpretative Provisions) Ordinance.[19] The ordinance was one in a series of ordinances enacted for the purpose of making technical changes to the wording of Hong Kong's existing laws so as to adapt them to Hong Kong's postcolonial status. This exercise of adapting the laws, together with another exercise of localizing the laws (i.e. re-enacting relevant British legislation originally applicable to Hong Kong directly in the form of local legislation, e.g. in the areas of intellectual property and merchant shipping), have in fact begun in the Legal Department years before the handover. They have generally been regarded as technical, non-political and uncontroversial in nature.

However, there was *one* provision in the Adaptation of Laws (Interpretative Provisions) Ordinance 1998 which generated heated debate in the community and intense criticism of the HKSAR government and the PLC. The provision relates to the adaptation to the post-1997 era of section 66 of the Interpretation and General Clauses Ordinance, which reads as follows:

> No Ordinance shall in any manner whatsoever affect the right of or be binding on the Crown unless it is therein expressly provided or unless it appears by necessary implication that the Crown is bound thereby.

This section was, in fact, no more than the restatement of a common law rule of statutory interpretation, which is also in force in other common law jurisdictions, such as Britain, Australia and New Zealand. In the pre-1997 era, the word "Crown" in section 66 would refer to the Queen, the British government, the British military forces in Hong Kong and the Hong Kong government. The use of the word "Crown" in Hong Kong law is clearly inappropriate in the postcolonial age.

Section 24 of the Adaptation of Laws (Interpretative Provisions) Ordinance substitutes the word "State" for the word "Crown" in section 66 of the Interpretation and General Clauses Ordinance, and the former ordinance also provides an elaborate definition of the new concept of the "State". The definition includes the HKSAR government, the central government in Beijing, as well as subordinate organs of the central government that exercise executive functions on its behalf but do not exercise commercial functions. Such subordinate organs would appear to include (and this has been admitted by the HKSAR government itself) not only the office of the Commissioner of the PRC Foreign Ministry in Hong Kong and the Chinese military forces in Hong Kong, but also the Hong Kong Branch of the Xinhua News Agency, which has been designated a work organ authorized to operate in Hong Kong by the central government.

Not long before this bill for adaptation of laws was introduced into the PLC, the Department of Justice's decision not to prosecute the Hong Kong Branch of the Xinhua News Agency for a possible breach of the Personal Data (Privacy)

Ordinance had already attracted much public attention. The alleged breach was that the agency did not reply within the time limit specified in the ordinance to an inquiry from Emily Lau (former LegCo member, also elected in May 1998 to the first LegCo of the HKSAR) regarding the personal data the Agency held on Lau.

There is a section in the Personal Data (Privacy) Ordinance expressly providing that it binds the government (meaning the Hong Kong government), but no provision to the effect that it binds the Crown. The effect of the Adaptation of Laws (Interpretative Provisions) Ordinance 1998 is that the Personal Data (Privacy) Ordinance would not be binding on agencies of the State (as defined in the former ordinance) other than the HKSAR government. Hence the Hong Kong Branch of the Xinhua News Agency would not be subject to the Personal Data (Privacy) Ordinance. Nor would it be bound by other Hong Kong legislation which does not expressly or by implication bind the State (even if such legislation expressly binds the HKSAR government).

The main criticism of the adaptative provision substituting "State" for "Crown" in section 66 of the Interpretation and General Clauses Ordinance is that it gives institutions, like the Xinhua News Agency in Hong Kong, special privilege which is inconsistent with article 22 of the Basic Law, which provides that all offices established in Hong Kong by the central government departments or by the provinces, and the personnel of such offices, "shall abide by the laws of the Region". On the other hand, defenders of the adaptative provision argued that the legal logic in substituting "State" for "Crown" is impeccable, and that the change is purely a technical measure of adapting the laws to Hong Kong's new status. It was pointed out that whether there is anything wrong with the substance of the original section 66 of the Interpretation and General Clauses Ordinance (which is the subject of the present adaptation exercise) in giving a special treatment to the "Crown" (now the "State") is a question of *law reform* rather than a question of *adaptation*. At the same time, the government undertook to review all existing laws, particularly those laws that already contain express provisions making them binding on the Hong Kong government, to see whether any of them should be expressly made binding on State agencies, such as the Xinhua News Agency in Hong Kong. And when LegCo enacts any new law in future, it can also consider whether the law ought to bind any State agency, and, if so, expressly provide so.

The debate generated by the Crown/State issue in the exercise of adaptation of laws provides a good illustration of the kind of political sensitivity, both local and international, that exists as Hong Kong experiments with life under "one country, two systems". The criticism voiced in the Hong Kong community of the stance of the HKSAR government and the PLC on this issue has attracted much international attention. Sceptics of "one country, two systems" find in this incident evidence of erosion of the rule of law in Hong Kong under the pressure of "one country". To be fair, however, it may be pointed out that the HKSAR government and the PLC have not sought to introduce any *new* rule into Hong Kong's legal system. The interpretative presumption in section 66 of the Interpretation and General Clauses Ordinance that legislation does not bind the Crown (unless it expressly or by implication does so) is inherited from the common law tradition, and it would be extremely difficult to justify to the central government in Beijing any abolition or curtailment of the presumption as part of an exercise in the adaptation of laws or even in law reform. The only remaining option would be to preserve the presumption while replacing the concept of the "Crown" by the equivalent concept of the "State". And this was the option adopted by the HKSAR government and the PLC.

# Immigration Legislation, the PLC and the Courts

One of the greatest legal challenge faced by the HKSAR authorities immediately after the establishment of the HKSAR was the problem of illegal migrant children from mainland China born of Hong Kong permanent residents. Before 1 July 1997, these children had no right of residence in Hong Kong, although they could apply (for a one-way exit permit from mainland China) to come to Hong Kong under the quota of 150 migrants from mainland China per day and, as it were, wait in a queue for many years before actually being allowed to come. However, under article 24 of the Basic Law, which came into effect on 1 July 1997, such children have the legal status of Hong Kong permanent residents with the right of abode in Hong Kong. Hence in the months before 1 July 1997 and the days following this critical date, some Hong Kong permanent residents with children in the Mainland arranged for their children to be smuggled into the territory, hoping that they could then jump the queue and exercise their constitutional right of abode in Hong Kong once they are physically in Hong Kong.

It was estimated that there were at least 66,000 such children in the Mainland. If all restrictions were to be lifted regarding their entry to Hong Kong, the social infrastructure and social services of Hong Kong could hardly cope with such a great and sudden influx. The strains put on Hong Kong's society and its government would simply be too enormous. The HKSAR government, with the support of the PLC, therefore, introduced amendments to the Immigration Ordinance on 9 July 1997 requiring children in the Mainland, of Hong Kong permanent residents, to prove their identity and apply to the mainland authorities for the usual one-way exit permit plus a certificate of entitlement to reside in Hong Kong issued by the Hong Kong authorities, before they can come to Hong Kong. The children's exercise of their right of residence in Hong Kong is, in effect, postponed until they have applied for and obtained the necessary documentation. If the children have already entered Hong Kong without such documentation before the enactment of the new legislation, the legislation requires them to be sent back to the Mainland, where they are supposed to apply to come to Hong Kong again, following the procedure set out in the ordinance.

In the famous case of *Cheung Lai Wah and others v. Director of Immigration*,[20] the legislation was challenged by lawyers acting for the parents of some of the children who had already entered Hong Kong before the enactment of the legislation on 9 July 1997. It was argued that the legislation was inconsistent with article 24 of the Basic Law which confers on these children the status of Hong Kong permanent residents with the right of abode in Hong Kong. Another argument concerned the legality of the Provisional Legislative Council (PLC) which enacted the legislation.

The issue of whether the PLC had been lawfully established and had the power to make laws for Hong Kong had been controversial for many months even before the immigration amendment legislation was passed by the PLC on 9 July 1997. When the Preparatory Committee for the HKSAR decided to establish the PLC in March 1996, critics already pointed out that insofar as the Basic Law and the related enactments of the NPC and its Standing Committee have not made any provision for any organ like the PLC, the establishment of the PLC was not properly authorized by law and, therefore, the PLC had no legitimate constitutional status and no legislative authority. Before the transition on 1 July 1997 but after the PLC started its work in Shenzhen in April 1997, legal action[21] was brought by a member of the Democratic Party in Hong Kong to challenge it on the grounds that its members were usurping the offices of the legislative councillors. However, the court refused to entertain the challenge on the grounds that the applicant did not have a sufficient interest in the matter (in the sense of being adversely affected by the actions which he complained about), and was "seeking to utilise the court to promote his own particular political interest". The court was reluctant to become involved in the Sino-British dispute regarding the establishment of the PLC, and it also pointed out that it had no jurisdiction over activities in mainland China where the PLC was operating.

Shortly after the establishment of the HKSAR, the issue of the PLC's legal status was litigated again. In *HKSAR v. Ma Wai Kwan David and others*,[22] a criminal case involving a charge of conspiracy to pervert the course of public justice, the defendants' lawyers argued that the common law (under which the conspiracy offence existed) had not survived the handover, and that the Hong Kong Reunification Ordinance (which provides for the continued operation of the common law after the handover) enacted by the PLC was invalid because the PLC was not lawfully established as a law-making body for the HKSAR. The issue was referred to the Court of Appeal for an authoritative determination. In a landmark decision delivered on 29 July 1997, the three-member court held unanimously in favour of the legality of the PLC. The court pointed out that as a local or regional court, it had no power to overturn an act of a sovereign authority, such as the NPC or its Standing Committee. Furthermore, after looking into the background to the establishment of the PLC, and, in particular, the derailing of the "through train" for members of the legislature before and after 1 July 1997 and the need for an interim legislative authority immediately after the HKSAR's establishment, the court concluded that the creation of the PLC was not contrary to the Basic Law, but was necessary for the purpose of implementing the Basic Law.

The legislative authority of the PLC was also challenged, as mentioned earlier, in the *Cheung Lai Wah* case where parents challenged the legislation restricting the right of entry into the HKSAR of children in mainland China of Hong Kong permanent residents. The case was first heard by Justice Keith in the Court of First Instance of the High Court. It was then appealed to the Court of Appeal. The Court of Appeal decided on 20 May 1998 that as far as the issue of the PLC's legal status was concerned, the court was bound by its earlier decision in the case *HKSAR v. Ma Wai Kwan*, and the issue could not, therefore, be re-opened.

We now turn to examine how the court dealt with the other major issue in the case, which was whether the immigration amendment legislation enacted by the PLC was contrary to article 24 of the Basic Law, which confers on the children concerned the status of Hong Kong permanent residents and the right of abode in Hong Kong. On this issue, the Court of Appeal in a judgment delivered on 2 April 1998 affirmed the decision of the Court of First Instance. The legislative scheme requiring the children to apply for and obtain the one-way exit permit and certificate of entitlement before they can come into Hong Kong was held to be valid and not inconsistent with the Basic Law. The court pointed out that the Basic Law is a constitutional document setting out basic principles, and detailed implementation is a matter left to the HKSAR legislature. In this case, the objective of the legislation is to provide for the orderly settlement in Hong Kong of the children concerned in phases over a period of time. The legislation, therefore, implements the Basic Law and is not inconsistent with it. The court emphasized that the restrictions placed on the children's right to enter Hong Kong immediately and without waiting for their applications to be processed are justified by article 22 of the Basic Law, which provides that people from other parts of China must apply for approval before they can enter the HKSAR. It was pointed out that articles 22 and 24 should be read together, and that such provisions in the Basic Law should be interpreted broadly and purposively.

Another part of the immigration amendment legislation denies the right of abode in Hong Kong to illegitimate children in the Mainland, born of fathers who are Hong Kong permanent residents. This legislation was also challenged in this case; the court held that the relevant provisions were, indeed, contrary to the Basic Law and hence invalid. The court held that they were inconsistent with the language of article 24 of the Basic Law, which contains nothing that discriminates against children on the basis of their status (i.e. whether they are born to parents who are married to one another).

There are two other cases litigated in the Hong Kong courts since the establishment of the HKSAR which concerned the interpretation of article 24 of the Basic Law. In one of these cases, the immigration legislation was also challenged on the grounds that it was inconsistent with article 24 of the Basic Law. In this case,[23] it was argued that Hong Kong permanent residents' children who had the right of abode in Hong Kong included not only persons who were born at a time when one of their parents was already a Hong Kong permanent resident, but also any person whose parent subsequently became a Hong Kong permanent resident. This argument succeeded initially in the Court of First Instance of the High Court, but was rejected when the case was appealed to the Court of Appeal. In the other case,[24] the Court of First Instance held that a Hong Kong permanent resident's step-child who was born in mainland China has no right of abode in Hong Kong.

In the *Cheung Lai Wah* case and the first of the two cases mentioned in the last paragraph (the *Chan Kam Nga* case), appeals were made to the Court of Final Appeal in January 1999. The two judgments rendered in these cases by the Court of Final Appeal, on 29 January 1999, became the most important and famous judicial decisions in Hong Kong since the 1997 transition, and had far-reaching implications for both the constitutional-political and the socioeconomic domains. The two judgments were those in the cases of *Ng Ka Ling and Others v. Director of Immigration*[25] (which was in fact the same case as *Cheung Lai Wah*) and *Chan Kam Nga and 80 others v. Director of Immigration.*[26]

In the judgments, the Court of Final Appeal affirmed the Court of Appeal's ruling regarding the right of illegitimate children to qualify for the right of abode under article 24 of the Basic Law. However, on the point raised by the *Chan Kam Nga* case, the Court of Final Appeal agreed with the view of the Court of First Instance and reversed the Court of Appeal's decision. It was subsequently estimated by the HKSAR government that the combined effect of the Court of Final Appeal's decisions on these two points is that 1.67 million mainland residents have qualified or will qualify as Hong Kong permanent residents under article 24 of the Basic Law.

What was even more momentous was that the Court of Final Appeal rejected the interpretation of article 22 adopted by the two lower courts. Consequently, the court held that the immigration amendment legislation of 9 July 1997 was unconstitutional (i.e. contrary to the Basic Law) and invalid, insofar as it required relevant mainland residents to possess the one-way exit permit issued by the mainland authorities (in addition to the certificate of entitlement issued by the HKSAR government) as a condition for entry into Hong Kong. These mainland residents have already become entitled to the right of abode in Hong Kong on the commencement of the Basic Law on 1 July 1997. The Court of Final Appeal held that as far as Hong Kong law was concerned, it would only be lawful to require such mainland residents to obtain the certificate of entitlement as a condition precedent for entry; it would not be lawful to deny them entry on the grounds that they do not hold a one-way exit permit. The certificate of entitlement scheme is for the purpose of and only for the purpose of verification of the applicant's status as a Hong Kong permanent resident under article 24, and the certificate should be issued without unlawful delay once the facts relevant to proof of the status have been verified.

In the Court of Final Appeal's opinion, article 22 does not apply to mainland residents who are Hong Kong permanent residents under article 24. Hence any restriction of their right of entry to Hong Kong on the basis of the one-way exit permit scheme would be an unlawful denial of their "constitutional right of abode", which the Court of Final Appeal regarded as a core right without which other rights guaranteed by chapter III of the Basic Law cannot be enjoyed. On the other hand, the Court of Final Appeal recognized that the mainland law on exit and entry of citizens on which the one-way permit scheme rests remains "fully enforceable" in the Mainland. The Court of Final Appeal also recognized that article 22 is a Basic Law provision that concerns the relationship between the central authorities and the HKSAR. Under article 158 of the Basic Law, the Court of Final Appeal is bound, before deciding a case, to refer such provisions to the NPC Standing Committee for interpretation if the court needs to interpret such a provision and its interpretation would affect the judgment. However, in the present case, the Court of Final Appeal decided that it was not necessary to refer article 22 to the Standing Committee because the "substance" of the case was such that article 24 rather than article 22 was the "predominant provision" being interpreted by the court.[27]

On the issue of the legislative authority of the PLC, the Court of Final Appeal held that the PLC had been lawfully established and its establishment did not contravene the Basic Law. However, the Court of Final Appeal's reasoning which led to this conclusion differs from that adopted by the Court of Appeal in the *Ma Wai Kwan* case. In fact, the Court of Final Appeal in its judgment expressly overruled the principle adopted in the *Ma* case that acts of the sovereign authority (the NPC or its Standing Committee) may not be reviewed by the Hong Kong courts. In what subsequently became the most controversial part of the judgment, the Court of Final Appeal declared that the Hong Kong courts have full authority (subject to the provisions of the Basic Law) to review the legislative acts of the NPC and its Standing Committee for the purpose of determining whether they are inconsistent with the Basic Law, and to declare such acts as invalid if they are determined to be so inconsistent.

This particular statement of the constitutional jurisdiction of the Hong Kong courts to review the validity of acts of the NPC and its Standing Committee provoked a strong reaction from the mainland government, thus precipitating the first constitutional crisis in Hong Kong since the 1997 transition. In a highly publicized seminar reported in Hong Kong and mainland media on 7 February 1999, four leading Chinese law professors, who were also former members of the Drafting Committee for the Basic Law and the Preparatory Committee for the establishment of the HKSAR, vehemently attacked the statement, even to the point of saying that it has the effect of placing the Hong Kong courts above the NPC, which is the supreme organ of state power under the Chinese Constitution, and of turning Hong Kong into an "independent political entity". After the HKSAR's secretary for justice Elsie Leung's visit to Beijing on 12–13 February to discuss the matter, it was reported that Chinese officials also criticized the statement as unconstitutional and called for its rectification.

The mainland reaction to the Court of Final Appeal's statement aroused international as well as local concern regarding the rule of law and judicial independence in Hong Kong. The British Consulate in Hong Kong, the US Consulate in Hong Kong and the US Chamber of Commerce in Hong Kong all issued statements expressing concern about the matter and support for the Court of Final Appeal and for judicial autonomy in Hong Kong. These were implicit warnings to the Chinese government against intervention. In this regard, it should be noted that under article 158 of the Basic Law, there does exist a lawful channel of intervention for the purpose of resolving a constitutional dispute between the HKSAR and the central government. This takes the form of an interpretation of the Basic Law issued by the NPC Standing Committee after consultation with the Basic Law Committee (a quasi-constitutional tribunal consisting of six mainland members and six Hong Kong members). It will not have retrospective effect in the sense of overturning court judgments which have already been delivered.

On 24 February 1999, the HKSAR government made the controversial move of applying to the Court of Final Appeal for the relevant part of the judgment of 29 January 1999 (containing the statement) to be "clarified" on the grounds that the matter was of "great constitutional, public and general importance". The application was heard on the morning of 26 February, and in a judgment issued on the afternoon of the same day,[28] the Court of

Final Appeal exercised its "inherent jurisdiction" to state that (1) the Hong Kong courts' power to interpret the Basic Law is derived from the NPC Standing Committee under article 158 of the Basic Law; (2) any interpretation made by the Standing Committee under article 158 would be binding on the Hong Kong courts; and (3) the judgment of 29 January did not question the authority of the NPC and its Standing Committee "to do any act which is in accordance with the provisions of the Basic Law and the procedure therein". It was generally accepted by the legal community and public opinion in Hong Kong that the Court of Final Appeal's statement of these additional points did not imply any retreat from its original position as defined in the judgment of 29 January 1999, but it only made explicit what was implicit in the original judgment.[29]

On 27 February 1999, the Legislative Affairs Commission of the NPC Standing Committee issued a statement referring to the Court of Final Appeal's "clarification" and pointing out that it had been essential. A comment made to the press the following day by Vice-Premier Qian Qishen indicated that the constitutional dispute had been brought to an end.

Critics of the clarification incident accused the HKSAR government of putting political pressure on the court to appease the central authorities, and of abusing court procedures in so doing (since the application for clarification of a judgment was unprecedented and did not fall within any recognized procedure in common law jurisdictions). They also criticized the secretary for justice for privately communicating with the chief justice on the two days immediately preceding the date of the application — the secretary's defence was that she only wanted to notify him about the forthcoming application so that he could expedite its hearing and arrange for Sir Anthony Mason, the non-permanent visiting judge (who participated in the original hearing as a fifth member of the Court of Final Appeal) to come to Hong Kong to participate in the hearing of the application.

On the other hand, it is possible to defend the clarification move by pointing out that it was a pragmatic solution to a crisis which originated, not from any political conflict between the central government and the HKSAR, but from a legal proposition made in the Court of Final Appeal's original judgment which the central government considered to be inconsistent with the true legal position regarding the relationship between the judicial power of the HKSAR and the central legislative power. It was, of course, possible and lawful for the NPC Standing Committee to make an interpretation under article 158 of the Basic Law overriding the Court of Final Appeal's statement. But in this event, a political cost will have to be paid, in terms of perceived or alleged "interference" with the HKSAR's judicial autonomy. Furthermore, such a move will be a severe blow to the authority and prestige of the Court of Final Appeal. Thus both sides will be losers. By contrast, the clarification seemed to have been effective in settling the conflict in a way that was "face-saving" for both the central government and the Court of Final Appeal. After all, if, as believed by some observers, the constitutional crisis had been due to a "misunderstanding" by the central authorities of the true meaning of the judgment of 29 January, then an explanation by way of clarification would be a natural and obvious way to dissolve the misunderstanding and hence to resolve the crisis.

# The Controversy over LegCo Rules of Procedure

Apart from the adaptation of law exercise and the new immigration legislation mentioned above, a third matter that raised a fundamental constitutional issue during the post-handover period was the Rules of Procedure of the Legislative Council. The Provisional Legislative Council had enacted its own Rules of Procedure, but after the first Legislative Council of the HKSAR was elected in May 1998, it began to draft a new set of Rules of Procedure.

Article 75 of the Basic Law empowers the Legislative Council to make its Rules of Procedure "on its own, provided that they do not contravene" the Basic Law. The new Rules of Procedure were adopted by the new Legislative Council (LegCo) on 2 July 1998, the day in which members of the new LegCo took their oath of office, amidst allegations on the part of the executive branch of the HKSAR government that some parts of the rules violated the

Basic Law. Daniel Fung, solicitor-general as he then was, spoke on behalf of the Administration on this matter and publicly criticized the rules for not being consistent with articles 48(10), 74 and Annex II, Part II of the Basic Law.

Article 74 of the Basic Law limits the right of LegCo members to introduce private members' bills to a greater extent than the limits prescribed by the previous colonial constitution. According to article 74, private members' bills may not "relate to public expenditure or political structure or the operation of the government". Furthermore, if a private member's bill relates to "government policies", then the written consent of the chief executive must be obtained before the bill can be introduced in LegCo.

The question arises in regard to who has the power to determine whether a particular private member's bill relates to public expenditure, political structure or the operation of the government (in which case it may not be introduced at all), or whether a bill relates to government policies (in which case it may only be introduced with the chief executive's consent). Following the approach used in the Standing Orders of the colonial legislature, the Rules of Procedure adopted by LegCo vest the power to make such determinations in the president of LegCo, whereas the Administration argued that according to the true interpretation of the Basic Law, it is the chief executive who makes such determinations.

Another point of contention concerns amendments (technically known as "committee stage amendments") proposed by individual LegCo members to bills originally introduced by the Administration. Under the LegCo Rules of Procedure, such amendments may be proposed without being subject to the limitations in article 74. The Administration's position, however, was that these limitations are applicable to amendments proposed by LegCo members to government bills in the same way as they are applicable to private members' bills.

Another controversy arose from the interpretation of article 48(10) of the Basic Law, which authorizes the chief executive "to approve the introduction of motions regarding revenues or expenditure to the Legislative Council". The LegCo Rules of Procedure now require that the chief executive's consent to the introduction of motions or amendments to bills which involve disposing or using "any part of the revenue or other public moneys of Hong Kong" (this language is in fact derived from Hong Kong's colonial constitution). The Rules also vest in the LegCo president the power to determine whether a motion or amendment falls within this category. The Administration argued that the formulation of the category in the Rules is unjustifiably narrower than that in article 48(10) of the Basic Law, which would also cover motions having the effect of increasing revenue or reducing expenditure. It also objected to the president's power to categorize a motion, arguing that it should be for the chief executive to do so.

The last area of dispute relates to LegCo voting procedures and the interpretation of Part II of Annex II of the Basic Law, which provides for different voting procedures for government bills, on the one hand (i.e. the passage of bills by a simple majority vote of members present), and private members' bills, motions and amendments on the other hand (i.e. the passage of bills by a simple majority of each of two groups of members present. Members elected by functional constituencies form one group, and members elected by universal suffrage and those elected by the election committee form the other group.) The question that arose was whether those members who are present but abstain from voting should be counted in the "denominator" for the purpose of determining whether there is a majority vote. The pre-1997 practice was that abstentions did not count, so that the required majority was determined simply by counting whether those who voted for the bill outnumbered those who voted against it.

The new LegCo Rules of Procedure depart from the pre-1997 practice because it was believed that the reference to members "present" (but not "present and voting") in Annex II of the Basic Law means that those who abstain from voting should be counted in the denominator for the purpose of determining whether there is a simple majority. However, the Administration was concerned that the change would make it more difficult for bills (particularly government bills) to get passed. Taking advantage of a minor linguistic difference (regarding the use of the Chinese character for "vote"), in the Chinese text of the Basic Law, between the provisions on voting procedures for government bills and those on voting procedures for private members' bills, the Administration argued that the Basic Law has preserved, in relation to government bills, the pre-1997 practice of not counting abstentions, and that the new system of counting abstentions in the denominator should only be applicable to the two-group voting for private members' bills. However, LegCo refused to accept the Administration's views in this regard, and the Rules of Procedure it passed provide for the same treatment of abstentions (i.e. those abstaining do count in the denominator) in relation to voting procedures for both types of bills.

Despite the differences of opinion between the Administration and LegCo, which already emerged when the Rules of Procedure were considered in draft form, LegCo went ahead to adopt the Rules on 2 July 1998 without any amendment on the points raised by the Administration. At the same time, LegCo established a committee on Rules of Procedure to give further consideration to the Administration's views. LegCo members publicly recognized the possibility of a revision of the Rules in future to take into account some of the Administration's concerns. At the same time, the Administration has not ruled out the option of applying to the court for judicial review of the Rules on the grounds of contravention of the Basic Law. At the time of writing this chapter, however, neither side has taken any action on this matter.

# The Case of Sally Aw

An account of major law-related events in Hong Kong in the period covered by this chapter cannot be complete without a mention of the extremely controversial case involving Aw Sian Sally, the chairperson of the group of companies that publishes the *Hong Kong Standard* and the *Sing Tao Daily News* newspapers. On 17 March 1998, the Department of Justice of the HKSAR government initiated the prosecution of one former and two current members of the senior management of the *Hong Kong Standard* newspaper. One of the charges was that they conspired with Sally Aw to artificially inflate the circulation record of the newspaper to defraud purchasers of advertising space in the newspaper. Although Aw was named in the charge, she herself was not prosecuted.

News of the case immediately caused an uproar in the Hong Kong community, and public opinion unanimously expressed serious concern about the matter (in view of the fact that Aw used to have close business ties with Tung Chee-hwa, the chief executive of the HKSAR; she is also a member of the National Committee of the Chinese People's Political Consultative Conference and is highly respected by the mainland authorities). Following precedents in the colonial era in which Attorney-Generals Michael Thomas and Jeremy Mathews affirmed the principle of accountability of the Attorney-General to the public through the legislature (even though the Attorney-General retains total independence in making prosecution decisions), Elsie Leung, the secretary for justice, appeared on 23 March 1998 to explain the matter at a special meeting convened by the Administration of Justice and Legal Services Panel of the PLC. However, the explanation was confined to general prosecution policy and the factors (such as evidential considerations and public interest considerations) normally taken into account in deciding whether to prosecute. Leung stressed that further comments and disclosure of details about the case (the trial of which was pending) would unfairly prejudice the persons concerned.

The subsequent trial for this case took place in the District Court and concluded in January 1999. On 20 January 1999, the three defendants were convicted of the offences of conspiracy to defraud and false accounting, and were sentenced to imprisonment for six months (in the case of the general manager) and four months (in the cases of the finance manager and the former circulation director). District Judge Peter Line found, on the evidence presented, that the three defendants had been involved in the conspiracy to defraud as charged. At the same time, the judge held that he had not found that any of the defendants conspired with Sally Aw.

Nevertheless, after the verdict, there was mounting pressure on the secretary for justice from the community to explain why she decided not to prosecute Aw in the first place. In particular, there was a feeling that the convicted persons were only employees, and Aw was the boss of the company. It could, therefore, be reasonably suspected that she might have been involved in the scheme of inflating the circulation figures of the newspaper. On 4 February,

Elsie Leung, the secretary for justice, appeared before the Legislative Council's Panel on Administration of Justice and Legal Services, and presented a statement on the non-prosecution decision in this case. In terms of the details provided, there had certainly been no precedent in Hong Kong's legal history. She also answered questions raised by legislative councillors immediately after the statement was read.

Leung cited both evidential considerations and public interest considerations in explaining her decision not to prosecute Aw. She pointed out that according to settled prosecution policy as published in the Department of Justice's booklet on *Prosecution Policy: Guidance for Government Counsel* (1998 edition), no prosecution should be launched unless the evidence suggests that there is "a reasonable prospect of securing a conviction". She referred to various items of evidence in this case and explained why she did not believe that the evidential test had been satisfied in this case. She then said that she also took into account public interest considerations as she had received written representations from lawyers acting for Aw regarding such considerations. The following passage in her statement should be set out in full since, in retrospect, it was of fatal significance:

> As a result, from the public interest point of view, I considered it not to be right to prosecute Ms Aw. At that time, the Sing Tao Group was facing financial difficulties and was negotiating restructuring with banks. If Ms Aw was prosecuted, it would be a serious obstacle to that restructuring. If the Group should collapse, its newspapers (which include one of only two English newspapers in Hong Kong) would, in all likelihood, be compelled to cease operation. I wish to add that several other newspapers had folded in late 1996, 1997 and 1998. Apart from the staff losing employment, the failure of a well-established and important media group at that time could have sent a very bad message to the international community. At a time when unemployment was on the rise, the prospect of a prosecution occasioning yet further widespread redundancies filled me with foreboding. It was my duty, in those circumstances, firstly, to consider the potential effects of a prosecution upon other people. Then, secondly, it was necessary to ask myself

whether the possible consequences of the prosecution were proportionate to the seriousness of the alleged offence. I decided they were not. The failure of an important media group at that time could have sent all the wrong signals to the international community, quite apart from the damage it would have done to local morale. Thus it was that I also decided that it was not in the public interest to initiate a prosecution of Ms Aw.

Leung's explanation of her decision not to prosecute Aw turned out to be counter-productive. A motion of no confidence in the secretary for justice was introduced in the Legislative Council by Margaret Ng, legislative councillor elected by the legal functional constituency consisting of all solicitors and barristers in the HKSAR. Such a motion of no confidence in a senior government official was unprecedented in Hong Kong's history. The motion was partly prompted by a strongly worded statement issued by the Bar Council (the executive committee of the Bar Association comprising all barristers in Hong Kong) on 10 February. In the statement, the Bar Council said it was "deeply disturbed by [the secretary's] interpretation of the public interest which is totally indefensible and contrary to her own published prosecution policy guidelines." The Council believed that the incident had seriously shaken the Bar's confidence in the secretary's ability and commitment to uphold the rule of law in Hong Kong. At the same time, the Council of the Law Society (representing all solicitors in Hong Kong) also expressed regret about the secretary's use of public interest considerations in this case. It did not, however, go as far as the Bar's statement which raised more fundamental questions regarding the wisdom of having the secretary remain in office.

On 11 March 1999, the motion of no confidence was debated at length in the Legislative Council. The secretary for justice, the director of public prosecutions and the chief secretary also spoke at the meeting. It was widely reported that the HKSAR government had mounted an intensive lobbying campaign targeted at councillors and their electoral constituencies (particularly the functional constituencies) before the meeting for the purpose of averting the passage of the motion. Many councillors elected from functional constituencies had also consulted their constituents on their views on the motion. In the course of these lobbying and consultative activities, the Liberal Party, which had ten members in the Council, switched from its original position of supporting the motion to that of abstaining from voting. After an intense debate in the Council on 11 March, the motion was defeated. However, the fact remains that 21 of the 59 members of the Council (excluding the president who does not vote) had voted for the motion, and another 8 members abstained instead of voting against the motion. The standing and authority of the secretary for justice had undoubtedly been impaired.

## The "Big Spender" Case

The nine-day trial, in October 1998, in the Guangzhou Intermediate People's Court attracted even greater and more prolonged public attention and debate in Hong Kong. The case involved Cheung Tze-keung, a Hong Kong crime boss nicknamed "the Big Spender", and 35 other accomplices, including 17 Hong Kong residents and 18 mainlanders. Cheung himself was a Hong Kong permanent resident. The case raised fundamental issues relating to the scope of the jurisdiction of the criminal courts in the Mainland and in the HKSAR with regard to Hong Kong residents. There was also concern that Cheung and his Hong Kong co-defendants were not given a fair trial in Guangzhou, in view of the fact that the trial was only open to selected individuals, and Hong Kong journalists were not allowed to attend the trial.

The public debate about the jurisdictional issue subsequently intensified when Li Yuhui, a mainland resident, was arrested by the mainland authorities (in Shantou) for the suspected murder of five Hong Kong residents at the Telford Garden residential estate in Hong Kong.[30] The question in the *Cheung* case was whether a Hong Kong permanent resident should be tried by the Hong Kong court rather than by a mainland court in respect of offences primarily committed in Hong Kong, while the question in the *Li* case was whether a mainland resident who is suspected of having committed an offence in Hong Kong should be tried by the Hong Kong court rather than by a mainland court. Both cases raised the issue of the extent to which Hong Kong should request extradition or rendition of suspected offenders apprehended in the Mainland to Hong Kong for trial. In both cases, critics accused the HKSAR authorities of being too timid in not putting forward any such request and thus failing to defend the jurisdiction of the Hong Kong courts under the Basic Law.

Cheung was the head of a criminal gang, comprising both Hong Kong and mainland residents, whom the Guangzhou court found guilty of a series of offences committed in the period 1991–98. Some of these crimes had been committed in Hong Kong, some in the Mainland, and many committed partly in Hong Kong and partly in the Mainland. The offences included the kidnapping of a Hong Kong tycoon and the son of another in Hong Kong (and thus involving ransom money in the order of hundreds of millions of dollars), cross-border smuggling and illegal trading of extremely huge quantities of firearms and explosives, as well as robbery in Hong Kong and in the Mainland. Cheung, together with four of the co-defendants, were convicted, sentenced to death and swiftly executed following the dismissal of their appeals by the Higher People's Court of Guangdong in December 1998. The court of first instance stressed that it had jurisdiction over the case since all of the offences concerned were either committed in the Mainland or had mainland elements, and none were committed entirely in Hong Kong without elements of planning or consequences in the Mainland. It also pointed out that the capital punishment was imposed with respect to the offences regarding firearms and explosives (which under mainland Chinese law are capital offences) and not the abduction offences (which are not capital offences under mainland Chinese law).

The secretary for security and the secretary for justice of the HKSAR government defended the government's decisions not to request rendition in both the *Cheung* case and the *Li* case. It was pointed out that in both cases, the suspected offenders were investigated and arrested (while they were in the Mainland) by the mainland authorities rather than the Hong Kong police, and the Hong Kong authorities had not gathered sufficient evidence for the purpose of prosecuting them. Indeed, in the *Cheung* case, victims of the kidnapping had not even reported the matter to the Hong Kong police. It was also argued that the mainland courts had jurisdiction to try the two cases under the mainland criminal law, and in the absence of a rendition agreement between the Mainland and the HKSAR, there was no basis for requesting their rendition even if they were cases over which both the mainland courts and the Hong Kong courts had concurrent jurisdiction.

Given the cross-border nature of the crimes organized by Cheung Tze-keung, there appears to be a firm legal basis for the exercise of jurisdiction over the gang by the Guangzhou court. However, the Li Yuhui case raises a more serious issue regarding the relationship between the Basic Law (which provides for the non-applicability in the HKSAR of the Chinese criminal code) and the mainland criminal law. In particular, the interpretation of article 7 of the PRC Criminal Code advocated by the Department of Justice of the HKSAR came under fire from the local legal community. The article provides for the application of the code to Chinese citizens who have committed crimes outside the territory of the PRC. The Department of Justice argued that in the light of the Basic Law, this article should be interpreted to mean that the code applies to mainland residents who commit crimes outside the Mainland as a jurisdiction, which implies that the code applies to mainland residents who commit crimes in the HKSAR. Critics argued that this would strain the wording of the article beyond reasonable limits.

In any event, the *Cheung* and *Li* cases underscore the pressing need for Hong Kong and the mainland authorities to enter into a judicial assistance arrangement, as originally contemplated by article 95 of the Basic Law, for the purpose of dealing with cases with cross-border elements. Part of such an agreement would define the respective limits of the jurisdiction of the Mainland and HKSAR courts to try criminal cases with cross-border elements, and provide for necessary rendition of fugitive offenders from one side to the other. At the time of writing, apart from an arrangement for the service of documents in civil litigation (which came into force on 30 March 1999), no other judicial assistance arrangement has yet been established between the HKSAR and the Mainland, although a number of such agreements are already in existence between the HKSAR and various foreign countries. Negotiations on civil and criminal judicial assistance (including reciprocal recognition and enforcement of arbitral awards and rendition of fugitive offenders) are, however, under way between the HKSAR and mainland authorities, and it is to be hoped that sound arrangements can be successfully established in the foreseeable future.

# Conclusion

Due to space limitations, it is not possible to discuss all aspects of and all developments in Hong Kong's legal system in 1997–99. We have only focused on what this author believes to be the most significant matters. On the whole, I believe that the legal aspects of the constitutional transition in Hong Kong have been reasonably managed by all parties concerned. The continuity of the pre-1997 legal system, including its laws, its judicial institutions and procedures, and, most important of all, the personnel who operate the system, has been maintained. The rule of law has survived. Indeed, the role of the judiciary — now the guardian of the Basic Law in cases involving constitutional judicial review as the immigration and flag cases mentioned above illustrate — has been enhanced. It is true that there have been a number of incidents which aroused public concern, and in this chapter, I have tried to describe them as impartially as possible. Understandably, different inferences and conclusions may perhaps be drawn from these incidents, but we can probably all agree that the Hong Kong community has proved to be vigilant in defending the rule of law and human rights. All government actions continue to be subject to a high degree of public scrutiny and potential public criticism. Freedom of the press, as well as freedom of association and demonstrations, have continued to thrive. Civil society is alive and well. There exists a vibrant pluralism of political parties, and democracy activists have been re-elected into the first Legislative Council of the HKSAR in an election by universal suffrage that achieved the highest voter turnout rate ever in Hong Kong's history. These, then, constitute the social and political foundations of the rule of law in Hong Kong.

## Notes

1. The phrase comes from the title of the book *Hong Kong: Borrowed Place — Borrowed Time* (London: Andre Deutsch, 1968) by Richard Hughes.

2. Paragraph 3(3) of the Joint Declaration.

3. For an English translation of the full text of this Decision, see *Hong Kong Law Journal*, vol. 27 (1997), pp. 419–24.

4. Ordinance no. 110 of 1997, sections 5 and 6.

5. Examples include the British Nationality (Miscellaneous Provisions) Ordinance (Cap. 186, Laws of Hong Kong); Army and Royal Air Force Legal Services Ordinance (Cap. 286); Royal Hong Kong Regiment Ordinance (Cap. 199).

6. The interpretative provisions concerned were sections 2(3), 3 and 4 of the Hong Kong Bill of Rights Ordinance. At the time of writing this chapter, the precise effect of their abolition has not yet been directly examined by the Hong Kong courts. However, given the existence of article 39 of the Basic Law, and in the light of the Court of Final Appeal's decision mentioned below (which relied partly on the human rights norms in the ICCPR) and the Court of Appeal's decision in *HKSAR v. Ng Kung-siu* discussed below, it seems that the status of the Bill of Rights in Hong Kong's legal system has remained unchanged despite the non-adoption of the interpretative provisions mentioned above.

7. The other features in the new version of the laws enacted by the PLC are technical changes to the existing law and do not take away any significant substantive rights which were enjoyed under the existing law. These features include the change from the system of notification to the authorities after the formation of societies to a system of registration of societies (but section 5A(6) of the new version of the Societies Ordinance provides that societies may still be formed and hold activities pending notification of the result of their application for registration), and the requirement of a "notice of no objection" in the case of public processions (but section 14(4) of the new version of the Public Order Ordinance provides that if the police do not expressly object to a proposed procession, they will be deemed by law to have issued the notice of no objection).

8. In December 1998, another law was added. This is the Law on the Exclusive Economic Zone and the Continental Shelf. See "Promulgation of National Law 1998", L.N. 393 of 1998, Legal Supplement No. 2 to Gazette No. 52/1998 (24 December 1998).

9. The National Flag and National Emblem Ordinance (Ordinance No. 116 of 1997).

10. See "Promulgation of National Laws 1997", L.N. 379 of 1997, *Government of the Hong Kong Special Administrative Region Gazette Extraordinary* No. 1/1997, Legal Supplement No. 2, p. B5; "Promulgation of National Laws (No. 2) 1997", L.N. 386 of 1997, *Government of the Hong Kong Special Administrative Region Gazette* No. 1/1997, Legal Supplement No. 2, p. B119.

11. Ordinance No. 116 of 1997.

12. A decision of the Court of Appeal dated 23 March 1999 in Magistracy Appeal No. 563 of 1998 (HCMA 563/98).

13. Ordinance No. 117 of 1997. Unlike the National Flag and National Emblem Ordinance, this ordinance is not based on any national law listed in Annex III of the Basic Law.

14. See also the PRC Criminal Code, article 299.

15. Ordinance No. 126 of 1997.

16. Ordinance No. 135 of 1997.

17. Ordinance No. 107 of 1997.

18. Ordinance No. 2 of 1998.

19. Ordinance No. 26 of 1998, passed by the PLC on 15 April 1998.

20. [1997] *3 Hong Kong Cases* 64, [1997] *Hong Kong Law Reports and Digest* 1081 (Court of First Instance), [1998] 1 *Hong Kong Cases* 617 (Court of Appeal).

21. *Ng King Luen v. Rita Fan* [1997] *Hong Kong Law Reports and Digest* 757, (1997) 7 *Hong Kong Public Law Reports* 281.

22. [1997] *Hong Kong Law Reports and Digest* 761, [1997] 2 *Hong Kong Cases* 315.

23. *Chan Kam Nga and 80 Others v. Director of Immigration* [1998] *Hong Kong Law Reports and Digest* 142, [1998] 1 *Hong Kong Cases* 16 (Court of First Instance); [1998] 2 *Hong Kong Cases* 405 (Court of Appeal).

24. *Lui Sheung Kwan and Another v. Director of Immigration* [1998] 1 *Hong Kong Law Reports and Digest* 265, [1998] 1 *Hong Kong Cases* 717.

25. [1999] 1 *Hong Kong Law Reports and Digest* 315.

26. [1999] 1 *Hong Kong Law Reports and Digest* 304.

27. For a critical analysis, see my essay "The Court of Final Appeal's Ruling in the 'Illegal Migrant' Children Case: A Critical Commentary on the Application of Article 158 of the Basic Law" (Paper No. 23, Law Working Paper Series, Faculty of Law, University of Hong Kong, March 1999).

28. [1999] 1 *Hong Kong Law Reports and Digest* 577.

29. For a critical analysis, see my essay "The Court of Final Appeal's Ruling in the 'Illegal Migrant' Children Case: Congressional Supremacy and Judicial Review" (Paper No. 24, Law Working Paper Series, Faculty of Law, University of Hong Kong, March 1999).

30. Subsequently, Li was tried by the Intermediate People's Court in Shantou and sentenced to death on 23 March 1999.

# List of Contributors

## Editors

**WANG Gungwu** is Director of the East Asian Institute at The National University of Singapore and Distinguished Senior Fellow at The Institute of Southeast Asian Studies, Singapore. He is also Emeritus Professor of The Australian National University. He has taught in the University of Malaya (1962-68) and the Australian National University (1968–86), and was Vice-Chancellor (President) of the University of Hong Kong from 1986–95. He is Honorary Fellow of the School of Oriental and African Studies (London), and Honorary Professor of Hong Kong, Peking and Fudan (Shanghai) Universities. Some of his publications include *The Nanhai Trade: The Early History of Chinese Trade in the South China Sea* (1958 & 1998); *The Structure of Power in North China during the Five Dynasties* (1963); *China and the World since 1949* (1977); *Community and Nation* (1981 & 1993); *The Chineseness of China* (1991); *The Chinese Way: China's Position in International Relations* (1995); *China and Southeast Asia: Myths, Threats and Culture* (1999).

**John WONG** is Research Director of the East Asian Institute at The National University of Singapore. He was formerly Director of the Institute of East Asian Political Economy (1990–96). His publications include *Land Reform in the People's Republic of China* (1973), *ASEAN Economies in Perspective* (1979), *The Political Economy of China's Changing Relations with Southeast Asia* (1986) and *Understanding China's Socialist Market Economy* (1993), as well as numerous papers on the economic development of China, ASEAN and the Asian NIEs. He also edited *China's Political Economy* (with Wang Gungwu, 1998).

# Contributors

**Johannes Man-mun CHAN** is Professor and Head of the Department of Law, University of Hong Kong. Some of his main publications include *General Principles of Hong Kong Law* (with Albert Chen and others, 1999), *Media Law and Practice* (with Kenneth Leung, 1995), *Human Rights and Public Law: A Hong Kong Sourcebook* (with Andrew Byrnes, 1993), *The Hong Kong Bill of Rights: A Comparative Approach* (with Yash Ghai, 1993) and *Human Rights in Hong Kong* (1990).

**Albert H.Y. CHEN** graduated from the University of Hong Kong (1980) and Harvard University (1982). He is currently Professor in the Department of Law and Dean of the Faculty of Law at the University of Hong Kong. He has published widely in English and Chinese. His books include *Hong Kong's Legal System and the Basic Law* (1986), *Human Rights and the Rule of Law* (1987) (co-authored), *The Workers' Compensation System in Hong Kong: Retrospect and Prospect* (1987) (co-authored), *Law and Politics in Hong Kong* (1990), *The Rule of Law, Enlightenment and the Spirit of Modern Law* (1998), and *An Introduction to the Legal System of the People's Republic of China* (1998). He is also the co-editor of *The Basic Law and Hong Kong's Future* (1988*)*, *General Principles of Hong Kong Law* (1999) and the *Hong Kong Law Journal*.

**Y.C. JAO** is Professor at the School of Economics and Finance, University of Hong Kong, where he has been teaching since 1969. His main research interests are money, banking and finance, in which he has published extensively. He has recently been invited to contribute to the "International Handbook of Financial Reform", to be published by Edward Elgar in 2000. In December 1997, the University of Hong Kong conferred on him the additional title of Honorary University Fellow, in recognition of his long and distinguished service.

**KUAH Khun Eng** is an anthropologist teaching in the Department of Sociology, The University of Hong Kong. Her main research interests include the relationship between Chinese overseas and their ancestral villages in China, the contemporary roles of Chinese voluntary associations, religion and politics, and women and politics. Her forthcoming book entitled "Rebuilding the Ancestral Village: Singaporeans in China" will be published by Ashgate (September 1999).

**KUAN Hsin-chi** is Professor in the Department of Government & Public Administration at The Chinese University of Hong Kong. He serves concurrently as the Director of its Universities Service Centre, a world-renowned research library on post-1949 China. His research interest lies in political culture and development. He has co-edited several volumes of *China Review* (1991, 1992 and 1997) and contributed articles to *The China Journal*, *The Journal of Commonwealth & Comparative Politics*, *Asian Survey*, *Hong Kong Law Journal*, *The Journal of Northeast Asian Politics* and *International Journal of Public Administration*.

**LAU Siu-kai** is Chairman, Department of Sociology, and Associate Director, the Hong Kong Institute of Asia-Pacific Studies, both at the Chinese University of Hong Kong. He graduated from the University of Hong Kong in 1971 and obtained his doctorate from the University of Minnesota in 1975. His research interests include political development of Hong Kong and comparative politics. He is the author of *Society and Politics in Hong Kong* (1982) and co-author of *The Ethos of the Hong Kong Chinese* (1988). He has contributed widely to academic journals.

**LEE Ming-kwan** is Professor and Associate Head of the Department of Applied Social Studies and Director of the Centre for Social Policy Studies at the Hong Kong Polytechnic University. He is co-editor of *Indicators of Social Development: Hong Kong*, a series of research monographs which report findings from territory-wide social indicators surveys conducted biennially since 1988, and has written various articles and essays on family and marriage in Hong Kong, the identity problems of the Hong Kong Chinese, class and stratification in Hong Kong, and the *Heung Yee Kuk*. His publications will also include *Beyond the Iron Rice Bowl: Chinese Occupational Welfare in Market Transition*.

**LIU Pak Wai** is Professor of Economics and Pro-Vice-Chancellor of the Chinese University of Hong Kong. He graduated from Princeton University and undertook both his masters and doctoral degrees in Stanford University. He is also Research Director of the Hong Kong Centre for Economic Research; Co-Director at the Hong Kong and Asia-Pacific Economies Research Programme, Hong Kong Institute of Asia-Pacific Studies; and the Secretary-General of the East Asian Economic Association. He plays an advisory role in a number of government departments, such as the

Central Policy Unit and the Economic Advisory Committee. His research focus is on labour economics and applied theory.

**SUNG Yun-wing** is currently Chairman and Professor of the Department of Economics, and Co-Director of the Hong Kong and Asia-Pacific Economies Research Programme at The Chinese University of Hong Kong. He is also Managing Editor of *the Asian Economic Journal*, Book Review Editor of *Pacific Economic Review* and Corresponding Editor *of Asian Pacific Economic Literature*. He obtained his doctorate in Economics from the University of Minnesota in 1979. He was Research Fellow at the Australian National University in 1985, Visiting Scholar at University of Chicago in 1985, Harvard-Yenching Institute at Harvard University in 1989–90, and University of Nottingham in 1996. His research interests cover international trade and economic development in China, Hong Kong and Taiwan. He has published widely in the area.

**TSANG Shu-ki** is Professor of Economics at the Hong Kong Baptist University. He graduated from the University of Hong Kong and obtained his post-graduate degrees from the Chinese University of Hong Kong and the University of Manchester. His major research interests include monetary economics, comparative economics and currency boards. He was a Hong Kong Affairs Advisor to the Chinese government before the 1997 transition and is now serving in a number of advisory committees of the Hong Kong SAR government. He is also Director of the Exchange Fund Investment Limited.

**WONG Siu-lun** is Professor of Sociology at The University of Hong Kong, and currently Pro-Vice-Chancellor and Director, the Centre of Asian Studies of the university. He graduated from The University of Hong Kong in 1971 and received his D.Phil. at the University of Oxford. In 1985, he was Visiting Scholar at the Harvard-Yenching Institute at Harvard University. He is the author of Emigrant Entrepreneurs: Shanghai Industrialist in Hong Kong (1988), and co-editor of Hong Kong's Transition: A Decade after the Deal (1995).